BOOKS BY MARK BEGO

~⌒~

I Fall to Pieces—The Music and the Life of Patsy Cline
Dancing in the Street: Confessions of a Motown Diva, with Martha Reeves
Country Hunks
Country Gals
I'm a Believer: My Life of Music, Monkees and Madness, with Micky Dolenz
Madonna: Blonde Ambition
Ice, Ice, Ice: The Extraordinary Vanilla Ice Story
Linda Ronstadt: It's So Easy
Between the Lines, with Debbie Gibson
Aretha Franklin: Queen of Soul
Bette Midler: Outrageously Divine
Cher!
Whitney! [Houston]
Julian Lennon!
Sade!
On the Road With Michael! [Jackson]
Michael! [Jackson]
The Doobie Brothers
Barry Manilow
The Captain and Tennille

~⌒~

I Fall to Pieces

I Fall to Pieces

The Music and the Life of Patsy Cline

Mark Bego

ADAMS PUBLISHING
Holbrook, Massachusetts

Published by Adams Media Corporation
260 Center Street, Holbrook, MA 02343

ISBN: 1-55850-476-1
Printed in the United States of America.

First Edition
J I H G F E D C B A

Library of Congress Cataloging-in-Publication Data
Bego, Mark.
    I fall to pieces: the music and the life of Patsy Cline / Mark Bego.
      p.   cm.
    Discography: p.
    Includes bibliographial references (p.) and index.
    ISBN 1-55850-476-1
    1. Cline, Patsy, 1932–1963. 2. Country musicians—United States—Biography. I. Title.
    ML420.C57B44   1995
    782.42'1642'092—dc20
    [B]   95-1536
                                                      CIP
                                                       MN

This book is available at quantity discounts for bulk purchases.
For information, call 1-800-872-5627.

Jacket design by Janet M. Clesse
Jacket Photograph Courtesy of Michael Ochs Archives/Venice, CA.

~⌒~

IN MEMORY OF AUNT JOJO:

Wild and unconventional,

you reminded me

of Patsy Cline

~⌒~

Contents

VIII

Acknowledgments

*T*he author would like to thank the following people for their help and assistance
in completing this book:

Donald Abare — David Andrew — Carlene Carter — Doug
Casmus — The Country Music Foundation — Mike Crawford —
Charlie Dick — Vince Gill — Katie Gillon — Roger Glazer — Sasha
Goodman — Mark Hall — Greg Hall — Anita Heilig — Tracy
Lawrence — Salli LeGrone — Pam Liflander — MCA Records —
Lorrie Morgan — Susan Nadler — Photographic Works, Tucson,
Arizona — Marc Raboy — Rhino Records — Bernard Schwartz —
Tony Seidl — Chris Skinker — Regina Stevens — The Tucson
Public Library — Mary Wilson

Introduction

BY CARLENE CARTER

My mother, June Carter, was one of Patsy Cline's best friends. Although I never met Patsy, I've heard all kinds of stories about her, and because of what I know, I really respect her. She never let anyone make her be something she wasn't. And, who in the world would want to change her anyway? In my mind, she was perfect!

I think that she was just the best female singer ever alive! Patsy Cline had it all. She had the courage and the heart to go on stage after her automobile accident, getting out there and singing after being disfigured, and having to go through all of the surgery she did.

I remember her going through all of that stuff, and years later I heard all of the stories from Mama.

Patsy basically didn't back down about anything, and wouldn't let anyone make her into anything she didn't want to be. Any time a woman has an opinion and says what's on her mind, and tells the truth, she's regarded as somewhat of a "bitch," particularly by men. Now, if men do that, they're regarded as "tough" and "good" and good in the business world. I just think that Patsy knew what she wanted, she knew how she wanted to do it, and she knew when bullshit was bullshit. She called it like it was, and there was nobody else like her at that time. I also remember that my Mom said that Patsy cussed like a sailor.

She took a lot of flak, and had a reputation for having "brass ovaries." I always think of her as "the Frances Farmer of country," in the sense that she's a little misunderstood. I think that all that Patsy wanted to do was sing, and that was it. Unfortunately, in this business there's just so many other things that come into play, and it sets up your reputation. I know that she was a sweet, sweet woman, and I know that my mother loved her so much, and she was devastated when Patsy died. I remember that.

All that Patsy had to do was to open her mouth and this beautiful voice came out. That was when—no matter what they might have thought of her, how they wanted her to "shut up and just sing"—they had to forgive anything that they didn't like or couldn't handle about her. She was labeled as "uncontrollable" in the "man's world" back then. She'd just say, "No, *this* is how I'm doing it! Sorry, this ain't me, I ain't doing this."

When I say these things, I'm pretty much speaking for all of the women in country music today, because all of us know that Patsy is what a lot of us would strive to be. Her singing, her sense of being true to herself, and her love for her family—she basically did it all! With her music, she did what all of us would like to do, which is to have your music without boundaries or categories like "country" or "pop" or "rock."

Thinking back, who else was as big a star as she was? Maybe Elvis. She just about blew all of the competition off of the list. She wasn't afraid of anything. Maybe inside she was a little jittery and scared, and thought, "Oh God, I'm gonna blow it! Oh, who cares!" But, she never let it show.

I really respect Patsy Cline, and whenever I'm in a situation where I might be kind of pushed around or controlled by the powers that be in this business, I always think, "Would Patsy Cline put up with all of this?" It's a good way to live. Like Patsy: Be true to yourself! That's all that matters, especially to us women. Men ought to listen to her a little bit too!

Patsy's music is timeless. Obviously the technology of recording is different, but, by the sound of it, Patsy could have been a huge star today. She would have been a huge star if she debuted in the year 2000, it wouldn't have mattered. There is no way you could deny her talent! In my mind, Patsy Cline was perfect.

Chapter One

THE CLINE

*T*here was only one thing that Patsy Cline truly craved: stardom. After a decade in the music business and six hectic years as a recording artist, she had earned the right to long for unqualified fame, and tonight it was undeniably hers.

～～

After a roller coaster of a year behind her, tonight she presented herself glamorously, in her prime. Her hair was done up in a meticulously coiffed brunette "do," with one delinquent curl falling on the left side of her forehead. She was suitably elegant in a form-fitting, custom-made dress of midnight blue lace, and above her left breast she pinned a large, white orchid corsage. It was conspicuously placed there as if this was the senior prom she had never had the chance to attend, and tonight she was its undisputed queen. This evening was not just another concert engagement—this was the magical night that was about to make up for a lifetime of disappointments and false starts.

When the appointed time came, she walked the short distance down a linoleum-covered hallway from her dressing room and came to the short flight of stairs leading to the stage. As she grabbed the metal handrailing and began to ascend the first step, she paused for a split second and wondered how many of her musical idols had grabbed that same handrailing before her. An inner glow of triumphant happiness emanated from within her at the realization of a dream becoming reality: Patsy Cline was playing Carnegie Hall, and nothing could possibly spoil this crowning achievement.

It was the week after Thanksgiving, and this was the frosting on the cake of a year that had its peaks and valleys of triumph and tragedy. The moment she stepped onto the stage, and the cheering from the crowd began, a rush of excitement came over her like an emotionally tingling wave. As she stepped up to the downstage microphone and into the spotlight, she was met with the outpouring of love and respect she had come to long for, the elements so lacking in her private life.

As she launched into her repertoire of country and pop hits and a list of sparkingly personalized standards, she knew that she had finally hit the big time. "Patsy just blew the end of the building out when she started to sing," one witness was later to proclaim. When she sang "I Fall to Pieces," the crowd went insane. Then, she introduced Manhattan to her masterful new single, "Crazy," and was mesmerizing when she launched into her own bluesy version of "Bill Bailey, Won't You Please Come Home?" She had come a long way from performing in the roadside beer joints back in rural Virginia, and now New York City was eating out of her hand. When she finished her set and received a standing ovation, a triumphant career victory was hers.

Only five short months before, she was lying in a Nashville hospital bed, recovering from injuries sustained in a near-fatal car crash. It had left her both physically and emotionally scarred. As she was recuperating from the accident, the first single release from her new deal with Decca Records—"I Fall to Pieces"—went all the way to the top of the charts and established her as country music's number one female star. In spite of the elusive evening of true glory she was now experiencing, within the next three weeks Patsy would record her emotionally chilling "She's Got You," and the very next day collapse from a nervous breakdown.

While this chain of events sounds like the kind of traumatic plotline that usually belongs to fictional soap opera heroines, this is the real life story of Patsy Cline. Her public worships her, her first record label cheats her, her second husband beats her, yet somehow she manages to create some of the most enduring songs in recording history. Welcome to the world of the most beloved and most famous woman in country music.

She struggled through several years worth of the pawing hands of patrons in smoke-filled bars, the early-age desertion of her abusive father, a passionless first marriage, a five-year ball-and-chain record contract that nearly derailed her career before it began, and a draining love/hate second marriage. Along the way, she truly earned for herself the right to sing the blues. When she sang heart songs like her signature hits "She's Got You," "Sweet Dreams," "Crazy," and "I Fall to Pieces," there was no question that she had firsthand knowledge in the kind of sadness that only the lonely can know.

However tinged with tragedy Patsy's life was, she would not want to be remembered with a tear. She would rather be recalled as someone who lived life to the fullest, like she sings in "Cry Not for Me." A hearty, mischief-filled laugh and a toast with a good stiff drink was more her style. In real life she was bawdy, liberated, jovial, aggressively fun-loving, confrontationally no-nonsense, and genuinely exciting to be around. She was known for her social drinking, chain-smoking, and her ability to tell raunchy jokes right alongside the boys in the band. No one who met her ever forgot her energy or her spirit.

Never one to cry in her beer, she was able to divorce herself from her troubles, and jokingly referred to herself in third person as "the Cline." Her friends and her co-workers were all lovingly referred to as "hoss." Aside from sounding like lingo from a wild west cowgirl, "hoss" is also a baseball term for a favorite team player. Among her peers in Nashville, she was known as a square-shooting team player all of her life.

While her early stage persona found her dressed like Dale Evans, and her stage patter was "aw shucks" folksy, Patsy was nobody's fool. When she finally emerged in the early sixties with her fashionable Patti Paige look, it was simply a matter of the butterfly emerging and fully realizing her glamorous potential.

When the late fifties and early sixties are rehashed, the sex symbol was Marilyn Monroe, the tragic Hollywood star was Judy Garland, and the voice was unmistakenly Patsy Cline—clad in skintight shirtwaist dresses, torpedo bras, and always chicly coiffed. She became such a respected pop star of the era that she once made a personal appearance with Elvis Presley and Ann Margaret, and was a guest star on "American Bandstand." After meeting her, one journalist from the era beamed, "Patsy Cline comes over like Ava Gardner, Marilyn Monroe, and Gina Lollobrigida all rolled up in one!"

Most importantly, she was an innovator. Patsy practiced women's lib years before anyone even thought of burning a bra. When it came to love, she called all the shots. When she saw something she liked, she went after it. Amid one concert tour in Canada, one of her buddies, Jimmy Dean, recalls that she walked up to a handsome uniformed Mountie and announced, "Hi, my name's Patsy Cline, and I'm gonna screw the boots off of you!"

The perpetual life of the party, Patsy never let social convention stand in the way of a good time. During the El Paso, Texas, stay, Patsy smuggled Roger Miller's marijuana across the border from Mexico for him—by stuffing it in her bra. Ages before the word "gay" had been attached to same-sex couples, Patsy got a "hoot" out of the unconventional lifestyles of her devoted homosexual fans.

On the other side of the coin, her girlfriends in the business remember her as having a heart as big as the state of Virginia itself. Loretta Lynn, Dottie West, Brenda Lee, and Barbara Mandrell all recall Patsy as a salt-of-the-earth kind of gal who would have given them the blouse off her back if they were ever in need.

Patsy lived large, and seemed to pack several extra decades into her all-too-brief thirty years. When the now-infamous plane crash terminated her vivacious existence, she was just finally beginning to enjoy the fruits of the fame she had struggled so hard to obtain.

Amazingly, America lost three living legends in the span of one year. Between the August 1962 death of Marilyn Monroe, and the November 1963 assassination of John F. Kennedy, the music world lost Patsy Cline. Like Marilyn and JFK, Patsy's fame and icon status has only magnified with time. In fact, in the 1990s she is an even bigger star than she was in the 1960s. Selling over four million copies since its 1967 release, the *Patsy Cline's Greatest Hits* album has had the longest continuous run at number one on Billboard magazine's "Country Catalog" album chart, beating out all of the contemporary competition. It is still the biggest selling solo female greatest hits country album ever released. Long before Wynonna and Reba there was Patsy.

Several of country music's biggest headliners—Trisha Yearwood, Lorrie Morgan, k. d. lang, and Reba McEntire—all list Cline among their top inspirations. According to Kathy Mattea, "The woman who embodied 'the Nashville sound' more than anyone is Patsy Cline." K. T. Oslin claims, "You believed what she sang. You believed what she was talking about. She had a style that *was* all her own, and still *is*."

She started out as a plain and simple country girl from the Shenandoah Valley, who dreamed about one day appearing at the *Grand Ole Opry*. Not only did she achieve stardom in Nashville, but before Patsy was through, she was acknowledged as the sexy and polished queen of country music, conquering the Hollywood Bowl, Carnegie Hall, and Las Vegas on her path to the top.

The public glory, the private hell—and ultimately the international superstar status of Patsy Cline: She made it to the top, but at what price? The following pages chronicle the making of a true singing legend, and how she mined her personal heartbreaks to yield several of the most memorable musical performances of the twentieth century. Unique, innovative, gutsy, bawdy, feisty, loving, combative, and finally worshipped, she was an exciting original who was able to emerge from the male-dominated country music scene, to tower over all the rest.

In 1980 a whole new generation of fans were introduced to

Patsy and her distinctive singing when Beverly D'Angelo played "the Cline" in the box-office hit *Coal Miner's Daughter*. The public's interest in Patsy continued to grow: Jessica Lange played Patsy in the 1985 film *Sweet Dreams*, devoted solely to Patsy's own career. As popular as each of these films were, they presented only the tip of the iceberg.

There are two ways to look at Patsy's story. On the one hand, it could be classified as a "tragedy"—the tale of a life cut short in full bloom. Or, it could be told as the inspirational account of someone who set lofty goals for herself and accomplished them through her own determination, moxie, and talent. She spoke her mind, made her own rules, and told off anyone who got in her way. This is the Patsy Cline that this book celebrates—the one who knew how to live life to the hilt.

She has touched souls with her emotion-charged singing, and there is nothing that can diminish the glow of her star—not even death itself. There is only one Patsy Cline—and this is her story.

Chapter Two

PATSY'S CHILDHOOD

Almost a premonition of what was to come, Patsy's childhood was full of ups and downs. Patsy was born on September 8, 1932, in the town of Gore, Virginia—just six days after her parents were married. Her father, Sam Hensley, at the age of forty-three, was literally forced by his family into marrying sixteen-year-old Hilda Patterson in a hastily planned "shotgun wedding," to avoid further scandal. For much of Patsy's young life, Sam Hensley behaved as if he blamed the young girl for ending his days as a bon vivant playboy. Her mother became her best friend and confidante.

The son of a once-wealthy Virginia landowner, Sam Hensley was a man who had faced several disappointments in his own life. Sam was born on August 16, 1889, the fifth of eight children. Because his four older siblings were all girls, for the majority of his life Sam rested on the knowledge that one day he would inherit the lion's share of the family fortune.

By the turn of the last century his father, Sol Hensley, owned over a thousand acres of prime farmland in the Blue Ridge Mountains near Elkton, Virginia. The Rockingham County property was so large that at one point it housed three separate farms. Sol was a hardworking man of Scottish-English descent who built his own impressive estate, which he immodestly christened "Solsburg." A mean bully of a man with a legendary temper, Sol was known in the area as "the Baron." Strongly self-motivated, Sol believed that Sam and his younger brothers should work as hard as he did. More often than not, they failed to match his expectations.

Sam went to school until he completed the seventh grade, which was as far as the Elkton school system went. The Baron made sure that all of his children had musical training as well. Sam and his siblings developed their musical skills at the local Shenandoah Conservatory of Music. While his younger brother Ashby became a proficient piano and guitar player, Sam could get by at the piano, but was best known for his gift at singing.

Having finished his formal education, the time came for him to learn a trade that would be useful for farm life, apprenticing with a blacksmith. He not only developed a talent for fixing metal farm tools and creating horseshoes, he was also a whiz as a machinery mechanic. Family members recall Sam's ability for disassembling, repairing, and reassembling motors and engines with ease.

Relatives, like nephew Herman "Punk" Longley, also recall that Sam not only inherited his father's interest in music, but also acquired Sol's legendary temper. As a teenager Sam developed a passion for fast cars, and he considered himself quite a lady's man. Dashing, young, eligible, and in line to inherit his family's wealth, Sam was quite popular.

When the United States entered into World War I in 1917, Sam enlisted in the Army, and fought in the bloody battle at Argonne Forest. The war instilled in him an edge of bitterness that he never lost, and a penchant for booze. Usually mild-mannered, whenever he drank his darker side came out.

After the war he married young Wynona Jones and for quite some time he seemed to be a happy family man. They shared an interest in music, as Wynona had also studied at the Shenandoah Conservatory of Music. Although their first baby passed away as an infant, they soon had a son, Randolph, and a daughter named Temple Glenn, whom everyone called Tempie.

Both Sam and Wynona made certain that both children also received formal musical training. Their teacher was an unmarried woman named Sally Mann, who Randolph and Tempie both adored. For a while, everything was in good order, and they had a marvelous life together.

Unfortunately, in the 1920s, things began to unravel for Sam and his family. Wynona, pregnant for the fourth time, was suddenly killed in an automobile accident. Despondent over the loss of his wife and the child he would never meet, Sam sent the children to live with their beloved music teacher.

Amid this personal catastrophe, all was not well at Solsburg. The Baron found himself embroiled in a scandal of his own when he got a fifteen-year-old Elkton girl pregnant. The girl's family was paid off to make the scandal go away, taking a large chunk out of the family estate. To make matters worse, southern agriculture was in its worst slump in decades when an unexpected drought had a disastrous effect on the family's income. Slowly, the Hensley empire had to be sold off acre-by-acre to make ends meet.

The October 1929 crash of the New York Stock Market took care of what remained. When "Black Friday" came, a forty-year-old Sam saw his inheritance fall with Wall Street. This sudden midlife crisis made Sam an embittered man.

Caring only for himself, he turned his back on his two children with chilling ease. He neglected to keep up his support payments to Sally Mann, and she finally ended up adopting Sam's children as her own.

Fortunately, Sam had marketable blacksmithing and mechanical skills, and he became a Depression-era drifter. He soon found himself driving from town to town, living here and there. For a while he worked on the railroad, then he was employed in a sand mine, and for one stretch he was employed as a "scab" worker at the Ford Motor Company's River Rouge plant in Detroit. He would move to a new town, get a job, run up a list of bills, and move on without warning to escape the financial obligation. Whenever things went wrong, Sam simply pulled up his stakes and fled in the night.

In 1931, Sam breezed back into Elkton, acting like the man-about-town he was before he was married. Driving a big car and acting as if the Depression meant nothing to him, Sam must have looked like quite a dashing guy to a love-struck fifteen-year-old girl like Hilda Patterson.

Hilda knew very little about men, or the games of deception they could play with a young girl's heart. Born Hilda Virginia Patterson on March 9, 1916, in the tiny town of Opequon, near Winchester, Virginia, her parents, James Arlington Patterson and Goldie Lavinia Newlin, were farmhands. James picked apples for $1.25 a week during harvest time in the local orchards. With two older siblings preceding her, Hilda was still a baby when her father succumbed to 1918's great flu epidemic. It was the final blow in a series of tragedies. He had recently survived a fall from a roof, which had resulted in him having to have his leg amputated. He was only thirty-three when he died.

Left a widow, Goldie was forced to seek work sorting apples at the National Fruit Company—and doing several other seasonal jobs. She later remarried, and with her new husband, Frank Allanson, she bore five more children. Hilda and her siblings were already hard workers by the time they reached their teens. Chores around the house, watching the younger children, and odd jobs for the neighbors occupied her days.

When Hilda first heard handsome Sam Hensley singing in the local church choir, he must have looked like a knight in shining armor. Seduced by Sam's charm and good looks, Hilda fell in love. Uneducated in birth control, it wasn't long before Hilda found herself in trouble. When Hilda was nine months pregnant, Sam married her merely to get his family off of his back, and to quell the scandal he had created. "Like father, like son," was a phrase he was getting used to hearing people say behind his back.

Less than a week past her wedding, Hilda gave birth to her daughter. She and Sam named her Virginia Patterson Hensley, derived from both parents' last names. Called "Ginny" while she was young, she used a shortening of her middle name, "Patsy," only once her career got rolling.

As a baby having a baby, Hilda must have seen Ginny as more like a doll or a sibling than a daughter. According to Hilda, "I was a sixteen years old when Patsy was born. All my life I had hand-me-downs, but when she was born, she was mine. We grew up together. We were hungry together."

For Hilda, marriage to Sam spelled escape from her hard life on the farm. When she and Sam and baby Virginia moved ninety miles south to Solsburg, she was expecting a better life. Instead, she found that she had departed the frying pan in favor of the fire. Widowed earlier that year, the Baron suffered a stroke which hampered his mobility—but not his demanding temper. Living with an irresponsible husband and a mean father-in-law she literally feared, Hilda soon found herself treated like a house servant instead of the lady of the house. For her it was a continuation of the same life, just a different floor to sweep. The only joy in her world was her baby.

Sam was quite demanding of Hilda, and he would insist that everything around the house be done his way. Hilda's sister-in-law, Marie Allanson, recalls being downright frightened of him and his temper whenever she would visit. From the time Ginny could speak, she learned to talk back to her father whenever he yelled at her. For much of Hilda's marriage to Sam, he was the common enemy. Whenever Sam would scream at Ginny, Hilda would defend her. Whenever Sam would direct his anger at Hilda, Ginny would rush to her mother's defense. Life at Solsburg was a perpetual domestic battlefield.

On a couple of notable occasions, Hilda packed her bags and left. Once, when she went to a Sunday school–sponsored picnic that Sam insisted she was not to attend, he tracked Hilda down with his brother in tow. Rifle-toting Sam must have been quite a sight when he demanded—at gunpoint—that Hilda get out of the swimming pool while the horrified church-going picnickers looked on.

At the age of three or four, Virginia learned to escape into the fantasy world of music and movies. After Hilda took her to see a Shirley Temple film, the girl was absolutely star struck.

II

According to Hilda, "Ginny idolized Shirley Temple. She would come home from the movies after seeing the pictures twice and say, 'Mama, I want to be a dancer like her.' I'd say, 'What! Now listen, Virginia …' but it didn't do any good. It wasn't too long before she was tap dancing all over the house. I'd stand there and watch her and shake my head. But I couldn't help but smile or laugh. She was something."

Ginny's fascination with show business dates back to an early age. She was four years old when her mother entered her in a talent show, and Ginny performed a self-conceived routine to the Shirley Temple song "The Good Ship Lollipop."

"To our utter amazement, she won!" Hilda recalls. "She took first prize! And Ginny had never had any formal training. At first, I figured she was going through a phase, but then I began to wonder. But I was right, because then she came to music. Not singing, but playing the piano."

It was Ginny's half-sister Tempie Glenn who became the key figure to steer the child toward the piano. Unsurprisingly, having been raised by Sally Mann, Tempie Glenn had become an accomplished pianist. Ginny would go over to her half-sister's house to visit, and would come back dancing "on a cloud," as her mother recalls. Having shifted her focus from dancing to the piano, young Virginia would insist to her mother, "I'm gonna play like that one day!"

Although Hilda explained to her that they couldn't afford to pay for the lessons let alone the piano, Ginny persisted. "Once I arranged to give her instructions. The teacher asked Virginia to sit at the piano and play something. In the middle of the composition the teacher looked at me and said, 'She's got a natural gift. You'll be wasting your money. She's terrific playing by ear. I don't think I could ever teach her to play the hard way.'"

With that, Sam and Hilda relented, and they gave Ginny a piano for her seventh birthday. Her love of music was by now deeply ingrained: she was constantly either playing music on the piano or listening to music on the radio. There were several country music stations in the area, and Ginny became fascinated with country music. According to Hilda, "From the time she was about ten, Patsy was living, eating, and sleeping country music. I know she never wanted anything so badly as to be a star on the *Grand*

Ole Opry. Patsy loved all the country stars—she didn't have one particular favorite. She adored them all, and she could tell you about each and every one of them. If she could help it, she'd never miss the *Opry* broadcasts."

Patsy would later attribute her incredible vocal range to a childhood case of rheumatic fever. "You might say it was my return to the living that launched me as a singer. In childhood I developed a serious throat infection, and my heart stopped beating. I was placed in an oxygen tent, and doctors brought me back to life. I recovered from the illness with a voice that boomed forth like Kate Smith's!" she recalled.

When Ginny started school, Sam's wanderlust was suddenly rekindled. A list of the schools Ginny attended from the age of five reveals either a nomadic soul, or a man trying to escape from his past. For whatever reason, the family moved nineteen times in fifteen years. First grade: Elkton; second grade: Lexington; fourth grade: Winchester; sixth grade: Portsmouth; seventh grade: Middletown; eighth grade: Gore; ninth grade: Hadley High School in Winchester, Virginia. For a while the family was also in Norfolk, where Sam was employed by the Naval Shipyard during World War II. Along the way, Hilda gave birth to Sam, Jr., while Ginny was in the second grade, and when she was in sixth grade, her sister Sylvia Mae arrived.

The only class she didn't get a "D-minus" in while in eighth grade was geography. Having moved all over the state of Virginia, Ginny had become quite adept at reading a map.

During the Depression, unclaimed empty homes were easy enough to come by. Amid this era the Hensley family's residences were all rundown, abandoned houses that Hilda became quite adept at decorating. She found that she could work wonders with a little bit of paint and some dime store wallpaper. Hilda's sister Nellie recalls, "We always looked up to them [the Hensleys] because they had everything nice, but they were up to here in owing. They would move sometimes two or three times a year into some big, old house that had sat empty. But Hilda was a great artist when it came to making a room quite livable. She'd make slipcovers for the sofa and chairs. She's a good carpenter. She wasn't lazy. She'd work her heart out."

What was it that drove Sam to move so frequently? Was it his drinking problem? Was it something that happened outside of the home that he was trying to hide, or was it something that was going on under his own roof that he wanted to hide from the gossiping townspeople?

According to several of Patsy's adult friends and confidantes, from the time she was eleven, she was forced to have sex with her father. Songwriters Mae Boren Axton and Don Hecht, as well as Loretta Lynn, all confirm that Patsy revealed to them the incestuous situation that haunted her. When filmmaker Bernard Schwartz was preparing his production of Sweet Dreams for the screen, Hilda opened up to him about the taboo subject of incest. She wanted to set the record straight so that people would fully understand the demons Patsy wrestled with during her young life. In a recent conversation with Bernard Schwartz, he confirmed that the rumored incidents were quite real in Patsy's life. According to Hecht, Patsy spoke in confidence to him of "frequent experiences." What an emotional weight this must have been for eleven-year-old Ginny to have to deal with.

Once Hilda realized what was going on, her bond with Ginny became even tighter. It was truly a matter of them against Sam, for their own protection.

Amid this personal trauma, Ginny kept her eye on her goals. According to her, "The one thing that I wanted to do more than anything was sing country music. One day I got real brave and decided it was time for me to do what I wanted to do."

By the time she was thirteen, she was obsessed with the idea of becoming a country singer. She already knew she could sing, as she had impressed the congregation at the Gore Baptist Church with her duets with Hilda. Through her quest to immerse herself in music, she had become an avid fan of a local Saturday morning radio program hosted by Joltin' Jim McCoy on Winchester station WINC. Although it was only a 250 watt station at the time, it was the only important station in the little town of ten thousand. From 9:00 A.M. until noon every Saturday, Joltin' Jim and His Melody Playboys would present a show comprised of hillbilly and cowboy tunes. Among the country stars Ginny would have heard on the radio in those days were Tex Ritter, Ernest Tubb, Roy Rogers, Gene Autry,

Bob Wills and His Texas Playboys, and Patsy Montana. As well as serving as one of the station's disk jockeys, McCoy had his own band with whom he performed live on the radio.

"I used to sing or hum along with the recordings I'd hear on the radio. One day I got real brave and walked into the Winchester radio station at the hour a hillbilly band was being featured," Patsy would later recount. "I found the musicians and asked who the leader was. This big fellow came out and looked at me and replied, 'I'm the leader. What can I do for you?'"

"You're Joltin' Jim McCoy?" she replied.

"Yes," McCoy answered, "Who are you?"

"Virginia Hensley from here in Winchester. I listen to your show all the time. I'm a singer and I want to sing on your show."

At first, McCoy couldn't believe her sense of bravado. He remembers, "I was impressed with her naïveté and determination—and nerve. I was polite and listened to what she had to say."

According to him, she answered, "If you give me a chance to sing with you on the radio, I'll never ask for pay."

When he answered, "Honey, you think you're good enough to sing with us live on the radio?" she looked him dead in the eye and replied, "Yes, sir."

Joltin' Jim decided right then and there that if this fourteen-year-old girl had nerve enough to ask him for her first broadcasting break, he was just daring enough to do it.

When Ginny opened her mouth and began singing, McCoy was astonished at what he had heard. He recalled, "As soon as I heard Patsy, I realized this girl meant business. I thought to myself, 'Someday this gal is gonna be a star.'"

Philip Whitney, the station manager at WINC found her to be a bit green, but her natural talent was undeniable. "When she first came to the station," he recalled, "she was just a youngster and very quiet, the wide-eyed type. She wasn't very good and her inexperience was obvious. But she was willing to work and she worked like the devil. She developed a good style and really labored on it. She always wanted advice and took it seriously."

Having pulled off this little stunt filled Ginny with a major boost of self-confidence. Already she had her sights set on bigger things. According to Patsy, "The way I looked at it, if I wanted to go to

Nashville and be on the *Grand Ole Opry*—the earlier I got started the better! So I used to sing or hum along with just about every song I'd hear on the *Opry* shows."

In 1947, things finally hit rock bottom in the Hensley household. Whether it was Sam's drinking, or the fact that Hilda finally caught on to Sam forcing Ginny to have sex with him, is unclear. Although Hilda would never talk about the specifics, sometime during Ginny's sophomore year in high school, Sam deserted the family. For Ginny and Hilda, this was a big relief. Faced with the prospect of having no family income, Ginny quit school so that she could earn money to help support the family. She was fifteen at the time, her brother only eight, and Sylvia was four years old.

According to Hilda, "I don't know what we would have done if it hadn't been for Patsy. It was terrible that she had to leave school, but there was no other way we could have made ends meet. Patsy considered it a family obligation."

At first Virginia had to lie about her age to gain employment. Her first job was slaughtering chickens at Rockingham Poultry down the road from where her family lived, a rundown section of Kent Street. She began work and was happy to have a job—until her true age was discovered and she was fired. When Ginny tearfully explained her plight, the foreman took pity on her and gave her two weeks notice to find another job.

Her next position was behind the counter at the local Greyhound Bus station. Not long afterward, she persuaded the owners of the neighborhood drugstore to give her a job. Hunter Gaunt and his wife knew Ginny and her family, and empathized with her plight. Much to her relief, the Gaunts offered her a position behind the soda fountain. She was paid seventy-five cents per hour for scooping ice cream and making cherry Cokes.

Dressed in her white outfit, rolled down white bobby socks and a pair of loafers, Ginny would serve customers, and talk with them about her career aspirations. She was a well-liked, fun-loving, wisecracking girl. One of her girlhood friends, Pat Smallwood, remembers Ginny announcing to her one day at Gaunt's Drugstore, "You know, I'm gonna be something one of these days. I won't be doing this for the rest of my life." That was for certain!

"Patsy was really dedicated to becoming a serious singer and worked at that goal without let up," Hilda recalled. She also remembered people warning Ginny what a hard road she had ahead of her if she wanted to entertain the idea of becoming a star. They told her of all of the potential disappointments that were likely to materialize, but she was undeterred: "That didn't faze Patsy," said her mother. "Knowing her, it probably made her all the more determined!"

There was no sense in arguing with her, so Hilda decided to help her daughter achieve her dreams any way she could. With Ginny's inner drive, there was never the need for Hilda to play "stage mother" to her daughter. More often than not, she found herself playing Ethel Mertz to Ginny's Lucille Ball.

Hilda figured that if her daughter was going to stubbornly insist on becoming a singer, it would be easier to assist her than it would be to talk her out of it. She knew of a Winchester piano player named Ralph "Jumbo" Rinker, who played in a supper club called the Melody Lane, just across the state line—in Martinsburg, West Virginia. One evening she and Ginny got dressed up and drove to Martinsburg and showed up at the Melody Lane. They walked in and walked up to the bar where Jumbo was sitting while taking a musicians' break. Jumbo had a distinctive look. Short, pudgy, and married, although he was only twenty-seven years old, his hair was thick, wavy, and prematurely white.

"You Jumbo Rinker?" Hilda asked him without missing a beat. "I'm Hilda Hensley and this is my daughter Virginia. Would you do me a favor? Would you play a couple of songs and let Virginia sing. She's trying to get in the music business."

Although he was a bit startled by Hilda's directness, he agreed. He didn't know any of the country songs that Ginny named for him, so she selected something that she knew from his song list. "Want to try that?" Rinker asked, "You have nothing to lose. Everybody's having fun—they won't care. I'll start out and you just jump in." That was all the encouragement Virginia needed. Although she wanted to sing country music, she felt confident with familiar pop standards as well. Her ability to sing both, and capture two kinds of audiences, was always one of the keys to her wide reaching appeal.

"On Saturdays I worked all day in Hunter Gaunt's drugstore in Winchester, and then at night, my mother drove me to Front Royal, where I sang pop tunes in a supper club from 10:00 P.M. to 1:00 A.M.," Patsy recalled of this era. "Mother would come and pick me up at work and take me whenever I could get a job. We only had the one car, so Mom either had to stay with me the whole night or drop me off and come get me later. Jumbo Rinker and Kenneth Windle played for me then, but Mother didn't trust anybody with me. Usually we'd get home about three in the morning—totally exhausted. A few hours later I was up and getting ready for work and Mom was fixing breakfast for the kids. And, you know something, we loved every minute of it!"

This became quite a pattern for Virginia. Her real money came from Gaunt's Drugstore, and her singing engagements were mainly for experience. Along the way, Ginny developed quite a crush on Jumbo. Since Jumbo was already married, Hilda felt confident that things couldn't get too out of hand between them. She was, however, wrong. What she didn't take into account was the fact that Ginny always attracted men. Ginny and Jumbo would carry on a secret, ongoing affair for several years to come.

In 1948, an amateur talent contest was held at the Palace Theater in Winchester. It was such a big deal that WINC broadcast the entire event live over the radio. The first prize was $5, the second $3, and third prize was $2. Ginny decided to enter the contest and sing her rendition of "Yankee Doodle Dandy." She wore a colorful creation that looked like something the Rockettes would wear in a Fourth of July spectacular. It consisted of a short red and white striped skirt, a cutaway jacket with tails and a striped collar, fishnet stockings, and high heels. To top it all off, she wore a top hat that was also red and white stripes. For Winchester in the late 1940s, this was a bit on the risqué side, especially for a sixteen year old, but that was Ginny—right down to the bright red lipstick. Evidently Ginny knew what was best for her: she took first prize that afternoon.

Later that same year, at Winchester's Capitol Theater, a regional audition for the national television show *Original Amateur Hour* was held. For this presentation Ginny sang a song from Show Boat, dressed in jeans and a western-style jacket. This time around a ten-year-old tap dancing whiz took first prize. However, Ginny knew that every performance was important when you are young and your heart is hooked on a dream.

Her next theatrical experience came at the annual Winchester minstrel show held at the local high school. She auditioned and immediately received a spot on the program, singing the song "Oklahoma." In addition to her passion for country music, Ginny also loved big, broad, show-stopping Broadway tunes. She began to make dramatic, Broadway-like song endings one of her main interpretive trademarks.

In addition to the theatricality of her singing style, Ginny also came to rely on her trademark flashy stage costumes. Since Hilda was an experienced seamstress, Virginia relied on her mother as her personal costumer. To help make ends meet, Hilda also took on sewing jobs that she could do in the house while keeping an eye on younger children.

In 1948, a Winchester man named Jack Fretwell came to visit Ginny and her mother at their house on Kent Street with a business proposition for the sixteen-year-old aspiring singer. There was a new nightclub on the edge of town called the York Inn, and the Jack Fretwell Orchestra was going to be the house band on Saturday nights. Jack needed a female singer to complete the act, and he had heard that Ginny was the best undiscovered vocalist that Winchester had to offer. Virginia and Hilda quickly accepted his proposition. To accomplish the proper effect, Hilda created a slinky outfit with a slit skirt, befitting a nightclub chanteuse. To top it off, Ginny wore her hair slightly draped over one eye in the "peek-a-boo" style of actress Veronica Lake. While the orchestra played, she'd sing songs like "Stardust" and "Embraceable You." However, it was "You Made Me Love You (I Didn't Want to Do It)" that was her real showpiece.

The owner of the club, Alfred deMazzon, was a classy restaurateur from Venice, Italy. He took an instant liking to Ginny, and he offered her additional money to be the club's "cigarette girl." She'd wear a skimpy costume, fishnet stockings, and high heels, and sell packs of cigarettes from table to table to the patrons. Then, when showtime came, she'd go and change her outfit, and come back as the featured singer.

Throughout all of these career-building experiences, there was only one person who always stood by her side, drove her to gigs, and looked out for her: Hilda. Ginny was the undisputed star of the family, but if it wasn't for her mother's devotion and encouragement, stardom might never have been hers.

Patsy was later to recount, "If I made a list of the people I admire, Mom would probably fill up half of it. She could do anything and everything. And she'd do it for me. She was the one person I could depend on. She never once let me down. I would never have gone anywhere if it hadn't been for Mother's faith and support."

Chapter Three

NASHVILLE

Hilda Hensley was busy making dinner, but she could tell that Ginny was up to something by the way she came up beside her and put her arm around her. Sure enough: "Mama, Wally Fowler's at the Palace and I'm going down to the theater and see if I can get on the show," she announced.

～〜

"What! You're going to do what?" she exclaimed. But she could tell by the tone in her daughter's voice that Ginny's mind was made up, so there was no sense in arguing with her.

Hilda was well aware of who Wally Fowler was. She had heard him enough times on the radio. Wally and his Oak Ridge Quartet were broadcast on WSM every Friday night from the Ryman Auditorium in Nashville. They had been *Grand Ole Opry* stars since 1945. Fowler was so well-known for his expressive forté—Southern gospel—that he was extolled as the "Gospel King." Fowler was also renowned for having written two of Eddy Arnold's biggest hits: "Mommy, Please Stay Home with Me" and "I'll Hold You in My Heart."

Ginny also knew from listening to the weekly broadcast of *Wally Fowler's All-Night Sing* that the star would often invite singers from the audience up onstage to sing. When she left the house and headed over to the Palace Theater that night, she was bound and determined to get herself onstage with Wally Fowler. When she arrived at the backstage door, she was rudely turned away by the stage manager. After all, Fowler was a big star and he didn't have time to be bothered between shows.

Ginny was quite familiar with the setup at the Palace Theater. She knew that there were six shows that day, and there would be plenty of time backstage where she could corner Wally Fowler.

Resourceful, young Virginia Hensley simply swung into action. She just happened to know one of the girls who worked as an usher at the theater, so she went into the lobby and explained to someone in charge that she had to get an important message to her friend.

When the friend came into the lobby, Ginny explained her plan and conned the girl into letting her into the theater. Somehow the usher swept Ginny right past the ticket taker unnoticed. That task out of the way, Ginny walked right through the "house" of the theater, up to the door that led backstage, opened it, and walked right in as if she belonged there.

Cool as a cucumber, Ginny had sense enough to stay in the shadows until the right moment came. Suddenly, there was Wally Fowler in the flesh, surrounded by an entourage. Wasting not a moment, she walked right up to him and tugged at his sleeve.

"My name's Virginia Hensley and I sing," she announced.

Fowler recalled, "I turned to the fellows: 'Hey, fellows, here's a young lady says she can sing.' I felt something about her. I knew she was a little cocky, but I figured she had real confidence. So I said, 'So you think you can sing.' She says, 'Yes sir, I sure can.' She was a very cute girl, a little bit chunky. She had a bubbling, outgoing personality."

He was especially impressed with the way she looked and the

way she presented herself. "No street clothes for that kid," he recalls. "She was dressed just as pretty as you ever seen. She came for the occasion. She knew she was going to get on that stage."

He asked her if she knew "I'll Hold You in My Heart."

"Oh yes, I love it!" she exclaimed. "I can do that one."

With that, Ginny launched into her rendition of the song Wally had composed. He was totally blown away by her bravado and her vocal delivery. "This girl sang anywhere anybody would let her onstage," recalled Fowler. "That was the story she gave me, and her mother, too, later. She just loved to sing and she wasn't bashful about it either."

The format of the sets was such that Wally's first act, a hillbilly band who went by the name of the Georgia Clodhoppers, would open the show and warm up the audience, then Fowler and the more famous Oak Ridge Quartet would make their entrance to a thunderous round of applause.

Standing backstage that evening, Wally asked Ginny if she wanted to sing the song she had just done for him, in between The Georgia Clodhoppers and the Oak Ridge Quartet. He didn't have to ask her twice. Through her own moxie, she had gotten her way!

"She absolutely captivated them," Wally distinctly recalled. "She went off stage with a thunderous applause and had to come back to take a bow. The band wasn't prepared to do another song, but she went on and sang another chorus of 'I'll Hold You in My Heart.'"

After the show, Fowler told her how impressed with her he was, and that he wished her good luck with her singing aspirations. Just beaming with excitement, Ginny asked the "Gospel King" to please come home with her, or her mother would never believe what just happened. At first he politely declined her offer, but she was so excited that he changed his mind and accompanied her back to the house on Kent Street.

Ginny left Fowler standing in the living room as she went upstairs, and quietly went into her mother's bedroom. Hilda was already in bed.

According to Hilda, "She came into my room and very quietly told me 'Mama, we got company.' I said, 'What! Virginia, it's eleven o'clock.' She told me what she had done. 'It's Wally Fowler.' I replied, 'Wally Fowler! You've got to be kidding.' I got up and put a robe on. I went into the living room not knowing what I was going to find. But sure enough, there was Wally Fowler, big as life. I nearly dropped dead."

Fowler recounted the incidents of that evening, and told Hilda how impressed he was with her daughter. As Hilda listened with amazement, Fowler said, "She wants to be a singer on the *Grand Ole Opry.*"

"That's right," Hilda replied.

"She has an amazing voice. I'd like to arrange an audition for her in Nashville with WSM radio."

Ginny was so excited she could hardly stand still, and poor Hilda didn't know what to make of all of this. She partially believed that—nice as he was—Mr. Fowler was just talking off the cuff, and nothing would transpire. When he left that evening he claimed that they would be hearing from him again.

Hilda was skeptical, but Ginny pinned her hopes on being invited to audition for the *Grand Ole Opry.* Hilda especially didn't want her daughter to be hurt if the call never came.

"If Mr. Fowler came over here from the theater, he must have liked the way I sing," Ginny kept announcing.

Finally, several weeks later, the phone rang. Wally Fowler wanted to know if Hilda could get Virginia to Nashville to audition for Jim Denny, the general manager of the *Grand Ole Opry.* Wally told her that he would call back with an exact date and time when Denny could see her. When he called back again, an upcoming Friday morning at 9:00 A.M.—sharp—was agreed upon. There was just one obstacle however. The family car could barely make it twenty miles to the West Virginia border. How was it going to get all the way to Nashville, eight hundred miles away?

Ginny's only dream was to become a professional singer, and Hilda recognized the fact that her daughter was indeed talented. She also realized that Ginny's singing career could be the financial salvation the family so desperately needed. Hilda was determined to make sure this was not a missed opportunity!

When Hilda explained the dilemma to a neighbor, the woman sensed the urgency in Hilda's voice, and volunteered to drive them there herself. Ginny took off a single day from the Gaunt's drugstore.

Unfortunately, there was no one to look after Sam, Jr. and Sylvia Mae—who were eight and four at the time—so they piled them in the car as well.

Patsy was later to look back on this comedy of errors and explain, "When I first came to Nashville in 1948, I drove in with my mother, sister, [brother,] and a friend of the family. We shared expenses. I didn't even have enough money to rent a hotel room. The night before we were to audition we stopped outside town at a picnic site and spent the night sleeping on a concrete bench."

They left on Thursday evening. The picnic area where Ginny and party stopped was just outside of the Nashville city limits. Laughs Hilda, "I have no idea what the poor people passing by at that hour of the morning must have thought. Looking back, however, it was funny. Then it was a mess! A real mess!"

After Ginny had her brief nap on the bench of a concrete picnic table, the five pilgrims continued on their journey toward the country music mecca of Nashville. When they got closer to their destination, they stopped at an Esso gas station and piled into the ladies room. The kids had to go to the bathroom and Ginny hastily changed into a nice dress and applied her make-up.

When the car arrived in downtown Nashville, Ginny caught her first glimpse of the famous Ryman Auditorium. She knew right then and there, that this was where she belonged!

Wally Fowler, who was not in Nashville that day, instructed them to be at Jim Denny's office promptly at 9:00 A.M. They followed his instructions to the tee.

Both Ginny and her mother were well aware of what a venerable institution the *Grand Ole Opry* was. Radio station WSM and the *Grand Ole Opry* each dated back to 1925. The radio station, which began broadcasting on October 5 of that year was, and is, owned by the National Life and Accident Insurance Company. Its call letters were derived from the company's advertisement slogan: "We Shield Millions."

In Chicago, on mega-station WLS, there was a country music program called *The WLS Barn Dance*. Since George D. Hay, the station manager of WSM, had previously worked at WLS, he copied the winning formula and christened a similar Nashville program, *The WSM Barn Dance*, which began broadcasting on November 28,

1925. Two years later, Hay jokingly referred to the popular program as *The Grand Ole Opry*, and the name has stuck.

The site that the *Grand Ole Opry* radio program originated from has changed several times over the years. At first it came directly from the broadcasting studios of WSM. However, the popularity and demand for tickets to attend the broadcasts grew so rapidly it had to be moved. A new studio that could accommodate an audience of five hundred was constructed especially for the *Opry*. It wasn't long before that too was outgrown. Three subsequent moves, and the imposition of a twenty-five cent admission fee, did not stop *Opry* fans from swarming. Finally, in 1943, a move was made to a former church, the Ryman Auditorium. Located on Fourth Avenue and lower Broadway, the Ryman was the broadcast's home until 1974, when it again moved to a larger facility. (Refurbished in the 1990s, the Ryman is still a Nashville landmark, actively used for entertainment events.)

In addition to weekly guests, the *Grand Ole Opry* had a list of regular performers Ginny was used to hearing every week. At the time they included comedienne Minnie Pearl, Roy Acuff, Mother Maybelle Carter and the Carter Family, Texas Ruby and the Fox Hunters, Whitey Ford, and the duo of Lester Flatt and Earl Scruggs.

Ginny's audition that day was set to take place on the fifth floor of the National Life Insurance's offices. The second hand of the clock had barely brushed past the number twelve at nine o'clock that Friday morning when Hilda Hensley asked the receptionist for Jim Denny. They were slightly taken aback when they were informed that Denny was involved in some important business and would be detained. Undeterred, the mother and daughter team had a seat, and began reviewing some of the music they had prepared for the much anticipated meeting.

Finally, Jim Denny, a stocky "good ole boy" of a man, arrived and introduced himself. Hilda immediately noted Denny's lack of enthusiasm, as though he had been roped into this obligatory "audition" as a favor to Wally Fowler. Wally was later to admit that this was indeed the case, and that the chances of this audition succeeding were small at best—especially since Ginny was under eighteen. However, Ginny was so excited, and gushed so enthusiastically about how honored she was to be there and how much the *Grand Ole Opry* meant to her, that Denny began to defrost.

He led Hilda and sixteen-year-old Virginia into one of the musician's rehearsal studios in the building, and introduced them to star piano player Moon Mullican. Ginny recognized his name from his *Opry* appearances. Billed as "the king of hillbilly piano players," he supposedly had the ability to "play the moon around anyone."

Well, Mullican had met his vocal match, because even at that early age, Virginia Hensley could assuredly sing rings around Saturn. She launched into several of her favorite songs, and obviously impressed Jim Denny. Not an overly emotional man, Denny admitted that he liked what he heard, but asked Hilda if she and Virginia could remain in Nashville a few days longer, so that some other people could hear her as well. Before Hilda could give him an answer, another gentleman appeared at the rehearsal studio door, inquiring as to who he had just heard singing.

Well, you could have knocked Ginny over with a feather, because that man was none other than country legend Roy Acuff! While she was singing, he had been in an adjacent room preparing things for his 12:00 broadcast of "Noon-Time Neighbors."

Mullican dove right in and said "Roy, I want you to meet Miss Virginia Hensley, from Winchester, Virginia. And, this is her mother. Ya'll this is Roy Acuff."

This was almost too much for the young, aspiring singer. Not only did Acuff tell her that she possessed one of the sweetest voices he had ever heard, he asked her if she would perform on that day's *Noon-Time Neighbors* program. Virginia graciously accepted, barely able to keep herself from screaming and jumping up and down with elation.

"Well, we nearly dropped. It was hard to believe. There we were talking to Roy Acuff!" Patsy was later to recount of her excitement at that very minute.

On Acuff's program that noon, Virginia Hensley made her WSM radio debut. To top it all off, Mullican again accompanied her on the piano. That event alone was worth the eight-hundred-mile roadtrip to Nashville. She couldn't wait to tell all of the skeptics back in Winchester about this!

When it was over Acuff congratulated Ginny on a job well-done, and wished her all the luck in the world. Jim Denny, although impressed, was not one to just sign new talent on the spot. He informed Hilda again that he would need some more time to assess Virginia's talent. Unfortunately, his compliments were not accompanied by phrases like "and we'll pick up the tab on a hotel room" or "we'll cover your expenses."

Seconds dragged on like hours as Hilda struggled to find some solution to the dilemma she now faced. Ginny had to be back at work at Gaunt's Drugstore tomorrow morning, and the neighbor had to return to Winchester that night as planned. She and Ginny could take the bus back home, but again there was the matter of no money. What could she possible do?

According to Hilda, "I was standing there attempting to sort out in my mind how Patsy might be able to stay the night so Mr. Denny would have the time to do what he needed to do. Everything looked so positive. It also looked like whatever Mr. Denny wanted to do would take a while. Things began to drag into the afternoon and still there was no definite word. It just did not appear possible for us to stay."

After discussing their options, Ginny and Hilda mutually agreed that they didn't have any choice. They simply had to get back in the car and return to Winchester as planned. After all, if Jim Denny was really that impressed, surely they would phone Ginny back in Winchester, and further arrangements could be made.

On the drive back to Winchester, Hilda was pleased to see how maturely Virginia had taken the news—or lack thereof. Over and over again she kept telling her mother, "After all, Mama: Wally Fowler, Moon Mullican, and Roy Acuff thought I was great!"

Days of waiting turned into weeks, and weeks into months. Unfortunately, this was the phone call that was never to come. In retrospect, it is easy to say that Jim Denny was the kind of man who wouldn't know a superstar-in-the-rough if one walked up and bit him. Not long before Virginia Hensley's audition, he had passed up the opportunity of signing an unknown named Hank Williams to the *Opry*. And, in 1954, following an *Opry* debut performance, he told an ambitious young man that he'd be better off going back to his job driving a truck. The aspiring truck driver's name was Elvis Presley.

"Nothing happened. No one volunteered to do anything," Hilda was later to sniff. "We never heard from anyone. Not a letter or call from Mr. Denny or anyone. They let us down. I guess we expected better treatment than that."

Never one to sit around and wait for things to happen, Virginia continued to work at Gaunt's Drugstore by day, and pursue her dreams of musical stardom at night. In addition to her other gigs in and around Winchester, she joined a musical group known as Gene Shiner's Metronomes. She was the lead singer for the group, for the four short months they performed together.

Of Virginia Hensley's song repertoire at the time, WINC disk jockey Jim McCoy recalls, "She wasn't country really. Her love of pop is what made her what she is today. There were very few songs she did that were strictly country."

Ginny continued to sing in nightclubs and roadhouses, literally anywhere there was a stage and an audience. Jumbo Rinker was still her most steady musical accompanist. Also, in spite of the fact that Jumbo was married, he continued his infatuation with Virginia.

By the time she was seventeen, Ginny was engaged for a short time to a childhood friend named Elias Blanchfield. Before that, she dated a boy by the name of Ray Horner. However, she always seemed to magnetically return to her on and off flirtation with Jumbo Rinker.

Jumbo recalls of this era, "I'd call Ginny up, 'Whatareya doin'?' 'Nothin'." I had an old piano and she'd come over and sing, and we'd cut up and have us a real good time. Then we got to smoochin'. We got to be real close buddies. Course I was still madly in love with my wife. But Ginny was filling in the void in my life. And we could relate through our music. She was very kindhearted. Did things for me that were uncalled for."

She'd do things like buy him a carton of his favorite cigarettes, which, considering her meager income, was pretty extravagant. To reciprocate, he'd take her out on one adventure after another. They'd go out riding motorcycles together, or he'd take her flying in a private plane, as he was an accomplished pilot. She never had a fear of flying in small private planes, especially if one of her buddies was behind the throttle. In addition to seeing Jumbo, occasionally she would go out with Elias Blanchfield. She had known him since childhood, and he was always a supportive friend she could trust.

Her mother recalls that Ginny was never afraid of performing in some pretty rough places, where amorous advances from liquor-fueled patrons were something to be on the lookout for. According to former Metronome bass player Johnny Anderson, "Patsy knew when to turn it on and when to turn it off. Oh, I heard her cuss people out. If some guy would come and try to make time with her, she'd tell him to go to hell and get lost. She didn't mess around."

Virginia had a genuine way of connecting with everyone in her audiences. With a great figure, and a flair for tight dresses, she was quite adept at catching men's eyes. On the other hand, her songs were so often songs of love and heartbreak, performed so sincerely that she held the women's attentions as well.

When 1952 began, twenty-one-year-old Virginia Hensley was still singing her heart out while listening to the *Grand Ole Opry* on the radio, but she was still singing pop songs and standards. Four years rolled by with Virginia continuing to sing in public every opportunity she had. She never once lost sight of her dreams of Nashville. Her next major break came not with the *Grand Ole Opry*, but with a bandleader named Bill Peer. He was the one who took her from floundering as a pop-singing chanteuse, and transformed her into a real "country" singer.

At the time there were three molds that female country singers and entertainers came from:

- "hillbilly comedienne" mode, which Minnie Pearl and actress Judy Canova personified,
- "homespun Appalachian gals" like Maybelle Carter, and
- "cowgirls" like yodeling Patsy Montana and Hollywood's glamorous Dale Evans.

It was Bill Peer who was responsible for orchestrating the distinctive first half of Patsy Cline's professional career, turning her into the original "rhinestone cowgirl." He changed her name, changed her look, and steered her into her first recording contract.

In 1952, a new singer named Kitty Wells came to Nashville with a huge number one country smash, "It Wasn't God Who Made Honky Tonk Angels." It was unique at the time, as it was the first country smash that expressed the woman's side of a love affair.

Suddenly a musical door opened up in early fifties, male-dominated country music. It was a door that Virginia Hensley became obsessed with walking through.

By day, Bill Peer was in the automotive business. Among other related positions, he was employed as a car salesman at the local Buick and Cadillac dealership in Martinsburg, West Virginia, where he lived with his wife, Jenny, and their two children.

By night Bill was the leader of Bill Peer and His Melody Boys and Girls. His music was defined as country swing, which is a lively, rhythmic, dance-oriented hybrid of country music, which grew out of the forties big band style. He also performed onstage in full cowboy attire, from the boots to the hat. Peer and his group performed all over the area—from West Virginia, to Virginia and Maryland. In the early 1950s Bill's gig was the every-Saturday-night engagement he had at the Moose Hall in Brunswick, Maryland.

Jumbo Rinker recalls that Virginia Hensley begged him to introduce her to Bill Peer. At the time, Peer was the biggest and most popular local bandleader. He had a solid reputation and a strong following. Jumbo knew Bobby Carper—who played the steel guitar in Bill's band—from his day job in a Winchester auto repair shop. Jumbo finally relented.

When Bill Peer first met Virginia Hensley he was impressed with her looks. He had heard she could sing. She didn't ask him for an "audition" per se; in her typical fashion she just asked him point blank if she could sing with his band. She also told him of her dreams of becoming a star on The *Grand Ole Opry*. He told her, "Okay, young lady, if you want to get to Nashville, I'll help you. First you get some material ready and then we'll get serious."

When Virginia Hensley showed up at the Brunswick Moose Hall on Saturday, September, 27, 1952, she came fully prepared, all the way down to the outfit. When she had sung "Yankee Doodle Dandy" in the amateur contest, she was all stars and stripes. When she was performing at the York Inn supper club, it was a slit skirt and a seductive hairdo. But at the Moose Hall that night it was cowgirl fringe, cowgirl boots, and the whole nine yards.

She arrived over an hour before the 9:00 P.M. music was scheduled to start. She walked right up to Bill Peer and said, "Hey there, you remember me?"

"I sure do," he said, visibly impressed.

"Well, I'm ready," she announced in her cocky fashion.

"We'll see about that," he replied.

When Virginia opened her mouth to sing she left no doubt in anyone's mind that she meant business. Bill Peer was totally impressed by what he heard that night. Right on the spot he asked her to join his band, and she accepted just as quickly.

However, he told her that she had to do something about her name, as it was totally devoid of any of that show business dazzle that a star should have. "Virginia" was too staid, "Ginny" to quaint. When he asked her what her middle name was, she said "Patterson."

Instantly, the image of Patsy Montana came to mind—cowgirl fringe and all.

"How about 'Patsy Hensley?'" Peer asked.

She agreed that she liked the sound, and from that point on she was always known as "Patsy."

Jenny Peer saw the whole thing from the sidelines. She had gotten used to the fact that her husband chased women. Just by the way Bill looked at Patsy she could tell what was going on, and so could all of the members of his band.

On the outside it was the old Pygmalion routine, with Patsy playing "Eliza Doolittle" to Bill's "Henry Higgins." He bought her western clothes and jewelry and made suggestions about her act and her singing. But underneath the tutor/student facade, Bill was falling in love with his young new creation.

Eleven years older than Patsy, there was no question that he was more in love with her than she would ever be with him. Patsy was no dummy. She knew that she was being actively pursued by an older man who was in a position to turn around her entire career. When Bill flirted, Patsy flirted right back.

Jenny recalled warning her husband. "I told Bill when she came along, 'Be careful. She's just going to use you. She'll stay with you until the opportunity she wants comes along.' But of course, he didn't listen. He just fell in love. And love is blind."

Two weeks after her debut with Bill Peer's ensemble, someone else who would change Virginia Hensley's name walked into the Brunswick Moose Hall. He was one of the most unlikely candidates for romance, but nonetheless, that's what Gerald Cline got when he encountered the newly renamed "Patsy."

She had just finished her first set with Bill Peer that night, and was on her break when a 220-pound man standing, five-foot-eight came up to her and said, "Hi, I'm Gerald Cline, and I think you're fantastic."

"My, you're quite a big man," Patsy fired back at him.

"Yeah, and I got a fast car," he said.

"Which of you is the fastest?"

"Want me to show you?" he asked.

Divorced and employed by his father's construction business, Gerald was a bit of a lazy dreamer. At the age of twenty-nine, Cline was an old man compared to a live wire like Patsy.

You might say that Patsy's "dance card" was quite full those last four months of 1952. Although she was not "in love" with Bill Peer, she relented to his sexual advances and began a physical affair with him because of what he could do for her professionally. Like Jumbo, Bill Peer was an unlikely Romeo. Skinny and not much taller than Patsy, Bill was known for being quite a ladies man. The fact that he was married—with children—did nothing to deter either of them from having an affair.

33

One of Peer's band members, guitar player Roy Deyton, confirms, "He kept chasing her and just got to her at a weak moment. He was a way to catapult her somewhere. We knew she was never serious about Bill. There was something else in her life and it was her desire to do music—she was so determined that she would use whatever means were at her disposal to get there. And she wasn't the type to hold back you know? If someone was willing to offer her help, I guess she was willing to go as far as she had to go, like a lot of girls in the movies. That's the way it was and she just did what she had to do."

Patsy's mother was furious with her for having an affair with a married man, even if it would advance her career. She refused to attend any of Patsy's appearances with Bill Peer at the Brunswick Moose Hall just to demonstrate her fury.

Even if two wrongs don't make a right, Patsy also began having an affair with Gerald Cline. He drove a big Buick, dressed nicely, and spent money like he had a good supply of it. In her mind, she could kill two birds with two stones. Both men were in love with her: one could advance her career and the other could support it financially.

Among other things, Gerald Cline represented Patsy's potential ticket out of Winchester, Virginia. By this point, she didn't exactly have a sterling moral reputation in her hometown. She had an on-and-off affair with one married man—Jumbo Rinker, was sleeping with another married man—Bill Peer, and was carrying on with a divorced man who was nine years older than her—Gerald Cline.

She admitted to her girlfriends that she was not in love with Cline, but the arrangement seemed to make sense and she figured that in time she would come to love him. Gerald was completely infatuated with Patsy. He even began working on charming her mother by showing up at the house on Kent Street with bags full of groceries. His plan worked. Hilda felt that her daughter was much better off with Gerald than she was carrying on shamelessly with Bill Peer.

In December 1952, Patsy made the startling announcement that she and Gerald were engaged to be married. By marrying Gerald she could buffer Bill Peer's affection toward her and gain some financial security. She was determined to make her career work, and these were the two men who were going to help her get what she wanted.

In an unelaborate ceremony held on Saturday, March 7, 1953, Virginia "Patsy" Hensley married Gerald Cline. The ceremony was performed by Ellis Watcher, who was the Circuit Court Clerk for Frederick County, Maryland. The couple rented a small apartment in Frederick, Maryland.

After the ceremony, there was a party for Patsy and her new husband at the Brunswick Moose Hall. That night Patsy got up to sing with Bill Peer's Melody Boys and Girls, just as if it was any other Saturday night.

Fay Crutchley and her husband were there that evening. Fay knew Gerald, but had never met Patsy nor had she seen her perform. Gerald sat down at the Crutchley's table, and they all sat mesmerized by the girl who was up onstage singing her heart out in the fringed cowgirl get-up.

"Who is that fantastic singer?" Fay asked Gerald. "You always know everyone—at least, all the pretty girls."

He turned to her and announced for the very first time, "That's Patsy Cline."

Chapter Four

A Cowgirl Singer

Caught up in a crazy love triangle, the whole dynamic of Patsy's marriage to Gerald was odd from the very beginning. It is obvious that the only reason she was interested in him was for her own security. Likeable and seemingly well-off, Gerald was a comfortable choice for her.

Her entire vision of men and marriage was already skewed simply by what the past had shown her. The experience with her own father made her feel like a victim. Now fully grown up, she made certain that it was she who was always in control of when an affair began, and when it ended. Gerald represented a safe father figure to her, and he fulfilled that role. It left her free to use her charms to keep Bill Peer interested in her, knowing that he could advance her career.

In a very real way, Patsy's marriage to Gerald made things quite convenient for Bill. On several occasions the Peers and the Clines went out together while Bill still carried a torch for Patsy. At the beginning of their marriage, Gerald would accompany Patsy on several of her out-of-town engagements. Everyone who met them as a pair around this time thought that they made the oddest of couples. Patsy was always so full of life and enthusiasm; Gerald was likeable but very low-key.

Since Nashville was Patsy's self-defined target, Bill felt that they might as well storm into "Music City" and make some noise to draw attention to her. On April 10, 1953, Jenny and Bill Peer and Gerald and Patsy Cline piled into Gerald's big Buick and drove the eight hundred miles to Nashville for the weekend. The two couples stayed at the Colonial Motel, and even had adjoining rooms. How convenient indeed, especially since Bill's affair with Patsy continued.

It would have been next to impossible for Gerald not to have known about Patsy's affair with Bill Peer. As time went on, he simply accepted it as fact and effortlessly turned the other cheek. This only served to make the whole affair all the more scandalous!

Anxious to please Patsy, Bill set up the whole trip. He just happened to know the famous Ernest Tubb from the club circuit, which entitled them to receive the red carpet treatment this time around. Not only was Ernest one of the stars of the *Grand Ole Opry*, but he also owned a famous Nashville record store. Saturday nights at midnight Tubb was the host of his own WSM radio show that was broadcast from the back of the record store. Bill turned their weekend in Nashville into quite a memorable trip. Not only did they get to watch the entire *Grand Ole Opry* show from the backstage wings, but afterwards they were ushered over to the Ernest Tubb Record Shop only a block away from the Ryman. To top it all off, Ernest invited Patsy to be his guest on that evening's broadcast of *The Ernest Tubb Mid-Nite Jamboree*; performing two songs on the show with him. It was a very successful "goodwill" trip for Patsy and her newly appointed manager Bill Peer.

When the foursome returned from Nashville, there were several weekends when Jenny and Gerald would join their spouses at the

Brunswick Moose Hall on Saturday nights. On a couple of occasions, after the evening was over and the band equipment was packed up, the Clines and the Peers would drive to an all-night Chinese restaurant in Hagerstown, Maryland. However, it wasn't long before Gerald totally lost interest and began to send Patsy on her own. Since Jenny had the two kids at home to take care of, her appearances at Bill and Patsy's club dates became less frequent as well. Jenny noticed that on several occasions when she didn't come along, Bill's story of what happened last Saturday night differed from what Patsy had told her. Jenny was later to admit that she was oblivious to what was really going on during this era. She should have talked to the Melody Boys.

In front of the band, Patsy and Bill weren't doing a very good job of covering up the fact that their affair had moved off the back burner, and was back in the forefront. At the time, Patsy's relationship with the members of Bill Peer's band was always very upbeat, and they recall her as being "just one of the boys." She was also blasé about any eyebrows she might have raised over her obvious affair with Bill Peer. Basically, she didn't give a damn about anyone else's opinion.

It wasn't long before Patsy's relationship with Gerald had cooled off all together. Although he bought her a two-toned red and white Buick Roadmaster Coupe—their marriage was going nowhere fast.

"I guess I thought I loved him or something, but he's so dull," she complained to her friend Pat Smallwood. He was completely indifferent as far as her "career" was concerned. "Gerald acts like he couldn't care less whether I make a 'go' or whether I do anything. It's like he's disinterested," she claimed. Gerald told her several times that he would much prefer it if Patsy stayed home and cooked his meals and ironed his clothes.

If she married him for passion, she certainly made a mistake. And, if she married him for his money, again the joke was on her. Gerald's "big wealth" was derived from his position on the payroll of his father's Cline Construction Company. While he claimed he had an important job at his family's construction business, his brother Nevin remembers that Gerald rarely even bothered to show up at the office, where he held the token position of "secretary."

While Patsy was gutsy, passionate, and full of life, Gerald was perfectly content to sit at home and quietly assemble model ships, or take apart clocks and watches which he'd repair and reassemble. Speaking of her own assessment of Gerald, Pat Smallwood recalls, "Dull. 'Dull' was the word."

Part of Patsy's reasoning behind marrying Gerald was to cool off the flames of her affair with Bill. Now, for lack of passion under her own roof, she again found herself sneaking off to Bill's arms. She began looking to Peer for the affection she craved and needed. The tables turned, and she began to seek out Bill to get away from Gerald's cold indifference.

With reference to Bill Peer, Pat Smallwood proclaimed, "Now there was a man that really loved her!" Pat often found herself dragged into the middle of things. Since they didn't have a washing machine of their own, Patsy would drive across the Maryland border to her mother's house to do her laundry. Or, sometimes she would do it over at the Smallwoods.

On one occasion, Bill Peer showed up at the Smallwoods with a large giftwrapped box. "When Patsy comes home, will you give her this and tell her it's from me," he asked her.

"Are you serious?" Pat answered with genuine surprise in her voice.

"Yes," he replied with a wink.

Patsy came over to visit Pat that evening as they had planned to, and Pat announced nonchalantly, "Oh, by the way, there's a gift here for you."

"Why here?" Patsy wondered, as Pat retrieved the box from where she had stashed it behind her sofa.

After she read the card that Bill included with the box, Patsy opened the package. Much to her surprise and delight, Bill had bought her a mink stole. According to Smallwood, Patsy cherished that stole and wore it for years. She may have been married to someone else, but she certainly didn't let that get in her way.

Peer also footed the bill for a demo recording of Patsy, which was done at WINC's studios. He had his sights on bigger and better gigs for Patsy, and he was determined to land her something else she was longing for: a record deal.

In the summer of 1953, Patsy entered the National Country Music Championship Contest. The competition, which took place every year at Warrenton Fairgrounds in Fauquier County, Virginia, drew a big crowd, and this was the third year it was held. The fans would come complete with picnic tablecloths and blankets and baskets of food, and usually numbered in the vicinity of twelve thousand. Each of the contestants would have their chance at centerstage, performing in front of the same backup band. That year the band playing behind everyone was Jimmy Dean and the Texas Wildcats.

That afternoon Patsy showed up in a new red cowgirl ensemble, trimmed with white fringe and white appliques. The song she chose to sing was one of her favorites, her up-tempo version of "Bill Bailey, Won't You Please Come Home." Although she delivered a red-hot version of the song, the winner that day was bluegrass fiddler Scotty Stoneman.

"We could see how great she was," recalls Marvin Carroll, the steel guitar player for the Texas Wildcats. "But, it was a pop song, and a singer against a fiddler in that part of the country? Well, everybody knows that Virginia is bluegrass country."

On September 8, 1953, Patsy Cline turned twenty-one. Hilda threw her a big party, and Gerald and Jenny and Bill and the whole crew came over. Now that Patsy was "of age," she could not only work in bars and taverns, she could now drink in them too.

For Patsy and Bill "the big time" beckoned them, and a necessary element to building up Patsy's career encompassed recognition in the big cities. Nearby Washington, D.C., was the closest hotbed of activity, and that became Bill's next target. There were several clubs in Washington at the time that featured live country music, and served as host to the live bands who played it. There was Harry's Tavern, Captain Guy's, The Famous, The Ozark, The Boondocks, and The Rendezvous, among others.

When Bill Peer booked Patsy and the Melody Boys at The Famous, it was time to make some changes for the big-city audiences. This was to be a totally different scene from the Moose Hall in Brunswick, which didn't serve liquor and catered to a family audience. The move "uptown" included a new eye-catching "look" for Patsy. She started wearing what the boys in her band referred to as "The Outfit."

When Patsy started working with Bill Peer, her first forays in western wear were fashioned right out of the television westerns, and were nothing that couldn't be viewed by the whole family. Her original western look was very close to what Patsy Montana had worn in 1936 when she released her million-selling hit, "I Want to Be a Cowboy's Sweetheart." There is a publicity still of Montana's from the 1930s in which she is standing in front of a perfectly shaped campfire, and she had one leg up on a log. One of Patsy Cline's first publicity shots stole the whole look, and featured her with one leg up on a barrel that had her name emblazoned across it in large letters. Even her cowgirl boots had her name tooled into the leather.

"The Outfit" took the look to a whole new eye-popping dimension. It included a pair of very short white shorts, a low-cut top with fringe lining it, white boots, and a pair of fringed wrist cuffs. Around her neck she tied a rakish white scarf. The top was so brief that it exposed her bare midriff.

Leo Miller, who was the piano player in the Melody Boys, said of "The Outfit:" "She'd come out there with those shorts on and she'd stand there and shake a little bit. Well, you can imagine—the audience just about jumped through the walls!"

It was one thing when she'd wear "The Outfit" in downtown D.C., but when she came onstage in it one Saturday night at the Brunswick Moose Hall she sure sent the tassels of their Royal Order of Moose fezzes a-spinning! When some of the Moose lodge members complained, Patsy was asked not to wear that costume there again.

Patsy knew that she was on the road to bigger and better things. She became more and more outspoken and self-confident, and she loved it that way. If someone from the audience ever heckled her, she'd just yell back, "I thought I left you in the parking lot!"

Johnny Anderson, a musician with Bill Peer's band, remembers seeing Patsy driving down the street with the top of her red and white Buick rolled down, wearing bright red lipstick, rollers in her hair, and a brilliant red bandanna wrapped around her head. When she saw him she laid on the horn, waved and yelled, "Hi hoss!" just as loud and bawdy as a ranch hand.

Patsy had a reputation around Winchester for being "fast" and wild. The dangling earrings, the bright lipstick, the eye-catching clothes, and the enthusiasm she displayed for everything she did was all a bit too much for some people—especially the men. In a rural town in the mid-1950s Patsy's fashion sense was looked upon as being provocative. Her close girlfriends, however, remember her as being warm, sincere, and generous with her time and herself.

On New Year's Eve at the Brunswick Moose Hall, both Jenny and Gerald were on hand to usher in 1954 with their respective spouses. It was like one big happy family. Of the Cline's marriage, Jenny was later to comment that through her eyes at the time, Patsy and Gerald seemed as if their relationship was just like everyone else's. They would fuss and argue, and then make up again like any other husband and wife.

Over the next couple of months Patsy and Gerald had quite a few disagreements. On several of those occasions, Patsy simply went over to stay at her mother's house.

That spring, Patsy didn't think too much of it the first couple of times that she woke up feeling ill. However, as the morning sickness recurred, her suspicions drove her to seek the opinion of her doctor. Sure enough she was pregnant.

One particular Saturday in June of 1954, Patsy was just not acting like herself. That afternoon at rehearsal at the Brunswick Moose Hall, she complained that she was simply not feeling too well, and claimed to be experiencing cramps. When Fay Crutchley took her aside to find out what was wrong, she recommended that Patsy go home and rest. Her logic was that the Melody Boys and the weekend partyers at the Moose Hall could surely live without her for one night. Always the trouper, Patsy replied, "Nah, hoss, it ain't that bad. I can't miss a night's work and let my public down."

She went onstage that evening and performed as scheduled, but friends noted that she didn't appear to be her normal exciting and energetic self. In fact she complained of stomach pains and spent a great deal of time in the ladies room. When she returned, she asked her old beau Elias Blanchfield to drive her home. To her concerned friends she claimed that she suffered a miscarriage. They offered her their deepest sympathies and accepted that explanation.

But losing her baby was only half of the story. In reality, Patsy had an abortion, which was performed by a woman in Winchester. She paid for it in cash, with a wad of $20 bills. Things were going too smoothly in her career for Patsy to be pregnant at this juncture. Besides, she couldn't be certain whose baby it was—Gerald's or

Bill's. No matter who the father was, having a baby now would have spelled sheer disaster for her.

In August of 1954, Patsy again entered the annual National Country Music Championship Contest in Warrenton, Virginia. This time she performed with Bill Peer and His Melody Boys behind her, and she sang the Bob Wills song "Faded Love." Dressed in another of her famous western outfits, she sang the song like there was no tomorrow, and won first prize in the competition. Not only was she awarded $100, but she also made a very valuable contact at the contest.

The emcee that afternoon was a local disk jockey and a very influential man named Connie Barriot Gay. In fact, it was Connie who organized and sponsored the event itself. He was very well-known, and quite well-connected in and around the mid-Atlantic area.

Connie Gay's radio show on WARL was called *Town and Country Time*, and it had quite a listenership. Connie also had lucrative contracts with the U.S. Army. He would record editions of his radio program on sixteen-inch diameter, $33^1/_3$-RPM transcription disks. They would be pressed in that format and distributed to 1,800 G.I. radio stations all over the world, and each side would serve as a self-contained fifteen-minute program, complete with a host who would introduce the guest stars. Usually the host of the show would be the recently established Jimmy Dean accompanied by the Texas Wildcats. Connie is in fact credited as being the first person to refer to the genre he loved as "country music," which previously had been called "hillbilly music." Very forward thinking, Connie had already produced several programs for local television, and his "Town and Country Time" television show was to country music what Dick Clark's Philadelphia-based *American Bandstand* was to rock and roll.

Patsy's rendition of "Faded Love" impressed Connie. In fact he couldn't stop talking about her. Country star Roy Clark was a guitar player with the Texas Wildcats back then, and he recalls meeting Patsy during that year. At first he found her to be shy, since she would always let Bill Peer do all of the talking for her. Although she would carry on a conversation if spoken to, she knew that this was business, and she'd rather not say anything than risk saying anything wrong.

Clark didn't meet her in Warrenton the day of the contest. He met her later at "The Famous" club in Washington, D.C., where Jimmy Dean and the Texas Wildcats were performing. Connie brought Patsy into The Famous, and said to Clark, "I have a girl singer who I want you to listen to and tell me what you think."

Roy Clark introduced Patsy Cline onstage and she told the band that she was going to perform the song "I'm Walking the Dog," which Webb Pierce made into a hit in 1950. She was wearing a black dress, and her hair was done up in a fashionable 1950s' hairdo. Since this wasn't her gig, she was dressed in a very contemporary fashion. She gave the band her key and launched into the song full force.

"Well, she literally blew the roof off the place!" Roy recalls. "She was so sure of herself—she was so good. Her singing was so positive and so powerful that you followed her. It was like we had been rehearsing forever. There was no hesitation—she led you to where she wanted to go and you wanted to go with her. She had this real gutsy sound, such a great communicating voice. I guess she sang like every girl wished she could, and probably every man."

Because of Connie's interest in Patsy, she soon had several new bookings. He hired her as the "girl singer" on dates with the Texas Wildcats, including another weekly D.C. gig at Rockwood Hall for their Wednesday night dances. He then asked her to become a "regular" on his daily three-hour radio program, which was directly followed by his daily half-hour television version of *Town and Country*.

Patsy was just what the television show needed. Lanky Jimmy Dean had a great gift of gab when you put a microphone in his hand. He handled all of the patter and the jokes, and did a great job of making his "aw shucks" kind of delivery sound genuine, although it was a bit on the corny side. Patsy's forté wasn't really in the unscripted dialogue arena. As Roy Clark pointed out, she was more comfortable letting her singing do all of the talking for her.

All of this was great for Patsy. Her guest appearances on Connie's radio and television versions of *Town and Country Time* gave her a nice base salary to supplement the $10 fee per performance she was paid with the Melody Boys and Girls. She was still supporting her mother and her younger brother and sister, so the $25 a day Connie paid her at first came in handy. Eventually she was given a raise to $50 a day for being on his radio and television broadcasts.

One of the best time capsules from that year was Patsy's first Army transcription disk that she recorded with Jimmy Dean and the Texas Wildcats. Never commercially released before, when MCA Records issued the boxed set *The Patsy Cline Collection*, they kicked off the first disk with two of Patsy's earliest recorded performances. The four-decade-old transcription disk included the following dialogue:

JIMMY: Well, sir, it's guest time here on "Town and Country Time." And, our guest is a mighty pretty girl that sings a real fine song. Here's a girl that's kind of just making a start here in country music, and sooner or later I know that you're gonna hear a whole lot about a real fine young'un by the name of Patsy Cline, and we'd like to say "hello" to her. Patsy, how are you, honey?

PATSY: Just fine.

JIMMY: You're lookin' real good.

PATSY: Why, thank you.

JIMMY: All the guys 'round here are standin' drooling down over the bibs of their overalls. As Lazy Jim Day would say, "My overall's are drawed up so my feet wouldn't touch the ground for three days." Patsy, what you gonna sing for the folks?

PATSY: I'm gonna walk a little bit of dog.

JIMMY: That's fine.

With that, Patsy launched into the peppy swing song "I'm Walking the Dog." This dialogue was typical of the "Town and Country Time" format. They kept it folksy and they kept the songs coming.

Patsy would freely choose her songs from the current country charts. "Faded Love" and "San Antonio Rose" were among her most familiar tunes. She would also pick such pop favorites as "Teach Me Tonight" and "The Wayward Wind."

With radio and television exposure now happening on a regular basis, the only thing that was missing was the elusive recording contract. That problem was about to be taken care of with the entrance of a man named Bill McCall. The good news was this was to mark the beginning of one of the most exciting recording careers of the era. The bad news was it was one of the worst deals she possibly could have signed.

In 1946, 4 Star Records, based in Pasadena, California, was on the verge of going under. It was already in "receivership" when Bill McCall plunked down $5,000 to take over the whole operation. Before he bought his way into the record business, McCall was involved in mining an element known as fluorspar, which was used in the manufacturing of inflexible shellac-based phonograph records. One of his accounts was 4 Star Records, and that's how he knew about the company as being an investment prospect.

Once he purchased the company, it didn't take Bill McCall long to learn that the real money in the record business is derived from the songwriting copyrights. Nashville was filled with struggling, young hopeful songwriters, as was Los Angeles and New York. There were dozens of aspiring Irving Berlin's out there, down to their last dime and more than willing to sign the rights away to their compositions for $25 or $30. Once McCall had a nice backlog of songs that he owned and licensed, 4 Star Records became an outlet for these songs. There were just as many struggling young singers out there dying to record their first sessions. Enter Bill Peer and his fresh young client—Patsy Cline.

In late 1953, Bill had begun paying for recording sessions for Patsy. They cut several "demo" disks meant to show off her voice. Bill sent several of them out to see if he could generate some interest from a record label. Bill McCall was among the few to even respond. He contacted Peer and offered Patsy her first recording deal.

On September 30, 1954, with Bill Peer as her signatory "witness," Patsy Cline signed her first recording contract, with 4 Star Records. Three pages in length and sixteen paragraphs in composition, it called for "a minimum of sixteen 78 r.p.m. sides, or the equivalent thereof ... and additional recordings shall be made at our election. The musical compositions to be recorded shall be mutually agreed upon between you and us, and each recording shall be subject to our approval as satisfactory." With very rare exception, that last sentence meant that Patsy was bound to only record those songs Bill McCall owned the publishing rights to.

The high standard royalty rate that was given at that time was 5 percent of the gross. There were several people who received "points" somewhere in the 2 percent to 3 percent range. Patsy's deal called for her to receive only 2.34 percent. Additionally, Patsy was to be paid $50 for each song she recorded. Several of the songs that she recorded under contract to 4 Star were done simply so she could receive her $50 check.

Two of the biggest hitches in the wording of the contract were the facts that the studio rental costs for Patsy's recording sessions and the cost of all of the musicians, were to be deducted from Patsy's percentage before she was paid. In addition, the songs were "joint accounted." In other words, if her first recordings lost money, later on down the line, when she finally scored a hit, the recording costs of the unsuccessful songs could be written off against the hit recording.

Patsy wanted nothing better than she wanted to become a singing star. When you're a hopeful singer with your heart set on stardom and you don't have a record deal, you're nowhere. Patsy wanted the opportunity to show the world her talent, so she grabbed the 4 Star deal, and at the time was glad to get it. Although she could record only 4 Star tunes, in concert she could still perform any song she cared to sing.

In late October–early November of 1954, Bill Peer, Patsy, Bill McCall, and a band of three hand-selected musicians all journeyed to New York City on a mission. Since the Melody Boys mainly had their own day jobs, Bill chose a trio to come along with them. The threesome was comprised of former Melody Boy Pete O'Brien, Leo Miller of the Legionaires, and ex-Metronome Gene Shiner. McCall wanted to go to the recording studio in New York to produce four Patsy Cline demos. The second piece of business was for her to audition for the national television program, *Arthur Godfrey's Talent Scouts*.

Bill Peer coerced the musicians into coming along on the roadtrip to New York City with the understanding that they were going to be part of the record deal, and that they were going to perform behind Patsy on the TV show. The trip was to pay for itself, because through his connections he had lined up several club dates Patsy and the band would play.

Driving in two cars from Nashville, they arrived in New York City. Bill Peer was away from his wife, so he simply reserved one room for himself and Patsy, and registered them as "Mr. and Mrs. Bill Peer." They stayed at the Dixie Hotel on 42nd Street, right in the middle of Times Square.

The first matter of business was the recording of the four demos. Bill McCall had gone to Paul Cohen, the Artists and Repertoire (A&R) director for the country division of Decca Records, to cut a licensing deal for Patsy's recordings. Paul was already famous in the country music world for signing Kitty Wells to the label. Although he had a very strong roster of male performers, he was a little bit light with women. The other two country gals he had under contract at that time were Goldie Hill and Wanda Jackson. He was impressed with Patsy's initial WINC demo, but he wanted to hear what she could come up with in a professional studio. So arrangements were made for her to lay down four songs at two of Decca's studios on West 57th Street and at 70th Street and Broadway, which was an old Knights of Pythian lodge hall that had been renovated.

Patsy and Bill Peer spent their first three days in New York reviewing the songs that Bill McCall had submitted for her to make her selections from. Not only would she be asked to record the songs as demos; she was also to learn, rehearse, and perform two of them for the Arthur Godfrey audition. The pair of songs she chose for the audition were "Turn the Cards Slowly" and "This Ole House." To reward her for all the work she was doing, Peer took her out shopping for something sophisticated and stylish to wear. The New York outfit that caused the biggest stir when she wore it back home, was a black, two-piece shoulderless number, trimmed in silver, with a dramatic chiffon sash.

Things weren't working out too well with the three musicians that Peer had selected. He had chosen them because he felt they could play the kind of country music Patsy wanted to perform. However, when they got hold of the material, they found them to be complicated pop songs rather than simple country bar band arrangements.

The TV audition was a crucial element on this trip. A spot on Godfrey's show could truly launch someone's career, especially since television sets were now in 50 percent of American homes. Already Godfrey had introduced several people to their first shot at national exposure, including Billie Holiday, Rosemary Clooney, Pat Boone, and Tony Bennett. In addition to the half-hour-long *Talent Scouts*, he also had another television program, the hour-long *Arthur Godfrey and His Friends*, which was simulcast on the radio.

It was the show's producer, Janette Davis, who personally judged the auditions. Those performers who made the final cut in front of Davis would be booked on the show, and then would compete against each other on the air.

When it came time for the audition, the musicians were still having some minor problems with the songs. They were especially having trouble following Patsy on the Rosemary Clooney hit "This Ole House," but seemed fine on the country boogie sound of "Turn the Cards Slowly." Davis took Patsy aside and told her that she loved Patsy's singing, but she hated the band. She thought that Patsy had a voice that could interpret blues and pop tunes as well as country, and that she was wasting her time with this band. She also told her that she could come back the next day and audition without the trio. Although Patsy wasn't too impressed with these musicians either, she was a "team player" all the way and announced that either she would perform with the band she brought, or she was going to pass on the opportunity. Janette Davis was sincere enough about her being impressed with Patsy's singing, and told her that the door was open for her to come back and audition for the show again—solo.

Through a booking agent that Janette Davis referred them to, Patsy and the trio picked up several more club engagements in New York City. One particular evening Patsy and the band set up and performed in the lounges of four different clubs, including the world famous Latin Casino. The agent, Richard Liselle, was also singer Theresa Brewer's manager at the time.

Ultimately, four songs were cut as demos during that eleven-day stay in New York City: the ballads "Three Cigarettes in an Ashtray," "This Ole House," and "Crazy Arms," plus the country swing number "Turn the Cards Slowly." The four songs were selected by Bill McCall and given to Patsy. The song "This Ole House" again presented the biggest problem, and Patsy insisted on twenty-seven "takes" until they had it correct. This caused a clash of egos and flaring tempers in the session.

The demos were for the sole purpose of arranging a little side deal Bill McCall was trying to cut with Decca Records. When Paul

Cohen reviewed the finished demos, he made McCall an offer to purchase Patsy's contract from him. Well, McCall wanted no part of that. What he wanted to do was continue to hold Patsy to her deal with 4 Star to record only songs that McCall owned the copyright on. That way he would have an artist on an important label like Decca, who would do nothing but plug the songs he controlled.

In the country music field, Decca was one of the major labels at the time. Although they also had Kitty Wells as part of their roster, they primarily had male acts. McCall was banking on their need for more female artists.

Paul was so impressed with Patsy's singing that he agreed to the deal. Unbeknownst to Patsy at the time, McCall's deal with Decca had them paying him a full 5 percent artists' royalty, out of which he would pay Patsy her 2.34 percent, less expenses. Then, on top of that, he would get the lion's share of the songwriting money.

One of Bill McCall's biggest scams came from the fact that he would purchase controlling rights to songs that struggling songwriters would compose, change a word or two of the lyrics, and make himself the song's co-writer. That way, the song's original writer suddenly had to accept only half of the copyright money. Just so he didn't look too obvious about this scam, he used his pen name, W. S. Stevenson. As his own personal joke, he took the "W. S." from William Shakespeare's initials, and combined them with Robert Louis Stevenson's last name.

Not long after the New York City visit, Paul Cohen and Bill McCall made a deal, and arrangements were made for her first recording session for 4 Star, which in turn was licensed to Decca. Although Bill McCall could dictate what songs Patsy would record, Paul Cohen retained the rights to select and hire the producer and the musicians. After hearing the group Bill Peer had hired for Patsy's four New York demo recordings, he wanted top-notch musicians on the sessions.

After Bill and Patsy returned from New York, a package was delivered to the Peer residence. It seems that Patsy had mistakenly left one of her coats hanging in the closet of the room at the Dixie Hotel. The coat arrived with a nice letter of concern from the manager of the hotel, which read:

Dear Mrs. Peer:

We are happy to inform you that the coat you and
Mr. Peer left behind in your room has been turned
over to this office. We are returning it herewith.
Sorry if your oversight caused you any inconve-
nience. It was our pleasure to serve you.

When Jenny confronted her husband with the evidence of his affair
with Patsy in New York City, he fabricated an elaborate excuse. But
Jenny was getting suspicious about what Patsy and her husband
were really up to.

Now that the Decca sublicensing deal was in place, Bill Peer
booked studio time at a radio station in nearby Fredricksburg,
Virginia. He decided to take a crack at the first songs Patsy had been
asked to record. He took the Melody Boys into the studio with Patsy,
and they recorded their own version of demos for four songs from
McCall: "Honky Tonk Merry-Go-Round," "Turn the Cards Slowly,"
"A Church, a Courtroom, and Then Goodbye," and "Hidin' Out."
The idea was to demonstrate that the Melody Boys could cut the
mustard with McCall's material, and that Decca would release these
four songs and everyone would get a contract out of the deal.

The following Saturday afternoon at a rehearsal at the
Brunswick Moose Hall, Patsy wanted to practice the new 4 Star
songs. She intended to give a couple of the songs a try with that
night's audience. When the band had problems playing the songs
during the rehearsal, she blew up in a fit of temper.

"Goddamn it, can't you guys ever get the beat on this song right?
Bill, can't you do something? They're awful!" she screamed.

The drummer, Grover Shroyer, yelled right back at her. He carried on about the fact that now that Patsy had gotten what she wanted—a big record contract—she could just go ahead and dump the
rest of them, like she was obviously going to do. Shroyer's ruffled
feathers were eventually smoothed out, and that night's performance
went without a hitch. He was, however, quite accurate in his pre-
diction of the future.

Bill Peer followed through with his plan, and bought plane tickets for Patsy and himself to Nashville. They personally flew there to present the demos at a special Nashville meeting with McCall and Cohen. The tapes were immediately dismissed. Cohen explained that they had their own way of doing things in Nashville, and their own professional session musicians with whom they work.

The height of Patsy and Bill's affair was reached in 1955. Her relationship with Gerald was pretty well over. They had simply drifted apart. It had gotten to the point where he'd be seen around town with his new girlfriend, whom he introduced to everyone as his "cousin." Patsy couldn't have cared less what Gerald did or didn't do at this point. There was only one thing that she cared about—her career.

Finally, after several months of anticipation, Patsy's first non-demo recording sessions were booked and set up. They were to take place in Nashville, on June 1, 1955, and would ultimately comprise material for her first two single releases.

In the spring of 1955, Bill Peer talked the car dealership he worked for into sponsoring him driving one of their black convertible Coupe de Villes in Winchester's annual Apple Blossom Festival parade. On the back of the car sat Patsy Cline, in black and white cowgirl regalia, waving and blowing kisses to the crowds. Things were finally starting to go her way. At long-last, she was on the threshold of becoming a bona fide recording artist. She had a lover who spent lavishly on her, and a husband who stayed out of her way. What more could she want?

While she blew kisses from the back of that long black Cadillac, unsuspecting Winchester hadn't a clue that it was about to witness the blooming of its wildest blossom.

Chapter Five

THE FIRST SESSIONS

*P*atsy's personality and demeanor had already fully developed. Although only twenty-two years old, she was a grown woman with an expressive style and a flamboyant exuberance to her every move. She could drink, smoke, and cuss, and her mere presence commanded attention and respect. Everyone seemed to agree: Patsy Cline was a fabulous broad!

It was in May of 1955 when Bill Peer and Patsy flew to Nashville to record her first 4 Star–Decca releases. It also marked the first time either of them had flown on a commercial flight. While Bill was uneasy about the plane ride, Patsy, in typical fashion, was perfectly calm and spent much of the air journey clowning around with the crew. As they prepared to land, the stewardess announced that the captain wanted everyone to get in their seats and fasten their seat belts. Always the clown, Patsy stood up in the aisle, straddled one end of her belt, and announced "All right ladies, you don't want to ignore the captain! Fasten your sanitary belts!"

The most important aspect of this trip was her introduction to and collaboration with Owen Bradley, the producer who would record all of her greatest hits. When Patsy Cline first met Owen he was thirty-nine years old. A talented pianist, he had been a staff musician for WSM, and worked his way up to become the leader of the studio orchestra. He had his own dance band, the Owen Bradley Quartet, and he once had been Dinah Shore's piano player. Just as Hollywood director George Cukor had made his mark in the movie business as the primo "women's director," Owen Bradley has built his reputation for being Nashville's best "women's producer." In addition to his work with Patsy Cline, he also scored with the likes of Kitty Wells, Brenda Lee, Loretta Lynn, and later, k. d. lang.

Together with his guitar-playing brother, Harold, Owen opened a number of recording studios in Nashville, moving from one to another in search of the perfect site. Finally, he bought a house in a rundown residential Nashville neighborhood. Paul Cohen was so enthused about helping Bradley in creating the ultimate studio for the sessions he wanted him to do, that he assisted in coming up with the $7,500 cost of the house. Owen and Harold ripped the first floor walls out of it, put offices upstairs and a recording studio in the basement. The Bradley Film and Recording Studio opened in early 1955 on the corner of Hawkins and 16th Avenue South. The idea was to create not just an audio studio, but one which could also accommodate the filming of kinescopes, the forerunners of today's music videos. It is of historic note that Bradley's became the first recording studio on what is now known as world famous "Music Row" in Nashville. When more space was needed the Bradley brothers simply added a military-style quonset hut to the house. Bradley's studio was thereafter dubbed "The Quonset Hut."

With the exception of two late sessions in New York City in 1957, Owen Bradley produced Patsy Cline throughout her entire recording career in that same studio. Speaking of his position in Nashville at the time he first met Patsy, Owen explains, "I worked for Paul Cohen as a musical director. I had no title. I was just friend/piano-player-man trying to get along. He was the director of the Decca Country Music department. A man named Bill McCall owned 4 Star Records and he came to town and worked out an arrangement with Paul Cohen to lease the masters to Patsy Cline on Coral Records, a subsidiary of Decca Records. Then McCall told me, 'I'm gonna send you a girl to record,' and says, 'She's mean as hell and hard to get along with.' I didn't know what to say.'"

The majority of Patsy's recording sessions had a similar pattern to them. She would go into the recording studio and record for three to four hours, yielding an average of four different songs per session. While working under her 4 Star contract, for every four songs recorded, she would exit the studio $200 richer, it would be left up to the record company's discretion to choose which songs were to be singles, which ones were for EPs and LPs, and which ones remained "in the can." Although now all of her recordings are available on compact disc, over thirty of the songs that Patsy recorded were not released during her lifetime.

When June 1, 1955, rolled around, Patsy had had the demos and sheet music to her first four songs for quite some time. They had been chosen by a committee of Owen Bradley, Paul Cohen, Bill McCall, a couple of 4 Star staff members, as well as Ernest Tubb. The songs they picked included two ballads and two up-tempo numbers. Two of the songs were written by Eddie Miller, but were co-credited to Bill McCall's pen name.

Since Patsy had already recorded the songs once with the Melody Boys (and "Turn the Cards Slowly" once before in the New York City demo session), she knew them by heart by the time she arrived in Nashville. This was musical history in the making, and Patsy arrived ready to roll.

When she reported to Bradley's studio on June 1, 1955, poor Owen didn't know what to expect, or what the results would be—especially with the warning that Bill McCall had given him about Patsy's temperament. According to him, "I was expecting someone to come in and just beat me to death, tongue lash me; but she didn't, she wasn't like that at all. Exactly the opposite. First trip she came down she didn't open her mouth. She did anything we asked."

Looking back on that first session, Bradley compares it to going to a strange doctor for the first time: you don't know quite what to expect. After the first visit, the element of surprise is gone, the sense of terror has vanished, and you can take your clothes off and be yourself. In her subsequent visits to Bradley's studio, Patsy relaxed and almost felt like she was among friends.

With the exception of this first session, up to 1958 Patsy would choose all of the songs that she recorded. From the 4 Star demos she was sent by Bill McCall, she selected the ones that appealed to her the most, and had an emotion she could identify with. According to Owen, "She'd just walk in and say, 'These are the songs we're going to do.' That's what we'd do. Then the pickings got worse and worse, and she'd complain."

Patsy would hand Owen the songwriters' demos—with other people singing on them—that she had received from McCall. They would play them in the studio, rehearse them a couple of times, and then turn the tape machine on and have a go at it.

Paul Cohen trusted Owen Bradley's taste. He knew that one of Owen's strong points came in his ability to assemble all of the right musicians for a session. He instinctively knew whom to hire, and how to orchestrate the sound he wanted. Paul had only three rules: no accordions, no vibraphones, and no yodeling. To him accordions turned a song into a polka, vibraphones didn't record well, and yodeling went out with Patsy Montana in the 1930s.

Right before the session started, there was a slight snag. Bradley took Bill Peer aside and asked him who was going to pay for the musicians. Peer told him that, according to the contract, this was to be McCall's responsibility. However, Bradley informed him that this in fact hadn't been done, and that the session couldn't start without the financial arrangements taken care of. They got McCall on the phone, and informed him that they needed $1,500 immediately or they couldn't proceed. McCall told Peer that if he fronted the money—in cash—he would be reimbursed. Not only was Peer upset, but Patsy was understandably upset as well. She finally said to Bill Peer, "Well, if you've got the money and want to go ahead, let's do it as long as he says he'll pay you back."

Up against the wall, Bill Peer pulled out a stack of $100 bills, and counted out the amount to Owen Bradley. "And don't forget my receipt!" Peer said, as he handed over the cash.

Other than the money confusion, things went quite smoothly

that day, and Owen ended up with four completed "sides." The only rule they bent for her that first day was the yodeling law. According to Bradley, "In the beginning, she had a tendency to yodel or growl, and we tried some of those things. Now some of the people think that's kind of cute, they like that."

"Hidin' Out"* [1], which was written by Eddie Miller (with McCall's "W. S. Stevenson" moniker attached to it), was a simple, pleasant, and straightforward country ballad. In content, the song could have been Patsy's own pen, as it is about a clandestine love affair. When she sings about holding no "legal claim" to the object of her affections, and how they were both married to someone else, it's about as autobiographical as you can get. The steel guitar and fiddle really sweetened this song nicely, as did Owen Bradley's mid-song piano solo which is quite effective in bringing this cheatin' lament to life.

"Turn the Cards Slowly" [2] is a peppy country swing number written by Sammy Masters. This is a great example of what Patsy must have sounded like in concert at that time, as she howls, growls, and yelps a lot of her lyrics. The intricate guitar work on the bridge makes it easy to understand why Bill Peer's New York trio had problems with it. A fun, fast-paced dance number, it finished off with a real "socko" ending that was one of Patsy's onstage trademarks. She sang the hell out of this song, and sounds like she was having a good time performing it.

By comparison, the third tune, "A Church, a Courtroom, and Then Goodbye" [3], is a bit maudlin. Penned by Eddie Miller and W. S. Stevenson, it is a slow-paced ballad about a sad marriage that ends in divorce. Patsy must have been thinking of Gerald when she sincerely sang this one. Technically, she did a great job on the song, yet she sounds a bit constrained with the material. To make up for it, she gave the tail end of the song a sweeping ending, with Patsy driving home that last note.

My favorite song from this session was the fourth one, "Honky Tonk Merry-Go-Round" [4]. A raucous rock-a-billy romp written by Frank Simon and Stan Gardner, Patsy sang it with hearty fire and conviction. The song is about being on a whirlwind bar-hopping

* The bracketed numbers that follow the song titles refer to the chronological order in which they were recorded, and coincide with their reference number in the detailed discography at the back of this book.

expedition. It's 100 percent Patsy party music, and is one of the most "fun" numbers she ever cut. Patsy got rowdy on the song, and she had a bit of a laugh in her delivery. Her vocal is clear as a bell, and you can definitely hear the power and the prowess of her early era voice. In my mind, "Honky Tonk Merry-Go-Round" should have been her first hit.

Of that session, Bradley recalls, "We had quite a problem recording Patsy at first, partially maybe because of the material. Maybe we tried too hard to make them sensational."

Right after the recording session, Patsy and Bill left for home, confident that she had done the best performances she could have with that first quartet of songs. Bob Gaines, who owned G&M Music Store, recalls Patsy returning to Winchester after that very first 4 Star recording session. The store was equipped with disk-cutting machines, where you could leave the shop with a record with your singing on it. Patsy came into the store several times after that to practice recording techniques and to rehearse songs.

Not long after the session it was announced that Patsy's first single would be released on July 20, 1955. It was to consist of "A Church, a Courtroom, and Then Goodbye" as the "A" side, and "Honky Tonk Merry-Go-Round" as the "B" side.

When radio stations were sent promotional copies of Patsy's first single, it was accompanied by a pitch letter from Bill McCall. It said in part: "We think Patsy Cline sings better than any female vocalist we have heard. Her diction, sense of timing and phrasings are exceptionally good. We hope that you will agree with us and give her first record a chance to be heard."

To launch the single in style, Patsy and Bill Peer returned to Nashville on Monday, June 27, 1955. Another significant date in Patsy's career, that Saturday night Patsy finally made her debut on *The Grand Ole Opry* radio show. Patsy had sought out Ernest Tubb's opinion about her first four recordings. Tubb liked "A Church, a Courtroom, and Then Goodbye." Also the host of one segment of the *Opry's* weekly broadcast, it was Tubb who invited Cline to perform on the program.

Bill and Patsy really did the town this time around. Bill went through his personal phone book, and called in every favor he could to launch his star client. She was not only his *only* client; she was also his lover, so he pulled out all the stops. They took Eddy Arnold out to lunch just so he could meet Patsy, and hopefully become interested in taking her under his wing. Arnold was impressed with Patsy, and he promised to keep her in mind as an opening act when he toured.

On Friday, July 1, an entourage of Patsy and Bill's friends from back home in the Winchester area arrived to witness her *Opry* debut. The gang included Fay and Harry Crutchley, Fay's sister Francis Null, and Patsy's ex-fiancé Elias Blanchfield. Bill took them all on a grand tour of "Music City," which included stops at Owen Bradley's studio, and an exciting backstage visit to *The Grand Ole Opry*.

The next night at the Ryman, Ernest Tubb introduced Patsy on *The Opry* with the warm greeting, "Here's a little lady with a powerful voice. I've been predicting big things for her. Make welcome Coral Records' newest star singing her debut recording, 'A Church, a Courtroom, and Then Goodbye.'"

Tubb was later to recall that this was the first and only time he saw Patsy nervous before a performance. She had anticipated playing at the *Opry* for so long that this was incredibly exciting for her. It was literally a dream come true.

The song only received polite applause, at which Tubb came racing out to milk the audience by announcing, "Folks: Miss Patsy Cline! Isn't she terrific?!" With that she won another more hearty round of applause.

Backstage that evening Patsy, Bill, and their friends met several of the stars of the country music world, including Kitty Wells, Hawkshaw Hawkins, Jeanie Shepard, Roy Acuff, and Minnie Pearl. This exciting night was capped off by Patsy appearing on Ernest Tubb's *Mid-Nite Jamboree*.

Ernest Tubb's manager, Gabe Tucker, recalls that Peer commented that he was going through a lot of cash promoting his star singer. Anxious to help, Tucker called up Roy Acuff's brother, Spot Acuff, who managed Roy's amusement park, Dunbar Caves. Through Tucker's wrangling, he booked Patsy for Sunday's show, for which she was to be paid $50. That way they would have more spending cash to help bankroll this week-long "launch" for Patsy's single.

On Monday, July 4, Bill and Patsy headed west to Memphis with their friends. Ernest Tubb was appearing in concert with singer Faron Young in an Independence Day country extravaganza. Cline and her manager-boyfriend showed up backstage, and Patsy cornered Ernest and asked him if she could perform a couple of numbers on that day's show—for free. He could never seem to say "no" to Patsy, so he agreed to add her to the bill. That day, in the one hundred degree heat, the crowd was estimated at fourteen thousand. According to Tubb, "They loved her!"

The following Saturday night it was business as usual at the Brunswick Moose Hall. However, friends, including Fay Crutchley, noted that things seemed somehow strained between Patsy and Bill. Perhaps it was the little surprise Molotov cocktail Jenny Peer had hurled in her husband's direction, by announcing that she was suing him for divorce on the grounds of adultery.

A woman of her words, the following Monday, July 11, Jenny formally filed the suit in Charleston, West Virginia. The hearing for "Virginia M. Peer vs. William Peer" was set for September 22 of that year.

Suddenly Patsy's relationship with Bill Peer was "strained" to say the least. Bill was talking about leaving his wife for Patsy. While Cline loved the attention he lavished on her, she wasn't in love with him. She did what she could to keep Bill interested in her career, while she attempted to cool off their affair. For the first time in months, Patsy made certain that Gerald was at her side for as many public events as possible, so she didn't look too obviously like "the other woman." Like the lyrics of the demo she had recorded in New York City, "Three Cigarettes in an Ashtray," it was she who was smoking the homewrecker's cigarette.

This was an emotionally frustrating period in Patsy's personal life. She was in a marriage she didn't want to be in. She was wrecking Bill's marriage to Jenny, yet she didn't have any desire to marry Bill. She was standing at the crossroads of two love affairs gone awry.

Ironically, following the lyrics of her debut single, "A Church, a Courtroom, and Then Goodbye," on September 22 the judge granted Jenny her divorce from Bill, and he was free to marry the woman he loved: Patsy. However, after the divorce was granted, Patsy informed him that not only was she not interested in marrying him, but that she was quitting the band as well. He was devastated.

Melody Boys' band member Roy Deyton recalls Patsy saying to him at the time, "Well, Roy, it's time I started moving on. I'm going to miss you. Staying on is not going to help matters any or help my career."

On Saturday, October 1, 1955, Patsy Cline made her final performance with Bill Peer and His Melody Boys and Girls, just like every other Saturday night at the Brunswick Moose Hall.

The band members were seriously worried that Bill was going to have a nervous breakdown. In a matter of several weeks, the two women who were the most important to him in his life had both dumped him. Not only did he lose Patsy as his girlfriend, but since there was no contract between them, he lost Cline as a client as well. The saga of Patsy and Peer was officially over.

In September of 1955, Connie Gay had launched his newest television extravaganza: *Town and Country Jamboree*. Three hours in length, it broadcast live in front of an audience of four thousand country music fans at Washington, D.C.'s, Turner Arena (oddly, it was best known as a wrestling arena). This was to become Patsy's new Saturday night gig. Patsy was paid only $50 a week, but she was on television, with a solid platform to promote her new recording career.

In November of 1955, back in Nashville, WSM sponsored its fourth annual Country Disk Jockey Convention. It was a chance to draw together all of the members of the country radio world. For an entire weekend they would eat, drink, party, and promote all of the latest singers, singles, and concert talent. Paul Cohen chose that weekend for the release of Patsy's second single for Coral Records. Although her first one garnered some good airplay and attention, it didn't hit any of the significant music charts. By promoting the new one that weekend, Patsy could actually "meet and greet" the disk jockeys and promote herself in person. In that way, her second single, "Hidin' Out" backed with "Turn the Cards Slowly" on the flip side, might receive the push that it desperately needed.

To buffer any talk about her personal or professional relationship with Bill Peer, for this trip Gerald was positioned securely on her arm. The convention was successful for Patsy on many levels. Not only did she meet several disk jockeys who would eventually assist her career, but she was given "star" treatment at the *Grand Ole Opry*—in the embodiment of two "all access" backstage passes. That way she could hang out with all the stars, and be viewed in Nashville as a star-in-the-making.

On January 5, 1956, Patsy was back in Nashville, for her second recording session. Again she recorded four songs in several hours.

"I Love You Honey" [5] is a silly, catchy little rock-a-billy tune that seemed tailor-made for Patsy Cline. In the context of the song, she sings about being enamored with someone for his: (a) love, (b) money, and (c) automobile. Written by Eddie Miller, it's the country swing version of Marilyn Monroe's "Diamonds Are a Girl's Best Friend." It is to the Patsy Cline songbook what "Material Girl" is to Madonna. A "gold-digging" gem, "I Love You Honey" is another of my personal favorites that should have been a hit.

Patsy's next song, "Come on in (and Make Yourself at Home)" [6], would become her signature song in concert and on television. Written by V. F. Stewart, this number is a bit on the cornball side. While the song is very upbeat and Patsy obviously had fun singing it, it's straight out of a "down-home" barn dance. This, however, was very indicative of how Patsy envisioned her own image at this stage of her career.

The third song was Bobby Flournoy's composition, "I Cried All the Way to the Altar" [7]. This song is another slow lament about lost love, which in content and pace is like "A Church, a Courtroom, and Then Goodbye".—Part II. There wasn't any space for Patsy to let loose on this number.

"I Don't Wanna" [8] is a song that Patsy was to record twice during her career at 4 Star. It's interesting to listen to both versions back-to-back, because this first one is a straightforward country tune, and the second one—complete with background vocals—was more of an exciting romp. A song about the declaration of love, Patsy claims to her beloved, "I Don't Wanna" love anyone but "you."

Her third single on Decca's subsidiary, Coral Records, was released on February 5, 1956. It consisted of "I Love You Honey" as the "A" side, and "Come on in (and Make Yourself at Home)" as the "B" side. Again it was met with mediocre airplay, and no chart action on a national level.

Directly due to her regional exposure from TV's *Town and Country Jamboree*, on March 18, *The Washington Star's* Sunday magazine carried a cover story on Patsy which was headlined, "Hillbilly with Oomph." The writer of the article claimed, "In one word, Patsy Cline's brought something new to hillbilly singing—oomph!" Connie Gay proclaimed in the same article, "Patsy has brought a brand of showmanship and rhythm to hillbilly music that's as welcome as a cool country breeze in springtime. We call her a country music choreographer. She creates the mood through movements of her hands and body and by the lilt of her voice, reaching way down deep in her soul to bring forth the melody."

Jimmy Dean, Patsy's TV show co-star, hit the nail on the head when he said, "When she punches out a hot tune, she sings all over!"

Although she was not a star in the record sales department, thanks to her radio and TV exposure, Patsy was becoming an "instant" local television star.

65

In addition to being her employer on television and radio, Connie Gay was also serving as Patsy's booking agent. He would send all of his stars out on the road, either separately or with a package. Other acts from the show, besides Patsy and Jimmy Dean, included Mary Klick and Dale Turner. George Hamilton IV was to join the show in the summer of 1956. Dale recalls that other agents wanted to book concerts for Patsy as well, but Gay's motto was that if he couldn't have 100 percent control, he didn't want to deal with you. For the time being, Patsy relied on him for all of her personal appearances.

By spring of 1956, Patsy was spending just about as much time residing at her mother's house in Winchester, as she did staying with Gerald. Gerald was involved in his other matters, and his marriage to Patsy was in name only at this point. Basically free of both Bill Peer and her husband, Patsy took the initiative to get back in touch with still-married Jumbo Rinker.

For a while she rekindled their affair, but she was so busy—between TV, radio, recording, and concerts—that they didn't get to spend too much time together. To replace the backup group that she had with Bill Peer's band, in 1956 she started touring with an existing band called the Kountry Krackers.

Jimmy Dean tells a story about a member of the band whom Patsy had the "hots" for. According to him, "She flirted with him incessantly and, finally decided she was going to have him. He talked about the way she was in bed for days, until one of us had to shut him up. He said that after they finished, Patsy looked him straight in the eye and asked, 'Now, hoss, wasn't that the best fuck you ever had?'" That was Patsy.

She was equally frank when it came to giving advice to people she considered friends. When nineteen-year-old George Hamilton IV came on the show, he was painfully shy. Patsy wouldn't have any of that. He had a gimmick of playing up the Roman numerals in his name, by having them embroidered on the front of his jackets. After that Patsy started calling him "Number."

During one of his first performances on the show, George wasn't making eye contact with the cameras or the audience, but was shyly looking downward. After he came off stage, Patsy walked up to him and gave him a piece of her mind. "Hey, hoss, I'm gonna have to light a fire under your goddamn ass! You're gonna have to learn to get out there in front of those cameras and hold your head up. Take charge when you're singing. You walk out there like you're embarrassed to be on that stage. Are you ashamed to be singing with us?"

"No ma'am," he shyly replied with his tail between his legs.

"What kind of singer are you? Ain't gonna go nowhere with that kind of attitude. That's not humility! That's a weakness. You gotta get up there and show 'em! You gotta get 'em to eat right outta your hands. You're a star. When you're doing your songs, take command, hoss!"

In her own straight-to-the-point way, Patsy had given him sound professional advice. If anyone knew about taking command of an audience, it was "the Cline."

When she went to perform at a concert in Elkton, Virginia, where she had once lived, she was treated like a long-lost daughter who had finally made good. This was in direct contrast to how people felt about her in Winchester. She told Jumbo that she had met several members of the Hensley family she never knew existed. When she sang the traditional hymn, "Just a Closer Walk with Thee" she had the audience in tears. During the first intermission, she went out into the lobby of the theater where she sold and auto-graphed photos for twenty-five cents each. She was shocked that she actually sold one hundred of her photos that evening.

The number thirteen is unlucky for some people, and decid-edly lucky for others. On the "Friday the 13th" of April 1956, an important figure walked into Patsy's life. While her friends found him an unlikely choice, for Patsy Cline, Charlie Dick was to become the love of her life.

Charlie grew up in Winchester, but had never met Patsy. Two years younger than Patsy, trim in build, and a likeable "party animal," Charlie was a guy who liked to have a good time. In 1956, Patsy was a woman who wanted to be shown a good time.

Charlie was the oldest of three boys. Charlie's father committed suicide with a rifle at the kitchen table one night. Charlie's two younger brothers were twins, and one of them was born mentally handicapped and had to be institutionalized. Charlie dropped out of school in the tenth grade, and not long afterward took a job at the local newspaper, *The Winchester Evening Star*. He held that same job, as a linotype press operator, when he meet Patsy.

As he tells it, "There was a band, a local band that played in honky tonks, armories, for dances and whatever: the Kountry Krackers, with a 'K.' And after Patsy started on the Jimmy Dean TV show in Washington, D.C., the band hired her to come and work some of their dates with them. And I had been going to some of their dances because I knew quite a few of the guys in the band. I had known them for years. And so Patsy came there to sing, and I met her at the dance—in Berryville, Virginia, at the Armory." For Charlie, it was love at first sight.

When the band took its first break, Charlie went over to his friend Bud Armel, who was one of the guitar players in the Kountry Krackers, and he asked him who the girl was who was singing with them. Bud told him that this was Patsy Cline, who was one of the star's of Connie Gay's *Town and Country Jamboree*. Charlie distinct-ly recalls, "She not only sang well, but she was a knockout!"

According to him, "I went up and asked her to dance. She said she couldn't dance while she was working. So, okay, I walked off and later on I see her dancing with somebody so I went over and asked her to dance again, and she said, 'No! I can't while I'm working.' I said, 'Well, hell, I just seen you dancing with someone. I thought you said you can't dance while you're working.' And she said, 'That's my husband.'"

However, there was something about Charlie that made her want to find the time to steal away, so she ditched Gerald for a few minutes and went out in the parking lot with Charlie. He remembers, "That was the night that I talked to her, and we went out to the car and sat down for a little while. And I took her to the Jimmy Dean show the next night."

Still seeing Jumbo Rinker occasionally, the following week Patsy announced to him, "I met a fellow last week and I been going out with him. I hope you're not mad. Hit me like a ton of bricks, Jum. I never thought it was going to happen. I hate to tell you this." From that point on—for better or for worse—she only had one man on her mind, and that was Charlie.

On April 22, 1956, Patsy and Owen Bradley were back in the studio for her third recording session. Two diverse directions were tried this time around. Since rock and roll was suddenly sweeping the nation, thanks to Elvis Presley, Patsy recorded her first rock song. Also, since Patsy was proving to be effective on religious music, she cut a pair of gospel tunes as well. In other words, they were still shooting in the dark.

"Stop, Look and Listen" [9] is Patsy's big rock and roll number. With Owen Bradley doing a Jerry Lee Lewis–style boogie piano, this wasn't far off from what Elvis Presley was releasing at the time. This is a perfect example of the different directions that were attempted while they searched for "the sound" that would launch Patsy Cline's recording career. In musical content, she sings about a "cool cat" who is "livin' fast," and how he should stop and smell the roses. Patsy rocked on this song by George London and W. S. Stevenson, which found her in an effectively exciting mode. This is a perfect "sock hop" song which musically evokes an image of bobby sox and poodle skirts.

"I've Loved and Lost Again" [10] by Eddie Miller is the first song that Patsy recorded which is close in style and performance to her 1960s' hits. Patsy sounded sincere and focused on the lyrics. Whereas on the similarly-paced "A Church, a Courtroom, and Then Goodbye," Patsy sounded hemmed in and constrained (like she'd rather be yodeling!), on this song she really connected with the lyrics, and sounded as if she seriously believed what she was singing.

The last two songs she cut during that second session were both written by V. F. Stewart, and were both gospel-themed. On both songs Patsy's singing is fine, but neither of these numbers are worthy of her full-throttle capacity. "Dear God" [11] is similar in context to Billie Holiday's "Ain't Nobody's Business (If I Do)." In it, Patsy confesses to being guilty of church-on-Sunday/sin-on-Monday behavior. But Patsy asks for forgiveness here, while in her song, Holiday tells her critics to "buzz off." That would have been much truer to Patsy's real-life character than this maudlin lament.

Similarly, on "He Will Do for You" [12], Patsy is lyrically on a guilt trip. Although the song finds Cline in excellent vocal shape, this record emerges as merely pleasant. This was one of Patsy's few recorded gospel numbers.

69

On several occasions, while Patsy was in Nashville she would be a guest on Wally Fowler's *All-Night Sing* program performing these and other sacred songs. Recalls Grant Turner, who was the *Opry's* main announcer during this era, "Wally presented her and she came out and she sang some gospel songs. I had thought of her at that time as a gospel singer. I never will forget that for each of these songs that she sang, she would always finish the song very tearfully and very emotional. And I thought then, 'This girl really feels this. She has a great feel for this work, and it's something that really gets down into your heart and soul.'"

Pop hits, country, sacred songs, rock and roll—she'd sing it all—whatever it took to find the right song that was going to "break" her career on a national basis. According to Jimmy Dean, he had never met someone so determined to become a star as Patsy. She claimed on several occasions that she knew she was going to obtain stardom, and she'd do anything it took to get there. She was soon to grab the bull by the horns.

On the television show Patsy could sing whatever she wanted, and she attempted all sorts of material. She would much rather have recorded some of the country and pop songs that she was able to perform on *Town and Country Jamboree*, *Town and Country Time*, and on Connie's radio show. Among the non–4 Star songs that Patsy sang in 1956 were several that were captured on sixteen-inch transcription disks. These performances include Cline versions of Webb Pierce's "Yes, I Know Why," Gogi Grant's "The Wayward Wind," and Sonny James' hit song "For Rent." What Patsy needed was to find the one true diamond-in-the-rough amid all of the demos that Bill McCall sent her. Fortunately, she was about to locate it.

Reminiscing about those first three recording sessions, Owen Bradley admits that it was frustrating working under the constraints of the 4 Star song catalog. According to him, "The problem we had for a long time was finding any songs that were any good. I think that all you have to do is listen to some of the old records and you'll see that they were sort of rewrites of whatever was happening in those days. That's about the best I can do, except for one song, 'Walkin' after Midnight.'"

Chapter Six

A Taste of Stardom

*D*ue to her weekly exposure on *Town and Country Jamboree*, Patsy was known locally as a television personality who also recorded, but was still searching for that elusive hit song that would make her a star. Although she was constantly working, she was far from rich, but she was able to support herself, her mother, and her two younger siblings. Poised for stardom, she still had a long way to go toward her dreams of fame and fortune.

In May of 1956 Patsy was again featured in Winchester's annual Apple Blossom Festival parade. Seated on the back of a two-toned Oldsmobile, she held court on the streets of her hometown. Connie Gay had sponsored her appearance that day, and provided the car—courtesy of his family-owned enterprise, Gay Oldsmobile of Warrenton, Virginia. Patsy invited her little sister Sylvia to ride on the back of the car with her. For maximum promotional effect, the car was festooned with banners identifying her as Patsy Cline of the hit TV show *Town and Country Jamboree*.

Wearing one of her red and white cowgirl outfits and a white cowgirl hat, she didn't feel like a star in her own hometown. She still felt that people were looking down their noses at her. Perhaps the townspeople of Winchester simply knew too much about the comings and goings of Patsy's apartment.

After the parade, Patsy went over to Charlie's house. She was sitting in the kitchen with Charlie's mother, when his little brother, nine-year-old Mel, came rushing into the house and stopped dead in his tracks. Here sat a boisterous woman dressed like a cowgirl. He recalls, "She seemed just bigger than life. She had ridden in the parade and she had fringe and she had boots. I never seen anybody like that in my life and I was afraid. She said, 'How are ya!?' and she had this big voice. I was startled. She just dominated the room, even then." As anyone who ever met her realized, Patsy dominated *every* room she ever walked into.

For the past couple of months things had been on-again then off-again between Patsy and Gerald, until finally she stayed with Hilda most of the time. That too caused living problems, especially since Charlie had become a fixture in her life. Patsy's mother did not care for Charlie at all, so he was not a welcome guest at the house on Kent Street. Anxious to have her own space, she finally packed up her things and moved herself into a trailer. It was located in a trailer park just outside of Winchester. Finally, she could come and go as she pleased.

Punk Longley, Patsy's cousin, recalls a car pulling up in front of his house late one afternoon. From inside the automobile came Patsy, Gerald, Hilda, Sylvia, and Sam, Jr. They had all been in the car, and Patsy and Gerald were in the midst of an argument. Hilda took her two younger children into the kitchen to "visit" with Punk and his wife, while Patsy and Gerald finished their "conversation." After a few minutes, Patsy came into the kitchen and announced that she and Gerald had finally agreed on something: divorce.

While Patsy was obviously in love with Charlie, none of her longtime friends could figure out why. According to Pat Smallwood, "A lot of people didn't like him. He drank a lot. I didn't care for him. He was crude, very crude."

"They don't look like a match," said Mary Klick, her *Town and Country* co-star. "She really must have fallen hard for Charlie to stop along the way and give *him* the time of day."

Johnny Anderson of the Melody Boys was even more opinionated when he said, "She associated with the wrong class of people. You don't pull yourself up associating with Charlie Dick."

Like him or not, he was to be a permanent fixture in her life. Many people from this era—and from recent times—have said that Charlie had a Dr.-Jekyll-and-Mr.-Hyde kind of dual personality, and that it was liquor that brought the belligerent Mr. Hyde to life.

The fighting and arguing between Patsy and Charlie went back as far as their falling in love. Somehow, the constant fighting and arguing was part of the dynamic of their relationship. Patsy loved him, she hated him, and then she loved him all over again. Although Charlie always loved Patsy, at the darkest end of his mood swings, he was known to become physically abusive.

It seems as if throughout her entire life, the one completely consistent string comes with the fact that everything that Patsy had, achieved, or accomplished in her life she had to fight for. It appeared that "love" fell into that same category.

On June 16, 1956, Patsy was back in Nashville to perform on the *Grand Ole Opry*'s Prince Albert Show—the segment of the show presented by Prince Albert Tobacco. She was introduced onstage and on the air by singer Little Jimmy Dickins. When she took the mike she told the audience that night, "Hi Jimmy. It's awful good to be back on the *Opry*, and to see you."

"Sing for us. Would you do that?" Dickins asked, in his twangy voice.

"I'd like to do my first record I ever made, 'A Church, a Courtroom, and Then Goodbye,'" Patsy announced.

With that, she launched into her first release. On the second half of the show she previewed a song from her latest recording session, "I've Loved and Lost Again."

On July 8, 1956, Patsy's fourth single was released. While the first three had come out on the Coral label, she was suddenly shifted to the main label, Decca Records. Symbolically, this indicated that the executives at Decca realized that one day soon, Patsy was destined to hit it big. This release carried "I've Loved and Lost Again" on the "A" side, and "Stop, Look and Listen" as the "B" side. Again, neither significantly charted on either the pop/rock or the country hit listings.

Throughout the year, Patsy kept very busy between all of her television and radio shows. In addition, Connie Gay was keeping all of his cast members active working their free evenings with *Town and Country* concert performances. Some of the most colorful memories that people have of Patsy come from the road stories of this era. She was riding in a car, on her way to a concert date with Mary Klick, when she suddenly wanted to pull off the road. The ladylike Klick discovered that it was Patsy's "time of the month" when Cline turned to her and bluntly said, "Hey, hoss, stop at the next fillin' station, will you? I got to change my firecracker!" Klick had never heard anyone talk like Patsy.

As outspoken as Patsy was, she was equally bold when it came to helping out a friend in need. Brenda Lee was just eleven years old when she met Patsy Cline. Lee had just been signed to Decca Records, having been discovered through various talent competitions, and had just released her first single, "One Step at a Time." On the same bill with Lee, Patsy came to her rescue. "I met Patsy in '56," Lee recalls. "I was doing a show somewhere in Texas, and the promoter ran out with all the money. And my mom and I didn't have any money to get home. And Patsy loaded us up in her car and brought us back to Nashville. That's how I met Patsy."

"I thought she was wonderful," recalls diminutive Brenda Lee, who was twelve years younger than Patsy. She considered Cline her "big sister." According to her, "I used to go over to her house and she would let me clomp around in her high heels and dress up in her stage clothes." For Brenda, Patsy was someone she would always look up to and admire.

This was an extremely frustrating time for Patsy. She was acknowledged as a singing star, but she had no trademark identity without a hit to call her own.

Besides that, Patsy's record deal called for her recording only sixteen songs. She had already recorded twelve, yielding four singles that went nowhere. She had one more session to come up with a hit, or she could possibly find herself without a record deal.

A songwriter named Don Hecht was the man who was to come to her rescue, though when she first met him, she didn't want his help. Hecht was nearly down to his last dime when he signed a contract with Bill McCall to doctor up songs already under contract, and to survey the company's artist roster and match them up to the right 4 Star compositions. The first time he played one of Patsy's records, Hecht immediately pinpointed what the problem was: she was a pop-oriented blues singer, and she was trying to force herself into a country mode. Instantly, he knew he had just the song for her. There was a tune that he had written with his friend Alan Block. It was a blues number which they had composed in 1954. Originally they had written it to submit to Kay Starr, but she turned it down.

Hecht raced into McCall's office, told him of his brainstorm, and played the demo to "Walkin' after Midnight" on the spot. Bill McCall immediately agreed that this could be a hit for Patsy, so he phoned her and played it for her long distance. After listening to it, Patsy complained in her no-nonsense fashion, "That song's got no balls!"

Patsy was due in California the following week to appear on several West Coast television shows. One of them included a program called *Town Hall Party*, which featured Tex Ritter and Merle Travis. McCall set up a meeting with Patsy while she was in town.

When Cline arrived at McCall's Pasadena office, she was introduced to Don Hecht for the first time. He recalls that, "She was not beautiful, but not plain. She walked like a dancer, and something played off of her that made her stand out from the crowd."

McCall played the song demo again for her, and she complained that she didn't like it because it was just a slow pop song.

Bill finally put his foot down, explaining, "Look, we've got to stop this bullshit, Patsy. It's not like I haven't let you do what you wanted to do. It hasn't happened. So let me do something now. It's my money you know." He then told her that every song that she had selected to record had bombed, and that he was reaching the end of his rope.

Finally he got tired of arguing with her. He told both Hecht and Cline that he was going to go out and get them coffee and donuts, and that he was going to let the two of them fight it out in his absence.

After Bill left, Patsy was the first one to speak. "Look, Mr. Heck," she began her argument.

"It's like 'Hector' without the 'o-r,'" he corrected.

By the time McCall returned with the coffee and donuts, they had a plan. Grabbing a donut and taking a bite, Patsy explained, "I'll tell you what we decided to do—me and Mr. Hector without the 'o-r'—we're going to put out a single, and we're going to put this nothin' pop song on one side and on the other side I get to pick a song that I like."

"What if neither side sells?" McCall asked.

"Then you just get yourself another singer," said Patsy. "Is it a deal?"

Tired of arguing, McCall agreed to the plan, and Patsy left the office with a demo to "Walkin' after Midnight." She still hated Don Hecht's song, but she had to admit that she liked him.

The first week in November of 1956, Patsy was in Nashville to attend the annual Country Disk Jockey Convention, and to complete her next, and possibly last, recording session.

When she arrived in town, she knew that she had agreed to record "Walkin' after Midnight," but she still wasn't convinced that she liked it. Throughout the week prior to the session, she kept playing the demo of the song for her friends in the business. Much to her dismay, they all seemed to love it. That only made her madder! Since McCall had agreed to let her put a non–4 Star song on the "B" side of the single, she spread the word that she was looking for material to record.

Two of the people she played the "Midnight" demo for were Native American recording artists Marvin Rainwater, and his disk jockey brother Ray Rainwater. Marvin had a record deal with MGM, and was about to release his biggest hit, "Gonna Find Me a Bluebird." He had appeared on *Arthur Godfrey's Talent Scouts* in

1955, and since then, both brothers had become chummy with Godfrey. He was friendly enough with the TV show host to sometimes suggest potential contestants to him.

As soon as he heard the demo to "Walkin' after Midnight," Marvin echoed everyone's opinion by telling her that it was a hit. In addition, he introduced her to songwriter Mae Boren Axton, who was to become another life-long friend. Mae had just scored a huge hit earlier in the year when Elvis Presley took her composition "Heartbreak Hotel" all the way to the top of the charts, thus launching his career. When Patsy complained about needing a hit, almost on the spot Mae and two of her writing partners penned a song especially for Patsy called "Pick Me Up on Your Way Down," just in time for her upcoming session. A song publisher named Al Gallico, whom she met and complained to, gave her the song "A Poor Man's Riches (or a Rich Man's Gold)," which she loved.

77

She was booked at Owen Bradley's studio on November 8, and she arrived with Bill McCall's choice: "Walkin' after Midnight," and three songs of her own choice from which the flip side of the single could be selected.

She took her song selections very seriously. As she once told Don Hecht, "It's like writing in your diary when you sing a song. I want to get it just right so that when other people see it, they see how it was and how you really felt."

From the second Patsy opens her mouth, the song "Walkin' after Midnight" [13] is absolutely irresistible. The wailing in her voice is the expressive longing of a woman in need of love. The funny thing is that Patsy wasn't even giving the song the kind of drama that she would later sing it with. Lyrically, it's about a woman walking down the boulevard in the middle of the night looking for her lover, and the defiant nonchalance in her singing makes it even more overtly "naughty." This song is truly a classic, and everybody—except Patsy—knew it the minute they heard her sing it.

Years before "Crazy" and "I Fall to Pieces," this early gem was Patsy's signature song. Although she was later to re-record it, this first version of "Walkin' after Midnight" has a simple charm all its own. There's a brief instrumental bridge on this song, but for the most part, the musicians are underneath her voice, expertly moving the song along without getting in the way of Patsy's determined singing.

Patsy was known among the musicians she worked with as a total professional. Don Helms, who was the steel guitarist on "Walkin' after Midnight" and played in concerts with Cline recalls, "One thing about Patsy Cline, she knew her material. When she got to the studio, or when she got to the stage to perform it, she knew it. She already knew what she was gonna do when she got there. I always admire anyone who is good at what they do—and Patsy was."

"The Heart You Break May Be Your Own" [14] is a nice pop ballad with a country musical accompaniment of a good solid steel guitar and fiddle. Patsy sang it well, and her a capella line at the end of the song, showed off the beautiful clarity of her voice.

"Pick Me Up on Your Way Down" [15] is one of Patsy's best recordings from her 4 Star years. Fully layered in sound, Owen's arrangement makes this sincere ballad a great country song. Lyrically, it is about leaving someone in the dust relationship-wise. Complete with steel guitar and fiddle touches, this is a great "two-stepping" song.

"A Poor Man's Riches (or a Rich Man's Gold)" [16] is a rock and roll ballad, featuring Owen's great 1950s' rock piano work. Singing about the age-old dilemma of being torn between "love" and "money," Patsy sang the hell out of this song with conviction and emotion. How fitting that this came from the writer who made Elvis a star! This recording is very similar to the kinds of songs that would make singers like Connie Francis and Brenda Lee stars in the next three years. An excellent recording, it was distinctively different in approach than the later version she would record in 1961 with strings and background vocals. Most important, the popular 1950s' dance called "The Stroll" could be done to this rock ballad.

After the session was over, Patsy again returned to the Rainwater brothers and played them the results. They both agreed that of the four songs, "Walkin' after Midnight" and "A Poor Man's Riches (or a Rich Man's Gold)" were the hits. Furthermore, Ray told Patsy that he wanted to put in a word to his friends at Arthur Godfrey's office, to submit her again for consideration on "Talent Scouts."

When she told him that she had already blown her shot at appearing on that show a year ago, he told her, "Timing is everything. Elvis Presley auditioned too, and they turned him down!"

Ray Rainwater made good on his offer to resubmit Patsy to the Godfrey show, and her next audition with Janette Davis was set up for the beginning of December. When she returned to New York City this time, she brought Charlie with her. He had taken off time from his job as a linotype operator at the local newspaper, *The Winchester Evening Star*.

Janette was very happy to see her again, and the audition went quite smoothly. She loved Patsy, and had, ever since their first meeting. It was pretty much a "done deal." All she had to do was wait until the producers called her to tell her when she was scheduled to appear.

According to Charlie, the scheduling wait drove Patsy crazy. "They told us, you know: 'Don't call us, we'll call you. We're set up at least two weeks in advance—or two months.' Something like that, the whole song and dance, and we figured, 'Well, that's the end of that.'"

Meanwhile, Patsy's father, Sam Hensley, surprisingly reappeared in her life. A longtime cigar smoker, he had developed throat cancer and was seriously ill. Patsy made the decision to go and visit him when he was in the hospital. Hilda accompanied her. A brief hospital visit couldn't erase all the missing years, nor the hurt feelings and wounded spirit of eleven-year-old "Ginny" Hensley. Although the incest issue was never mentioned—nor the emotional scars it had caused—Patsy "made her peace" with her father, and saw him in time to properly say goodbye. He died on December 11, 1956.

While all this was happening, she was still waiting for her phone call from *Arthur Godfrey's Talent Scouts*. To save money, Patsy had since given up her trailer, and had moved back into her mother's home on Kent Street in Winchester. One afternoon in the beginning of December the phone rang, and Hilda picked it up. On the other end of the line was someone calling from *Arthur Godfrey's Talent Scouts*. Excitedly, Hilda called out to Patsy to pick up the phone, telling her who it was.

Trying not to act too available, Patsy took her time coming to the phone. "Let them wait a few minutes. They let me wait a few weeks. Tell them I'm next door."

"What!" Hilda exclaimed. "Patsy, you come to the phone! Are you crazy?"

Finally she came to the phone and listened to what the person on the other end was telling her. When they inquired about the band they had seen with her the previous year, much to their relief she told them that they were no longer a part of her act.

In the context of the show, they also needed an official "talent scout" who introduced each individual contestant to Godfrey on the air. They could be a friend or acquaintance of the contestant, and they would present them to the audience as well.

"Who will be your talent scout?" they asked her on the phone.

"My mother," said Patsy. When they informed her that it couldn't be a parent, because that could prejudice the audience, they pressed her to come up with someone else. She thought for a moment, and told them that she would bring "Mrs. Hilda Hensley."

"Is she a friend?" they inquired.

"Yes, my *best*. She's known me all my life!"

Her mother couldn't believe that she'd tell such a deceptive lie, and she especially couldn't believe that Patsy would expect her to go on television and repeat such a lie to the entire country as well.

As she had known all along, there was no sense in trying to talk Patsy out of something once she had made up her mind. This was to be another one of the grand schemes she roped her mother into.

Patsy's appearance on the program was set for January 21, 1957, and she immediately began making plans. While the television show was going to take care of her plane ticket and hotel room, it did not make provisions for a plane ticket for Hilda. Patsy called up Al Gallico, the song publisher who had given her "A Poor Man's Riches (or a Rich Man's Gold)" and asked him for a favor. Since he had a vested interest in her success, he agreed to grant Patsy her wish, and he paid Hilda's airfare.

In the meantime, Patsy's relationships with Connie Gay and Jimmy Dean were quietly eroding. First, there was the matter of her bringing Charlie to the Saturday night telecasts: their arguments got on everyone's nerves. On January 5, 1957, Patsy phoned the studio to inform Jimmy that she was going to be late for that day's rehearsals. She had spent the night with Charlie and after a night of heavy drinking and partying, Patsy and Charlie both overslept.

Jimmy was less than amused when she told him that she was simply running late. He was already unhappy about all the time she had been taking off for her Arthur Godfrey auditions, and the upcoming appearance on *Talent Scouts*. Instead of listening to her excuse, he simply informed her, "If you can't make it on time for the rehearsal, there's no need for you to come down for the show, because there won't be a spot to put you in. Consider yourself fired!"

On that night's broadcast, Jimmy really drove his point home when he announced on the air, "Patsy Cline is not here tonight. My advice to you, Patsy, is you better be good to us on your way up, 'cause you're gonna need us on your way down." To further emphasize his point, he then went into his own version of Mae Boren Axton's song "Pick Me Up on Your Way Down," which Patsy had just recorded.

Free of all of her possible scheduling conflicts, Patsy was able to fully concentrate on her upcoming national television debut on *Arthur Godfrey's Talent Scouts*. Patsy and Hilda arrived in New York City on Friday, January 18, and ironically checked into the Dixie Hotel. They connected with Al Gallico and the three of them went out to dinner. He later recalled her as being nervous with anticipation. Having just been fired by Jimmy Dean and her record contract almost expiring, she had a lot riding on her performance on Godfrey's show on Monday.

On the day of the show, Janette Davis met with Patsy early and began going over potential material for her to perform on that evening's program. Davis was among the first people to encourage Patsy Cline toward singing more pop ballads. Patsy brought along the music for about a dozen of her country songs. She also had "A Poor Man's Riches (or a Rich Man's Gold)" with her. Davis still didn't hear the right song—until they came to "Walkin' after Midnight."

"That's it!" she announced. Patsy argued and whined, but to no avail. Janette had found the song, and there would be no further discussion.

Patsy called Don Hecht up and started yelling at him on the phone. "You son-of-a-bitch, hoss!" she began. "I fought you all the way down the line. They've gone through every song I ever sang and recorded and they picked 'Walkin' after Midnight.' You guys are a bunch of jackasses, but you got the people in New York agreeing with you."

This was a crucial moment in Patsy's career. This show could make or break her. The matter of what she was to wear was still another important decision. Patsy was all set to wear one of her trademark cowgirl outfits, but again Janette Davis interceded.

"You're not just another hillbilly singer," Davis sincerely told her.

"What's wrong with being hillbilly?" Patsy asked defensively.

"Oh my goodness, nothing, Patsy!" she replied. "But look at it this way, you've got the potential to reach a far vaster audience."

Ray Rainwater went out shopping with Patsy, looking for the right dress to replace her cowgirl outfit. From store to store she tried on dozens of dresses. At long-last they decided on a simple dark blue linen dress that would look good on television. It was tight in the waist, and around her neck she tied a white scarf, the ends of which hung down fashionably in front.

Everything seemed so strange to her that evening. She was going to be singing a song she hated, wearing a dress that she wouldn't have chosen if left up to her own devices, and she also had to worry about keeping her mother's identity a secret. However out of her element she may have felt, she made up for it that evening the second she opened her mouth to sing.

That evening when Patsy's mother was introduced on the show, she presented her "friend" Patsy Cline. Godfrey then announced, "We would like very much to present for your entertainment, a talented young woman from Winchester, Virginia. She's very talented and very popular these days in the record jukeboxes and in nightclubs around the country, her name is Patsy Cline."

Backed by Arthur Godfrey's studio orchestra, she launched into "Walkin' after Midnight." The song received a totally unique big band rendition complete with a horn section. Patsy sang it sincerely, giving the song everything she had. When she was finished with it, the applause she garnered was deafeningly enthusiastic, and the applause meter that appeared on everyone's television screen had its indicator stuck at the highest end of the scale.

Patsy was absolutely stunned by the audience's response, as tears dampeneed her beautiful brown eyes. She was joined on stage by Godfrey, and the following dialogue was exchanged:

Virginia Hensley of Winchester, Virginia, dreamed of one day appearing on the *Grand Ole Opry*. Yet beyond her wildest fantasies, she became the legendary queen of country music: Patsy Cline. (Photo: Michael Ochs Archives Venice, CA)

LEFT: Patsy's first attempt at adopting a "country" image came across as decidedly "hillbilly." (Photo: BMI Photo Archives/ Michael Ochs Archives Venice, CA)

ABOVE: Although she switched back and forth between country and pop music throughout her career, Patsy had a vision of herself as a cowgirl, just like Dale Evans and Patsy Montana. (Photo: Country Music Foundation)

ABOVE: Patsy's stage accessories usually included bandannas and fringed gloves. She made a hobby out of collecting earrings like these tiny silver cowgirl boots. (Photo: Country Music Foundation)

RIGHT: Patsy took this pose directly from a 1930's still of Western singer Patsy Montana. With her mother sewing all of her stage costumes, Cline became known for her sequins and fringe. (Photo: *Movie Star News*)

LEFT: Patsy's first trademark song was the folksy "Come on in (And Make Yourself at Home)." She sang anywhere she could find an audience. (Photo: Michael Ochs Archives Venice, CA)

ABOVE: Appearing regularly on television shows like Washington, D.C.'s *Town and Country Jamboree* gave Patsy her first wave of local stardom in the mid-1950s. (Photo: MJB Photo Archives)

ABOVE: Discussing the record business with some of her Decca label mates. (L to R): Rex Allen, Justin Tubb, and Arlie Duff. (Photo: Country Music Foundation)

RIGHT: These early television performances often found Patsy either depicted as the cowgirl sitting around the campfire (*top*), or singing her heart out directly to her television fans (*bottom*). (Photos: MJB Photo Archives)

Patsy singing "Walkin' after Midnight" on TV's *Arthur Godfrey's Talent Scouts*, January 21, 1957. That smash single, and this television appearance, made her a recording star. It was Godfrey who insisted she leave her cowgirl outfits behind and dress in a more sophisticated mode. (Photo: MJB Photo Archives)

In 1994 the album *Patsy Cline: Discovery!* was released, featuring 17 of her performances from Arthur Godfrey's TV and radio programs in 1957 and 1958. (Photo: Lost Gold Records)

LEFT: When "Walkin' after Midnight" crossed over to the pop charts, Patsy began to adopt a more contemporary look. Her form-fitting dresses became her new trademark. (Photo: Michael Ochs Archives Venice, CA)

ABOVE: Patsy in Bradley's famed Quonset Hut recording studio in Nashville, 1957. (Photo: Country Music Foundation)

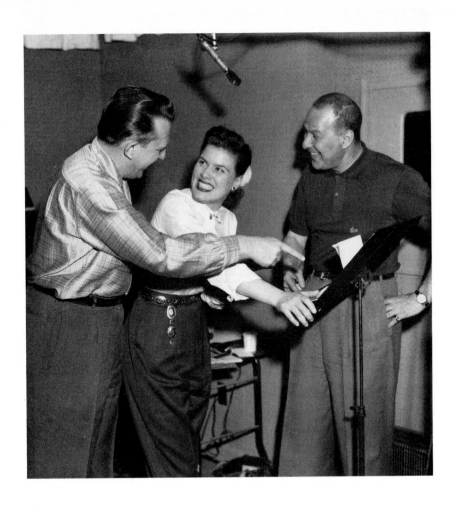

ABOVE: In the recording studio with Owen Bradley (left) and Decca's Paul Cohen (right). It was Bradley who produced the majority of Patsy's recordings, and all of her major hits. (Photo: Country Music Foundation)

RIGHT: An accomplished piano player since she was a child, Patsy tried her hand at songwriting in the mid-1950s. "A Stranger in My Arms" was one of the two songs she composed and recorded. (Photo: Michael Ochs Archives Venice, CA)

Harry Silverstein of Decca Records presents Patsy with her first major award, naming her as *Billboard* magazine's "Most Promising Country and Western Female Artist of 1957." (Photo: Michael Ochs Archives Venice, CA)

ARTHUR: Patsy Cline, "Walkin' after Midnight!" Don't go away Patsy—you done won this! You thank all those nice people out there.

PATSY: (sobbing and barely audible) Thank you!

ARTHUR: Bless your little heart. Sit down, sit down before you have a heart attack, sit down here.

PATSY: (still sobbing)

ARTHUR: (to the audience) Patsy Cline ... they sure did knock the thing out! (to Patsy) Calm yourself.... How many of these [contests] have you won?

PATSY: This is the first.

ARTHUR: Is this the first one? Is that the first record you made?

PATSY: No, I've got four records made.

ARTHUR: Have you had any hits?

PATSY: No.

ARTHUR: You know, I've got a hunch this one is.

PATSY: Oh, I hope so.

ARTHUR: Oh, this one's commercial. (to the audience) Isn't it, isn't it commercial? [huge round of approving applause]

83

Putting his arm around her, Arthur Godfrey said to Patsy, "Well, little lady, you sure know how to sing! Will you do another song for us?" She then performed her stand-out version of the Hank Williams' hit "Your Cheatin' Heart." Again she drew a wave of thunderous applause when she was finished.

Hilda was later to beam, "That certainly had to be one of the most memorable occasions of my life, not to mention Patsy's."

In front of his millions of viewers, Arthur Godfrey announced to twenty-four-year-old Patsy, "You're the most innocent, the most nervous, most truthful and honest performer I have ever seen. There is surely stardust on you."

Winning the competition on the Godfrey show was almost too much for Patsy. Not only did she get all of the glory that evening, it also meant that she would be Arthur's guest star for an entire week of his daily radio broadcasts, and she'd be making a return visit to the prime time show the following Monday as "last week's winner."

The following day, Hilda and Patsy were to meet with Arthur Godfrey in his office. They had both made up their minds to confess their "talent scout" charade before any more time lapsed and they were consumed with guilt. Before they could blurt out their confession, he let them know that he and his staff had already figured out the obvious identity of Mrs. Hensley.

At that meeting, Arthur Godfrey mapped out Patsy's further performances on his various programs. Hilda returned to Winchester and Patsy remained in town with a whole week of scheduled events. On the following day, she was to appear on the Wednesday edition of Godfrey's morning radio show. That afternoon she was expected in Paul Cohen's office at Decca Records.

When she arrived there, she was welcomed as the conquering hero. The record label had been deluged with requests for copies of "Walkin' after Midnight," and there were none pressed! Patsy's next single, with "Walkin' after Midnight" on the "A" side and "A Poor Man's Riches (or a Rich Man's Gold)" on the "B" side had to be rush-released on February 11. She finally had a hit. In April, it found itself reaching number two on *Billboard* magazine's country music chart, and number twelve on the pop chart.

In addition, the "flip side"—"A Poor Man's Riches (or a Rich Man's Gold)" also became a hit on the country chart, where it climbed to number fourteen. Not only was Don Hecht a master at picking a hit song, but Patsy's choice for a "B" side wasn't bad either.

When Patsy's new single hit the stores the week of February 11, Billboard magazine covered Patsy's breakthrough record—"Walkin' after Midnight"/"A Poor Man's Riches (or a Rich Man's Gold)"— with a glowing review. It read, "Miss Cline, heretofore identified mainly with the country field, makes a strong bid to break pop-wise. Both readings have had strong exposure via thrush's performance of them on Arthur Godfrey's TV airings. The 'Walkin' side has a fine bluesy flavor and the flip is loaded with reflected sentiment set to a rock and roll pace." Patsy was clearly on her way to the big time!

Arthur Godfrey was more than a little impressed with Patsy's singing talent, and both he and Janette Davis kept telling her that she had a huge future as a pop singing star. They both told her in no uncertain terms to give up on Nashville, and go for the big time in New York. However, it would take a couple more years before she would give up her cowgirl-Nashville dreams and go with a more mainstream image. She felt that she knew herself better than any-one else, and she strongly resisted people trying to change her.

Before one of the television broadcasts that week, Arthur said something to her that kind of rubbed her the wrong way: he told her to shave her legs. Since she had light leg hair, and usually dressed either in pants, or in medium length skirts with high boots, no one had ever asked her to do such a thing. She didn't dare argue with Godfrey, she simply shaved her legs as she was told, but it became indicative of how she felt that people in New York City wanted to change her.

Patsy Cline was still a diamond-in-the-rough, and although her first single made her an "overnight" star, she wanted to keep some of her rough edges intact. She kept needling Janette Davis all week about wearing her cowgirl clothes on at least one of the TV pro-grams. Finally they relented, for just one of the shows. So that Patsy didn't stand out like a sore thumb in her cowgirl get-up, they gave the rest of the show a western theme. They saw the broad-based appeal in Patsy that she herself was still unable to recognize. In her mind, the *Grand Ole Opry* was the end-all and be-all for her. Little did she know that she was destined to become a bigger star than she had ever dreamed.

Although New York City still frightened her, the entire trip was one big fairy-tale journey. When she returned to Winchester, she found that the telephone wouldn't stop ringing. She was sud-denly inundated with congratulatory calls and job offers. Interviewed by *The Washington Star* for their February 9, 1957, issue, Patsy was quoted as saying, "I'm not making up my mind about anything right now. Things are happening so quickly for me, and I'm still in the thinking stage."

She wasn't given too much time to stand still and just think about things. For Patsy, her honky tonk merry-go-round was sudden-ly spinning faster than ever before.

Chapter Seven

1957

Patsy had not only returned home to find the fame and glory that comes from having a hit on the charts, she also returned to find out that Gerald had formally filed for divorce. This was a mere formality to Patsy, as this marriage had ended ages ago, and Gerald had merely become a friend who escorted her to public events. With reference to her marriage to Gerald, Patsy was later to tell Nashville singer Del Wood, "Oh, hoss, it was like a bad dream with no tunes in it."

⌒⌒

The only relationship she really cared about patching up was with Connie B. Gay and Jimmy Dean. Patsy apologized for her habitual lateness, and they invited her back onto *Town and Country Jamboree*. Although the three of them aired their differences and "buried the hatchet," an even bigger disagreement was about to erupt between them. Patsy made a handful of *Town and Country Jamboree* appearances in February and March, but this reconciliation was temporary.

To further complicate matters, there was a simultaneous "battle of the giants" in the country music television world. When news hit the street that CBS-TV was planning on pulling the plug on its 7 A.M. weekday show starring cowboy star Will Rogers, Jr., there was a mad scramble to find a replacement program for that time slot. CBS specifically wanted a show with country music, and the network executives were most interested in simply signing on a pre-existing program as opposed to producing its own from scratch.

Among the contenders were WSM's *Grand Ole Opry*, Chicago station WLS's *National Barn Dance*, Shreveport station KWKH's *Louisiana Hayride*, Springfield's *Ozark Jubilee*, and *Town and Country Jamboree*.

Patsy was on the original schedule to be part of the live audition that *Town and Country Jamboree* was doing on February 3 and recording it on kinescope. However, she didn't show up. She had just returned days before from her triumphant streak of appearances on all of Arthur Godfrey's programs. Everybody seems to remember a different version of the exact course of events.

The most prevalent story is that Patsy missed *Town and Country's* special audition, but was featured on *The Grand Ole Opry's* quickly-put-together demonstration film. This fact reportedly angered Gay, and when he found out, that was the last straw in their professional relationship. That is certainly possible, since she was in Nashville the third week in February. Patsy's cousin, Punk Longley, swears that he saw her when she returned from New York City, and that she had a bad case of laryngitis—causing her to miss the *Town and Country* show. Connie Gay later recalled that when CBS found her missing from the *Town and Country* telecast, she was branded by the network as "unreliable" and passed on including her in the contract. There is also the theory that Arthur Godfrey flexed his muscle with the network, and wouldn't allow another in-house CBS show to steal his new discovery, as he had plans for her on his show. Charlie Dick's version is that it was simply one big "misunderstanding."

The exact facts constitute a moot point. Whatever it was that happened, CBS retooled the *Town and Country* program, retitled it *The Jimmy Dean Show*, and debuted it as a weekday morning show on April 8, 1957, sans "the Cline."

"I thought she'd be a stand-out," Connie Gay was later to lament. "Just when I was counting on her most, Patsy Cline let us down. Maybe the chain of events was uncontrollable; nevertheless she did let us down." Gay also complained that Patsy had showed up to do too many of his Saturday night telecasts with alcohol on her breath, having just done "cocktail hour" with Charlie. When "The Jimmy Dean Show" went national, and Gay became irritated with her, their working relationship fell apart, never to be patched up.

While Connie Gay spoke of Patsy drinking too much on occasion, her co-workers recall that as an exaggeration. George Hamilton IV recalls, "She was always professional. Patsy could take a drink with the best of us. She could hold her liquor, as they say. But I never can remember ever seeing her mess up a show or miss one. I never even saw her drunk."

Hurt and disappointed by Patsy's "deserting" him and his show, Gay may have been prompted to complain that liquor was one of Cline's problems. Not only did she not become part of his network television dreams, but upon her return from New York City, she had also just turned him down flat when he offered her a management contract—a deal which would cut him a proposed 50 percent of her income. She literally laughed at his proposition. Although Elvis Presley was stupid enough to sign that exact same 50 percent deal with Colonel Tom Parker, Patsy was too smart to fall for that kind of an arrangement. While Connie was busy complaining that Patsy drank too much, it was he who was a self-proclaimed alcoholic, and his personal life was in shambles. In her inimitable fashion, Patsy told him point blank that he could take his 50 percent deal and stuff it. Now that she was popular, everyone wanted a piece of the pie. She wasn't about to let Connie—or Arthur Godfrey, for that matter—control her or her career.

All of a sudden, Patsy's professional plate was full and she couldn't seem to be in enough places at once. Arthur Godfrey wanted to maintain some degree of control over her national television exposure. When Godfrey got wind that Patsy was booked to appear April 7 on the program of his arch-rival, Ed Sullivan, Godfrey put his foot down and cancelled that. Sullivan's Sunday evening show was also broadcast on CBS, and Godfrey certainly had more clout with the network. As it was, Patsy had already made a deal with Godfrey to appear on his program several times during the rest of the year, when her schedule permitted.

Things began to spin faster and faster in both Patsy's career and her personal life. On March 28, her divorce from Gerald became final. Only days later Charlie received his "greetings" from Uncle Sam, and was told to report to basic training at Ft. Bragg, over six hundred miles south of Winchester in Columbus, Georgia. Although she was upset about him being drafted, Patsy had her own hands full at this point, and didn't have time to concentrate on her relationship with Charlie.

For nine years Patsy had sacrificed everything for a career that was exciting and demanding. The year 1957 was when it all suddenly started to move faster and faster. Her personal life was suddenly taking a backseat to her newfound stardom.

Because of the instant success of "Walkin' after Midnight," both 4 Star Records and Decca Records were in a big hurry to come up with enough material to release the first Patsy Cline album, to capitalize on the popularity of the single. None of her previously recorded material could—or would—even be considered.

There was an immediate scramble for suitable material. Since Bill McCall had won his song-selecting wager with "Midnight," Patsy was even more tightly bound to record only 4 Star compositions. Riding high on her first hit, option clauses on her existing contract were signed, and she was now obligated to continue to record under the 4 Star–Decca sublicensing deal for an additional three years. It was 4 Star's "Walkin' after Midnight" that had just made her an overnight star. Why should she tamper with a formula that was working? Patsy began listening to dozens of demos that Bill McCall sent her. Since "Patsy Cline mania" was sweeping the country, she would record eighteen new songs in 1957.

In March of that year, Patsy was on the West Coast to tape several television appearances. She was a guest star on *Town Hall Party* and on CBS's *The Bob Crosby Show*, which was hosted by Bing's bandleader brother.

While she was in Los Angeles taping those programs, she was staying in a motel in Pasadena. The owner of the motel had a sister who was a poet who'd had her writing published in several woman's magazines, including *McCall's* and *Good Housekeeping*. When he told Patsy that his sister, Mary Lou Jeans, was trying to branch out into songwriting, he offered to show her one of her first attempts. It was a song that Jeans wrote with a friend of hers named Charlotte White called "A Stranger in My Arms." Patsy loved the lyrics, which were about the end of a love affair. All it needed was to be set to music. Patsy had always wanted to get into songwriting, so she decided that this could be her chance. She took the poem and drawing upon her ability to play the piano, set it to music. According to an interview in *The Winchester Evening Star*, this was her debut songwriting foray, and she was quite pleased with the results. When she finished, she placed a call to Paul Cohen and sang him the results over the phone. He loved it. The lyrics of the song included the lines,

> *Through the years your love will haunt me,*
> *And I'll dream about your arms,*
> *Still I know you'll never want me,*
> *You're a stranger in my arms.*

When Bill McCall went to have the song published by BMI, they informed him that there could be copyright problems, as the first six notes were identical to Rodgers and Hammerstein's "Some Enchanted Evening" from *South Pacific*. McCall slickly turned to Rodgers and Hammerstein's publishing company, Chappel Music, and registered it there. It would be rather ridiculous for Chappel Music to sue itself for copyright infringement!

Patsy was thrilled and encouraged by the results of her song-writing debut. She got back to the Washington, D.C., area, and recalled that another friend of hers, Lillian Claiborne, also wrote songs. When she told Lillian about her songwriting debut, she showed Patsy an R&B song she had written called "Don't Ever Leave Me Again," already published by 4 Star. Claiborne suggested re-working it with Patsy, and making it more of a torch song for Cline to record. Claiborne and her co-writer, James Crawford, gave her songwriting credit on that one as well. Excited by this new career tangent, Patsy made plans to record both songs in her very next session. They each carried her songwriter's credit under her birth name: Virginia Hensley.

But back in Los Angeles, Patsy was receiving all kinds of additional career offers as well. At one point, a movie deal was even proposed. Mae Boren Axton recalls speaking to Cline during this era, and her expounding upon how a film producer had spoken to her about doing a screen test. "Do you think I can do it?" Mae remembers Patsy asking her. Axton immediately warned her about the nature of the movie business, and how it was a real "hurry up, and wait" process on a movie set. Rock and roll movies were suddenly the rage, and everyone wanted in on the action. Another new rock-a-billy star on the scene, Elvis Presley, had just signed to do his first film role, so why shouldn't Patsy get in on the action too? At this point in time Patsy and Elvis were both in their initial streaks of success, so they had a lot in common. When Axton was later to quiz Patsy about whatever happened to the film offer, her reply was, "Well, I'm just too busy." It was quite an accurate answer.

Touring steadily to promote her hot new hit, in late March she played several dates in the midwest. Not only was she performing at country venues, but she also headlined at several pop-oriented "sock hops" as well. In April, she toured South Carolina, Georgia, and Florida on the bill with country artists Ferlin Husky and Faron Young.

Having become popular on TV's *Louisiana Hayride*, Young made his movie debut in 1956 in a film called "Hidden Guns." The character he portrayed was "the young sheriff," and Patsy would refer to him as "lil' sheriff"—and refer to his "gun" as a sexual innuendo.

Young recalls Patsy singing for him the two new "compositions" she was working on. Sitting in the back of a car, riding to the next town, the pair sang each other's songs, and they actively discussed songwriting. Patsy sang him "A Stranger in My Arms," and was thrilled that he encouraged her to continue to pursue this new writing phase.

Patsy returned to New York City in the latter half of April, where she made another appearance on the Godfrey show. Her sudden star stature in the rock and pop arenas further confused the question of what direction her career should take: "country" or "pop" or "rock?" This was to be a career-long dilemma for her.

Patsy went into the recording studio in New York City for two more four-song sessions on April 24 and 25. The studio records of who produced these tracks and played on these sessions are all lost. They are assumed to have been produced by Paul Cohen himself, and most likely took place at Decca's studio's in the former Knights of Pythias building on Broadway. She recorded four songs a day for two days. The first day she sang with an unknown male vocal group behind her, and on the second day she was accompanied by the Anita Kerr Singers.

What a quandary everyone must have been in when Patsy returned to the recording studio on April 24 to record a follow-up single to her first genuine hit record. First of all, "Walkin' after Midnight" was still on the charts while her next eight recordings were made. Decca was in search of a follow-up single, as well as needing eleven more cuts to compete the album that would frame her already existing hit.

"Today, Tomorrow and Forever" [17] was a good choice for starters. Much more upbeat and lighthearted than "Walkin' after Midnight," this song of true devotion set the tone for her next thirteen recordings: no yodeling, no steel guitars, no barn dance numbers, and absolutely no country. A breezy song about the devotion of love, written by Don Reid, on it, Patsy sounded excellent, and it was to become her next single release.

"Fingerprints" [18] has an ethereal male chorus at the very beginning, which catapults Patsy into the lyrics. It is a beautiful ballad carried with a classical-sounding fiddle played violin-style. A sincere song about an unforgettable love affair, it was written by Don Hecht (with W. O. Fleener and W. S. Stevenson). A beautiful tune, Patsy sang it in a heartfelt fashion, yet it lacks the exciting "oomph" that "Walkin' after Midnight" had. On this song, it is fascinating to hear how Cline's vocal instrument is note-for-note every bit as lush and emotion-filled as the mournful fiddle.

Warmed up by the first two numbers, Patsy was in fine form when she came to the third selection of the day—her own music on the beautiful ballad "A Stranger in My Arms" [19]. When she sang about a love so memorable that it haunts her—she sang it with gusto and conviction. Buoyed throughout by the all-male backup group, this forgotten gem is one of her best songs from the 4 Star era.

Her second writers' credit came on "Don't Ever Leave Me Again" [20]. Listening to the four songs that she recorded that day in chronological order, she clearly saved the best for last. Her voice opened up and was full sounding as she drove home this blues number with a "last of the red-hot mamas" fervor. A song about devotion and desertion, Patsy sounded gutsy and exciting throughout.

The following day, April 25, Patsy went back to the studio in New York and laid down four more tracks. This was the first of four consecutive sessions she recorded with the Anita Kerr Singers. A quartet comprised of two women and two men (Anita Kerr, Dottie Dillard, Louis Nunley, and Gil Wright), the group had also been "discovered" on "Arthur Godfrey's Talent Scouts," and it has been hypothesized that the idea of Patsy working with them may have been Godfrey's.

"Try Again" [21] is a light jazz–pop number that Patsy sounds absolutely fabulous on. With guitar accompaniment and the Kerr Singers unobtrusively behind her, this is the kind of number someone like Doris Day might have recorded at the time. A surefire pop standard, Patsy excelled on this one.

Bobby Lyle's composition "Too Many Secrets" [22], is one of the most fun songs that Patsy ever recorded. A pop–swing number, it tells a story in its lyrics, and Patsy literally wails on the choruses of this song. Finally, she really unleashed the unbridled power in her voice on a real "socko" ending. Amid the plot of the song, Patsy sings about going to get a pack of cigarettes and encountering a girl next to her who has her boyfriend's picture in her wallet.

On Bobby Lyle's "Then You'll Know" [23], the Kerr Singers come more into the forefront to trade off chorus lines with Patsy. A sorrowful ballad about the end of a love affair, the results are lush and tasty.

The final song of the day was the sheer Cline classic, "Three Cigarettes in an Ashtray" [24]. Written by Eddie Miller and W. S. Stevenson, it tells the tale of a couple in a small café, smoking and drinking. Suddenly, an interloper comes by, sits down, and puts her burning cigarette in the ashtray, and promptly leaves with the boyfriend. At the end of the song, the other woman is left at the café, smoking her cigarette alone. An impelling song of love lost, Patsy turned it into an unforgettable and effective pop jewel.

On May 3, she was again in Winchester's Apple Blossom Festival Parade, on the back of a convertible. This time around, Patsy went for a contemporary new look. She had her hair swept fashionably upward, and she wore a shoulderless dress with a long boa of chiffon she chicly draped around herself. This year the banners draped over the side of the car read,

"Walkin' after Midnight"
PATSY CLINE
Decca Record Artist and Recording Star
"A Winner All the Way"

The next day Patsy was in Iowa for concert engagements in Dubuque and Des Moines. In Dubuque on May 4, Patsy sang with Tony Pastor's band, with whom Rosemary Clooney began her career. In Des Moines, she was the opening act for Webb Pierce ("Bye Bye Love," 1957), who had his own radio show on KWKH. They played at the Des Moines Auditorium. After Patsy's set, someone backstage told her of a fourteen-year-old fan of hers who had purchased a ticket to see her favorite singer—Patsy Cline. Unfortunately, young Shirley Nelson had been whisked to a local hospital to undergo emergency surgery instead. "What hospital?" Patsy asked, "I'll go and sing for her." And, that's exactly what she did! That was the kind of person Patsy was.

Patsy's diary entry for Saturday, May 4, 1957: "Plane ticket $120 ... Paid $700." She had yet to see a cent of royalties from her hit single, but she was making good money from her concert appearances.

Jumbo Rinker recalls a flood in the Winchester area that washed away several poor people's homes. Although she was far from rich, Patsy went out and bought groceries, and had Rinker help her deliver them to the flood victims.

On May 15, Patsy was in a Washington, D.C., studio recording a series of radio commercials. Then on May 23, she returned to Nashville to work with Owen Bradley on eight new songs, each a potential cut for her first album.

Patsy cranked out six songs that day in Nashville with Bradley holding the reins. Bill McCall was present at the session and drove everyone nuts. He claimed that he hated two of the songs that were recorded in New York, so he demanded that she record six that day to make up for it.

Patsy and the Anita Kerr Singers sounded wonderful trading off lines on the first song of the day, "That Wonderful Someone" [25]. However, this pop/gospel number is so saccharine that Patsy's great singing was totally wasted on this gooey confection.

Swinging right out of that somber mood came two back-to-back blues rockers written by Eddie Miller and W. S. Stevenson. "In Care of the Blues" [26] begins with a twangy guitar, and is carried by Owen's subtly-placed piano work. Patsy virtually growled some of her lyrics on this one, giving the song excitement and verve.

Likewise, when Patsy declared on the next number that she's "Hungry for Love" [27], you really sit up and take notice. Lively and rocking, it features Hank Garland's great rock guitar work, which sounds like vintage Chuck Berry.

On the next three songs, Patsy reflects the negative feelings both she and Bradley must have felt towards McCall's interfering presence that day, as they all have the words of refusal in the title: "can't," "don't," and "ain't," respectively. "I Can't Forget" [28] slowed down the pace of the session a bit. A piano bar type of a ballad, Patsy sang effectively about an absent lover, and her painful memories. The results were, however, decidedly dull.

"I Don't Wanna" [29] is a remake of her eighth recording. This livelier version is kind of fun, yet the Kerr Singers' silly "ooh-bop-a-doo" backgrounds come across like corn still on the cob. Patsy's singing on this number was again electrifying.

Likewise, "Ain't No Wheels on This Ship (We Can't Roll)" [30] finds Patsy wailing, and the Kerr Singers bopping, but this ship never quite gets off of dry land. Patsy was seriously beginning to feel the pinch of having to select her recording material from 4 Star's limited songbook.

The day after the marathon recording session, on May 24, Patsy rushed back to Winchester to celebrate Charlie's twenty-third birthday. After cutting the birthday cake, he had to hurriedly return to

Ft. Bragg. Patsy and Hilda spent the evening working on some new stage costumes for Patsy.

May 25 she left town for a tour with Porter Wagoner, and her new little friend Brenda Lee, who had just recorded her trademark single, "Dynamite." After that Brenda was known as "Little Miss Dynamite." While she was on tour, Patsy's next single, "Today, Tomorrow and Forever"/"Try Again" was released May 27, from the New York sessions. Unfortunately, neither song ever made the charts.

With the money she was making from personal appearances, both on television and in concert, Patsy was able to accomplish something she had longed to do for quite some time: move her mother and her siblings out of the dilapidated old wooden Kent Street house and into something better. Oddly enough, Patsy didn't move them a long distance. Her friends were surprised that she didn't transplant them to a better neighborhood as well. What she did do was relocate them to a more sound brick house on the very same street. Buying this house for her mother was a great accomplishment for Patsy, and she was thrilled to do it.

It was on a flight from New York City to Nashville in 1957 that she met someone who was to become one of her dearest friends, June Carter. A member of the country music institution, the Carter Family Singers, June had launched an acting career and now performed as a country comedienne. Whenever Patsy was feeling down, June was one of the people she would turn to and discuss her problems.

One of her biggest problems was the fact that while she was now one of the year's hottest newcomers, the kind of money that should be coming from her recording career simply wasn't there. While she had sold between 750,000 and a million recordings of "Walkin' after Midnight," her account with 4 Star was "in the red," due to the studio costs from a dozen songs that didn't sell. When she received her first post-hit royalty statement, she was appalled to find that instead of being due a check, McCall claimed that she had a negative balance. The worst part was the fact that in return for three cash advances, she had signed three additional one-year contract extensions with 4 Star. Patsy was furious once she realized what Bill McCall was doing to her under the terms of his recording contract.

She was now stuck until 1960, recording only 4 Star songs. Her frustration with this deal only mounted with time.

In early July of 1957, Patsy found herself on the road doing an all-country tour with Ray Price, Faron Young, Hank Thompson, Ferlin Husky, and Johnny Cash—who was in his rock-a-billy phase. That was the dramatic thing about Patsy Cline's career: from the minute that "Walkin' after Midnight" became a hit, she was usually the only woman on the bill with all of the men. Because of her one hit single, she was one of the first women in country music to become a star. It was male country stars who dominated the field until Patsy Cline came along. Kitty Wells was the only other major female in the business, but her songs were mainly "nice" tunes like "I Heard a Jukebox Playing" and "Cheatin's a Sin." Patsy was raucous, bawdy, flamboyant, and exciting—and audiences loved that about her. Looking back on this time, she was the one who single-handedly opened the door for all of the young and independent-minded female country singers of the 1960s.

Only days after completing the country tour on July 26, Patsy was in New York City as one of the headliners on Alan Freed's ABC-TV four-week summer 1957 series, "The Big Beat." Rock impresario Alan Freed was famous for his rocking multi-star extravaganzas at the Brooklyn Fox Theater. This is what he staged for the brief run of his own short-lived but exciting half-hour series. This was one of the first network programs devoted exclusively to rock and roll—and Patsy was part of it.

She invited her sister Sylvia, and her friend Dale Turner from the *Town and Country* show, to join her in New York to keep her company. Patsy figured that her sister would get a big kick out of all of the rock stars, and although Dale was a network TV star, she had never been to New York City. The three of them packed their bags and took the train from Washington, D.C., to Manhattan.

The show that Patsy was on included Fats Domino ("Blueberry Hill"), Clyde McPhatter ("Treasure of Love"), Dale Hawkins ("Susie-Q"), Jimmy C. Newman ("A Fallen Star"), and her friend Marvin Rainwater ("Whole Lot a Woman"). Everyone performed one of their hits, with a bit of theatrical staging.

Fourteen-year-old Sylvia was thrilled beyond belief. Backstage she shared a piano bench with Fats Domino, and as a gift he took a piece of gold-plated piano wire and using a pencil, he curled it into a "G clef" musical note. Meanwhile, Dale was charmed by one of the agents who was responsible for Patsy's appearance, and took off on a tour of the city while Cline rehearsed her number.

"I brought you here to be company for me, and you're running around!" Patsy hollered at Dale when she returned. According to Dale, "We could talk to each other that way."

On the broadcast that night, wearing a blue chiffon cocktail dress with an off the shoulder cut, Patsy looked suitably dreamy as she performed a lip-sync version of "Walkin' after Midnight." She sang while she walked across a footbridge, up a flight of nearly a dozen steps, and then back down again. She looked every inch the lovely young pop star that she was.

On August 5, 1957, Patsy's self-titled debut album was at long-last released. Composed of a dozen of her new pop-flavored songs, it was met with moderate success. The "Patsy Cline" album featured "Walkin' after Midnight," "Fingerprints," "Don't Ever Leave Me Again," "Too Many Secrets," "Then You'll Know," "Three Cigarettes in an Ashtray," "That Wonderful Someone," "In Care of the Blues," "Hungry for Love," "I Can't Forget," "I Don't Wanna," and "Ain't No Wheels on This Ship (We Can't Roll)."

On August 10, Patsy appeared back in a country music context on ABC-TV's *Country Music Jubilee*, which was hosted by Red Foley. Seated in a staged café setting, Foley announced, "The young lady who has come to visit us this week is the one who made such a hit with her song 'Walkin' after Midnight.' Here with a brand-new tune, 'Three Cigarettes in an Ashtray' is pretty Patsy Cline."

When her new single was released on August 12, "Three Cigarettes in an Ashtray" was on the "A" side, and "A Stranger in My Arms" was on the "B" side. Like "Today, Tomorrow and Forever" before it, it too failed to hit the charts.

It was only after the single's release that Patsy discovered the song she had written, "A Stranger in My Arms," was credited as having been "arranged" by Ethel Bassey—Bill McCall's wife. Patsy was duped again, and received only one-third of the royalties. Jeans/White as a lyricist team received one-third, and in the name of his wife, McCall stole the remaining one-third. Patsy was so angry with McCall after that that she would never go out of her way to plug "A Stranger in My Arms."

September was a time of celebration for Patsy. Not only was her twenty-fifth birthday on the eighth of the month, but she and Charlie had set their wedding date for the fifteenth. The night before, Patsy and Charlie and several of their friends went out and partied until the early hours.

The next afternoon, Patsy and Charlie were married at a ceremony held at Hilda's new Kent Street house. Surrounded that Sunday afternoon by a crowd of fifty friends and family, they took their vows. Charlie was on leave, and Patsy was in heaven. She was marrying the man she truly loved.

The bride wore a two-piece pink knit suit with a calf-length skirt and a large white corsage on her left side. Wearing high heels and a white feathered hat, Patsy radiated happiness that afternoon. Charlie wore a beige suit, a striped tie, and a carnation in his lapel. The reception directly thereafter was held at the Mountain Side Inn in Winchester.

There was no planned honeymoon, as both Patsy and Charlie were in the midst of the busiest year of their lives. Several days after the ceremony, Patsy was back in New York City to appear on Arthur Godfrey's show. When Godfrey congratulated her on her wedding, he asked her if she was happy about the marriage. Quipped Patsy, "I sure am. Just as happy as if I had good sense!"

Patsy left Winchester, and she and Charlie found a modest house on Pool Drive in Fayetteville, North Carolina, not far from Ft. Benning where Charlie was now stationed. It was a strip of identical modest houses built for servicemen and their families.

On the weekend of November 15, Patsy and her military-uniformed husband ventured to Nashville for WSM's birthday bash and annual Country Disk Jockey Convention. She dressed movie-star glamorous that weekend, and she walked away with just about every award she was eligible to win. *Billboard* magazine named her 1957's "Most Promising Country and Western Female Artist." *Music Vendor* magazine named her recording of "Walkin' after Midnight" the year's "Greatest Achievement in Records." And, *Country and Western Jamboree* magazine crowned her the "Best New Female Singer of 1957."

Decca released Patsy's eighth single on November 18. It was comprised of two cuts from her debut album. "I Don't Wanna" was the "A" side, and "Then You'll Know" was on the flip side. Again, it was met with no chart action.

On December 13, 1957, Patsy was back at Owen Bradley's recording studio in Nashville, with the Anita Kerr Singers, to lay down another four tracks. "Stop the World (and Let Me Off)" [31] is a tasty blues-rocker with a nice beat. Patsy dives right into the lyrics like she is delivering a sincere plea. Giving it all she's got, Cline's performance crackles with energy. Although the song itself is only mediocre, the singing is top-notch. This was one of the first songs where Patsy's voice cracks: she is so emotion-filled. This was to later become one of her most successful techniques.

"Walking Dream" [32] is one of my all-time favorites, and it really should have been a huge rock hit for Patsy. Exciting in its innocent but rambunctious 1950's rock and roll sound, this song has the same fun flair that Bradley injected into Brenda Lee's tracks during that same year. This is Patsy in full rock gear, and she was every bit as effective as Elvis Presley and Ricky Nelson were with their songs that were hitting number one that very year.

Don Hecht and Jack Moon wrote "Cry Not for Me" [33], which is quite an appealing rock ballad. While it is easy to give a blanket excuse as to why Patsy's career was so "hit-and-miss" during this year, she still managed to come up with several gems. Many of the 4 Star songs were "turkeys," but the effectiveness of "Walking Dream" and "Cry Not for Me," makes one wonder if Decca didn't promote her incorrectly. This pair of bluesy rockers should have been smashes, but were not because no one could figure out how to market her talents. Was she "country" or "pop?" This was an ongoing dilemma.

The last session of the day was "If I Could See the World (Through the Eyes of a Child)" [34]. It is a maudlin gospel-flavored ballad. While Patsy's singing was full of poise and grace, the number was dull, dull, dull. Although the song is forgettable, you can hear how effective Patsy was becoming at really getting into the mood and the message of a song, even if the material was less than perfect. Listening to her songs in the order in which they were recorded, you can hear her honing her craft tune-by-tune, and appreciate her chameleon-like ability to go from rock to blues to gospel—all in one afternoon.

The next day she returned to the *Grand Ole Opry*, and was introduced onstage by Ray Price. Said Price that evening, "We're always glad to have you with us at the *Grand Ole Opry*, and before any more time gets away from us, I want to ask a favor."

"Well, you just name it," Patsy answered.

"Walkin' after Midnight," he replied.

"It's a date boy," said Cline in a happy fashion as she launched into the song that would always be identified as one of her most beloved numbers.

To top off an exhausting year, at Christmastime Patsy announced her own little secret to Charlie: she was pregnant and expecting the following summer. It had been a twelve-month whirlwind, but as 1957 came to an end, Patsy had a new husband, a new home, her first huge top ten hit, and a new identity: as a genuine singing star.

Chapter Eight

PATSY AND CHARLIE

The year 1958 was one of mixed emotions for Patsy. Like the first line of Charles Dickens' "A Tale of Two Cities," for Cline, "It was the best of times, it was the worst of times."

Patsy had worked so hard to obtain that elusive goal in the music business: a huge hit record that was so exciting and appealing that it was too big for just one music chart. However, the whole experience was turning sour. Due to the awful 4 Star Records deal, the most money that she ever received from Bill McCall for "Walkin' after Midnight" was $900. Even worse was the fact that she had already recorded what she considered "the best" of the songs McCall owned. In concert she could still sing whatever she wanted, and to compensate for some of the mediocre material she was forced to record, she performed an interesting assortment of Top 40 songs from both the "country" and "pop" charts. Thankfully, several of

Patsy's live recordings from this year exist on transcription disk from the *Grand Ole Opry* and various other shows. Among the non–4 Star material she mastered during this era included: Connie Francis' pop hit "Stupid Cupid," Webb Pierce's "Yes, I Know Why," Sonny James' "For Rent," and Gogi Grant's huge number one smash "The Wayward Wind."

Her personal life also had two distinctively different sides to it. On the one hand, her new identity as a wife and expectant mother gave her a fresh outlook on life. She felt focused, and was happy that she had an identity apart from her career. However, that too was to have its downside. Instead of being supportive of her career and her pregnancy, Charlie would do everything he could to erode whatever career achievements and happiness she experienced.

Throughout her pregnancy, Patsy and Charlie fought constantly. Verbal shouting matches were one thing, but there were several physical battles as well. Charlie would have several drinks, they'd get into an argument, he'd smack her around, storm out of the house, and carry on with other women. Patsy's friend Pat Smallwood saw her at various phases of her pregnancy, back in Winchester. According to Smallwood, "It wasn't a happy time for her. She was constantly running back home here to her mother. He just wouldn't quit drinking and he'd party with other girls in his life—he had a couple girls besides Patsy."

Charlie was later to state, "We did argue quite a bit, but it moved fast—it ended as fast as it started. We didn't go around with a chip on our shoulder. If a stranger walked in the door and didn't know what was going on, they might think we'd be going after the shotguns or something like that."

When the film *Sweet Dreams* was released in 1985, actor Ed Harris—as Charlie—was seen slapping around pregnant Patsy (Jessica Lange). When *People* magazine queried Charlie about the domestic violence depicted on the screen, he stated, "Patsy and I were really worse than they made us look in the film."

If he expected Patsy to put her career aspirations aside, he was sadly mistaken. According to Charlie, "She was what you'd call a career gal today. Patsy said to me before we got married, 'Someday I'm gonna be a famous singer, and if you want to be beside me, then let's do it!' From then on it was one show, one record, one dollar after another." And, that's exactly how it was to be.

Exhausted and confused, Patsy had earmarked 1958 as the year she was going to put her career on "hold" and turn her focus toward being a wife and expectant mother. It didn't exactly turn out that way. As the year progressed and her dream marriage turned less than perfect, she began to focus with a vengeance on her career again.

Without the guidance of Connie Gay, or anyone else managing her career, Patsy began working with a talent agent by the name of Xavier "X" Cosse. He had done some of her bookings in late 1957, and in the January 13, 1958, issue of the trade publication, *The Music Reporter*, it was announced that Patsy was signed to be managed by him. Chet Atkins, Boots Randolph, Ferlin Husky, and gospel singer Martha Carson were all represented by him, so he seemed like a good choice.

It was also in January of 1958 that *Opry* singer Jeanie Shepard recalls having a conversation with Patsy in the ladies room of the *Grand Ole Opry*. "She was stomping and raving and just a-cussing," Shepard recalls.

"Goddamn it, Jeanie," Patsy whined. "I'm pregnant."

Miffed by Cline's reply, Jeanie offered her congratulations, and told her that this was wonderful news.

"Wonderful? It's horrible! Damn it! It's not great," ranted Patsy. "Here I am just coming off a big record and I go and get pregnant. I won't be able to go out on the road. This is really gonna tie me down. No road and no TV appearances!"

However, show business was in her blood, and slowing down wasn't something she took too easily. On February 13, she was back in the recording studio in Nashville with Owen Bradley and the Anita Kerr Singers. They produced six new tracks, which turned out to be Patsy's only recordings for the entire year of 1958.

The first song they tackled was "Just out of Reach (of My Two Open Arms)" [35]. Written by V. F. Stewart, Patsy delivers a great pop performance on this blues number, which remains one of the best of her 4 Star recordings. The Anita Kerr Singers offered a strong vocal accompaniment, and Patsy sang with a great deal of passion. Kay Adelman's "I Can See an Angel" [36], is almost identical in content, tempo, and execution to "Just out of Reach (of My Two Open Arms)." Again, Patsy sang with conviction and excitement in her voice.

Patsy had been using her song "Come on in (and Make Yourself at Home)" to open her concert performances. However, the first version she had recorded in 1956 was a down-home hillbilly rendition. Her re-recording of "Come on in (and Make Yourself at Home)" [37] was decidedly different in approach. Not only were the harmonic Kerr Singers added to the track, but the steel guitars and fiddles were gone, and a brass section was added to give the song a lively new "party" music effect. Much more rousing and fun than the first version, this is the superior recording of a true Cline trademark number.

Patsy recorded the next three numbers solo. The fourth song tackled that day was the rousing rock-a-billy number "Let the Teardrops Fall" [38], which is an excellent example of Patsy really rocking out. With nothing more than guitar, drums, and bass, this is another tune of Cline's from this era that should have been a hit for her. She comes across again like a female Elvis Presley, so she should have gotten more of a pop-rock promotional push when this was released as a single later that year. Unfortunately, it was buried on the "B" side of her new version of "Come on in (and Make Yourself at Home)"—a big mistake on the part of Decca's marketing department.

Continuing on a rock and roll bent, next came "Never No More" [39], an excellent jazzy-bluesy ballad. Floyd Cramer's piano work was a stand-out, and Patsy's delivery was nothing short of perfection. This is another one of her songs that should have been a huge chart hit for her, but it too ended up buried on the "B" side of one of her singles.

Unreleased during her lifetime, the ballad "If I Could Only Stay Asleep" [40] finds Patsy in a blue mood. With drums, guitar, piano, and bass lushly playing behind her, this was Cline's finest straight jazz number. Listening to this song, it is hard to imagine that this superb chanteuse round is from what is known as her commercial "slump" period.

Patsy made a television appearance February 21 on *Country Music Jubilee*, and much to her delight, in March she was booked on a concert tour in Hawaii. Playing to military personnel on bases all over the soon-to-be fiftieth state, she was featured along with head-liners Ferlin Husky and Faron Young, as well as newcomer Jerry Reed. Patsy was enthralled by the lush tropical islands, and when she shipped local flowers back to Hilda, they were accompanied by a note that read, "You've got to see this!"

Performing before an audience of Marines, Patsy announced onstage, "I played with Arthur Godfrey for about a year and a half." When their response was laughter—as though she meant she had "played around" with Godfrey sexually—she became upset. "Them sons-of-bitches," she complained to Faron Young. The next time that same line of onstage patter drew titters from the soldiers, she turned the joke around and quipped, "Well, I guess you all took that the wrong way. Only me and Arthur Godfrey will know!"

Patsy's association with Arthur Godfrey came to a close after she made an April 27 appearance on his show. Godfrey continued to press her to be managed by him, but she had her own concept of the kind of singer she wanted to become. Because of Godfrey, in the last year and a half she had become a nationally known name, but she disagreed with his ideas. She saw herself as a Nashville-based coun-try star. If Godfrey had his way, she'd have to move to New York City and become a pop singer, like Rosemary Clooney. Now it was time for Patsy to move on.

Unfortunately, her being aligned in business with Xavier Cosse was also short-lived. Cosse was married to singer Martha Carson, and when Carson was signed to an important nightclub contract in New York City, he decided to cease managing country acts. Again the steering wheel of her destiny was returned to Patsy's own hands.

The *Grand Ole Opry* was becoming a regular outlet for her talents as a guest star, and in June she was again booked for an appearance. Very pregnant—at seven months—Patsy came rushing into the ladies dressing room at the Ryman Auditorium brandishing a waist-cinching corset. Like Scarlett O'Hara being laced up by Mammy in *Gone with the Wind*, she intended on wrestling her way into the decidedly non-maternity outfit that she had in mind. Waving the corset at Jeanie Shepard, Patsy asked the singer to help lace her into it.

Shepard argued that putting a tight corset on in her condition went beyond vanity, and refused to help her. Undaunted, Patsy turned to Essie, a helpful and beloved black woman who worked backstage at the show, to help lace her up. Even Essie argued back at Patsy, but Cline was insistent, and so the woman relented and helped her struggle into it. When Patsy went out onstage that evening and performed, the audience had no idea of her condition. Nothing was going to stop Patsy Cline from looking her best onstage.

This incident was so typical of Patsy. She was very conscious of her looks, and her sex appeal. She knew that she had an expressive voice, but in her mind her looks were half of her act. The same held true for her song choices. She never sang a song in which she was a wife or a mother. Her songs were always about love—but her role in them was always as the narrator, the girlfriend, or the jilted lover. That night at the *Opry*, her fans came to see Patsy Cline the sexy star—not Mrs. Dick, the pregnant wife.

With the benefit of an empire-waisted dress, in July, Patsy was invited by the town of Elkton, Virginia, to help them celebrate their "Golden Jubilee." As the Grand Marshall of the parade, now eight months pregnant, Cline proudly sat atop the back of a convertible, waving at all of her adoring fans. While Winchester still looked at her as a woman of questionable reputation, Elkton lovingly considered her their prodigal daughter.

Tired of arguing with Charlie, in August Patsy moved back to Hilda's in Winchester. He took a leave of absence from the Army toward the end of the month, so that he could be with his expectant wife. The night of April 25, when Patsy went into labor, Charlie was out drinking, and Hilda had to take her daughter to the hospital.

It was at Winchester Memorial Hospital, where Patsy herself was born, that she gave birth to her daughter Julia Simadore Dick. The interesting middle name came from one of Patsy's favorite movies, *Samson and Delilah*. In the film, Delilah's beautiful sister, Simadore, was played by Angela Lansbury. Ever since Patsy saw the 1949 movie, starring Victor Mature and Hedy Lamar in the lead roles, she had been in love with the unusual name. Although her formal first name is "Julia," Patsy's daughter has always answered to "Julie."

Right after the baby was born, Patsy returned to her career—full speed ahead. She immediately went on a diet and turned her energies toward her big "comeback." Although she was a doting mother, her first love was her career, and neither Charlie nor her newborn baby was going to become an obstacle. "Sitting around the house playing the wife and mother is driving me crazy," she announced to Charlie. She also informed him that she had absolutely no desire to return to the little tract house on Pool Drive in Fayetteville. With that, he gave up the house and moved back to Ft. Bragg, until he completed his term of military service. Having worked at the newspaper in Winchester, he was given similar duties in the Army, running their presses. He only had a couple more months in the service ahead of him, so he would soon be back in Patsy's life on a permanent basis. But was this really what she wanted?

If Charlie had his way, Patsy would have quit the business and devoted her life to being a full-time wife and mother. How was it that she twice ended up married to men who saw her as a mere cook and housekeeper? Nothing could have been further from Patsy's intentions. She was going to return to her career like gangbusters—and as usual nothing was going to stop her!

Most of Patsy's fights with Charlie had to do with his desire to see her start acting like Mrs. Charles Dick, and put her career as "the Cline" on ice. To make his opinion known, he especially liked to get drunk and embarrass her from the audience while she was onstage. This was just what she didn't need—a drunken husband who would heckle her and call her a "bitch" and a "whore" while she was earning money to support him.

One of these occasions came in October of 1958. Slimmed down, corsetted in, and looking sexy, Patsy was booked to perform in Gaithersburg, Maryland, at the Agricultural Exposition Center. Roy Deyton, who had known Patsy when they both performed with Bill Peer's band, showed up to see her at that particular show. He recalls being shocked to see Patsy and Charlie amidst one of their famous public rows. "Charlie was stumbling around, and Patsy was high [on liquor]," he recalls.

Before her performance, Charlie was insisting that Patsy give up show business right then and there, and she calmly told him that if she didn't sing, she wouldn't get paid. Then Charlie argued that she ought to behave like his wife, and how he could support her. "I heard you, but I'm a going," she announced. When she attempted to get up from the table they were sitting at, Charlie grabbed her by the arm and proceeded to dump a drink all over her.

After a moment of dead silence, Patsy pulled her arm loose. While her horrified friends looked on, she turned sharply and headed for the dressing room. She simply changed her clothes, and headed for the stage to perform. When incidents like this occurred, it only strengthened Patsy's career convictions. She was going to become a star, and no one—not even Charlie—was going to stop her.

By the time Patsy returned to the recording studio in January of 1959, there had been several changes made at Decca Records. Most notably, Owen Bradley was promoted to the post of A&R Director, the position previously held by Paul Cohen. Now this would give him the freedom that he needed to take both Brenda Lee and Patsy Cline to their greatest recorded successes. With Cohen and McCall to answer to, Patsy's recording career was being run by committee. Now, much to Owen's pleasure he was in control. Explained Bradley, "By now Cohen had been promoted to a higher position. He was promoted in 1958, and at that time I took over the job that he had. Now it was my problem—my responsibility for all the artists. So, we fumbled along. We had a couple of almost hits with her [Patsy], but not quite."

Although Patsy had been absent from the recording studio for the last ten months of 1958, Decca released five new Cline singles. Unfortunately, none of them made the charts. They included: "Stop the World (and Let Me Off)"/"Walking Dream," "Come on in (and Make Yourself at Home)"/"Let the Teardrops Fall," "I Can See an Angel"/"Never No More," "If I Could See the World (Through the Eyes of a Child)"/"Just out of Reach (of My Two Open Arms)," and "Dear God"/"He Will Do for You." Meanwhile, the walls between rock and roll and country were disintegrating as crossover artists enjoyed popularity on both the pop and country charts. Patsy's "Walking Dream," "Let the Teardrops Fall," and "Never No More" were every bit as exciting as the hits of several of the country-rock artists, but somehow none of these releases made it onto the charts. Instead, Carl Perkins' "Pink Pedal Pushers," Johnny Cash's "Ballad of a Teenage Queen," Elvis Presley's "Wear My Ring around Your Neck," and Patti Paige's "Left Right out of Your Heart" were the big hits of 1958.

In January 1959, Patsy returned to Nashville for two days of recording. These were quite historic sessions, because it marked her first work with the Jordanaires. As a quartet, the Jordanaires were known around Nashville for their gospel harmonizing, as well as their background recording work. They had been working behind Elvis Presley, both in concert and in the studio since the 1956 New York City session that produced "Hound Dog" and "Don't Be Cruel." The original individual members of the Jordanaires were Gordon Stoker, Hoyt Hawkins, Neal Matthews, Jr., and Ray Walker. They were to record on all but one of Patsy Cline's twenty recording sessions from 1959 to 1963.

Patsy connected with the Jordanaires through Owen Bradley. Since Bradley now held the reins at Decca's Nashville A&R Department, he made the decision that Patsy should be working with the group Elvis was working with, in the hope that some of the magic that had taken Presley's career to the top of the charts would rub off on Cline.

Patsy, however, had a fit when she found out that she was going to have to record with an all-male chorus behind her. She had found working with the Anita Kerr Singers obtrusive enough for her taste. "I don't want no four male voices covering me up!" she protested. However, Bradley was insistent that she at least give them a try.

In a three-and-a-half-hour session that began at 5:00 P.M., on January 8, 1959, Patsy and the Jordanaires recorded three new songs. The first one they did was "I'm Moving Along" [41], a medium-tempo ballad about pulling up one's stakes and leaving town to escape the blues. Although the very first lines were sung by the Jordanaires, the song is clearly Patsy's. The male chorus' lilting harmonies were so tight that it actually allowed Patsy the space to drive the end of the song home with a lot of gusto. The effect was that of a nice contrast between the two vocal styles: the Jordanaires' smooth harmonies, and Patsy's powerfully gruff delivery.

The next song they tackled was "I'm Blue Again" [42], which found Patsy in excellent voice. Cline's phrasing is full of warbling emotion. When she hits the high notes on this one, you can hear her utilize some of the vocal acrobatics that would highlight her strongest later work. This was one of the finest recordings to date.

On "Love, Love, Love Me Honey Do" [43], they picked up the pace for this rousing rock-a-billy number. Patsy's yelping excitement provides a great juxtaposition with the Jordanaires. Obviously, Cline was stretching out from cut to cut, and by the time she got to this one, she was revved up to full throttle. Another Cline classic, this one is another of her best 4 Star outings.

The following day, at 2:00 in the afternoon, the same troupe gathered at Bradley's studio to record another pair of songs. They began with "Yes, I Understand" [44], a mid-tempo ballad, which was merely pleasant, and ended up with the much more exciting "Gotta Lot of Rhythm in My Soul" [45]. The second number was close in feeling and excitement to Bill Haley and the Comets' 1955 smash "Rock around the Clock," and the Jordanaires were moved farther into the background to let Patsy soar on this rocker.

No one was more astonished than Patsy at how effective her work with the Jordanaires was. "After the first session we did with her, she liked what we did so well that she said she wanted us on everything," Gordon Stoker recalls. With Owen Bradley now the A&R Director of Decca's Nashville operation, and the Jordanaires backing up, the right elements were all falling into place for Patsy to achieve her greatest success. The only element that was missing was the right material. She still had one more year to go before her restricting 4 Star deal ran out. Then she would be free to lend her voice to any song she chose to sing.

Another subtle, yet significant change that took place when she started recording with the Jordanaires, was that all of Cline's songs from this point on were not only recorded in mono, but in stereo as well. Recalls Owen Bradley, "Along about 1957, stereo came in. We bought our first stereo machine, I believe in 1957. We just heard about it, and we thought it was sensational. So I thought I'd like to get one of those. And I called Ampex and we got the first one around here [Nashville]."

On February 23, Decca released a single with "Yes, I Understand" on the "A" side, and "Cry Not for Me" on the "B" side. Although she now had a great formula going in the studio with the Jordanaires, her music still was missing the mark on the radio. The company had now released nine singles since her smash "Walkin' after Midnight," and none of them had made a dent on either the country or the pop charts. Patsy was very unhappy about the lack of promotion that "Cry Not for Me" received from 4 Star, as she felt that this was one of the best songs she had ever recorded.

In a March 1959 issue of *Music Reporter* magazine, it was reported that Patsy had just signed a booking deal with another Washington, D.C., disk jockey–television host by the name of Don Owens. He had a TV program called *Don Owens' Jamboree*. Connie Gay had retired from the scene at this point, having sold his rights to Jimmy Dean's career to CBS in 1958, and having confronted his own problems with the bottle.

It was Patsy herself who approached Owens about working for him. "I got me a hit record and I ain't never made a cent from it,'" she complained to him.

Of course he knew of her from the Godfrey show, and her success with "Walkin' after Midnight." He confessed that he was not wealthy enough to offer her anything more than "scale" for her appearances. She told him that she would be happy making the $50 he was willing to pay her for television appearances and live concert dates. Charlie had just gotten an early discharge from the Army, and although he resented her career, she was basically supporting her whole family. Eager to earn as much money as she could, Patsy took every gig she could get her hands on.

Although she was heartily welcomed on Don Owens' TV show, and in concert with his decidedly "bluegrass" band, it was becoming increasingly clear that she had to break out of the regional Washington, D.C., market, if she was ever going to make her income reach the potential of her vocal talent. Friends remember her as being increasingly more and more frustrated during this era.

Since Charlie had left the Army in February, Patsy and Julie had moved out of Hilda's house, and they rented a place near Winchester. Although they only paid $30 a month for the place on Valley View Road, and Charlie returned to his job at *The Winchester Evening Star*, these were depressing times for her.

Johnny Anderson was one of the musicians Patsy worked with during this era. He recalls one gig that Patsy headlined at a country fair near Philadelphia. He was appalled by Charlie's behavior, and amazed at Patsy's ability to ignore him. "She was really excited," says Anderson of Patsy's anticipation of the gig. She even made fried chicken for the band and her entire entourage. "Charlie went with us," he recalls. "That's when he showed his ass up there and walked up and down in front of the stage, cussin' her and callin' her 'a whore' and 'a bitch' and everything else. Yeah, he got drunk and walked up in front of the bandstand just hollerin' at her and cursin' the hell out of her the whole time she was doing that job."

On July 3, 1959, Patsy was back in the recording studio with the Jordanaires and Owen, for a session that found her at her lowest emotional point yet. Frustrated beyond belief, she could not find a single song in 4 Star's catalog that she cared to record. And yet, she was absolutely desperate for the immediate check that came from Bill McCall for every song she recorded.

Ray Walker recalls, "She'd come off 'Walkin' after Midnight' a two-and-a half-million seller and she didn't have a dime to show for it."

Owen Bradley distinctly recalls this particular session. "She came in and she was pretty much down," he explains. "We couldn't find anything out of the stack that he had sent her or they had sent to me that we thought was any good at all. I said, 'Patsy, why don't you just come back another time. These are not any good at all.' Then, she started crying. She said, 'I don't have any money, Owen. I'm really up against it,' she said. 'He won't give me any money unless I record.'"

Industrious Bradley thought for a moment, and came up with a suitable solution. Several traditional songs written before the turn of the last century were not covered by copyrights, and were considered to be in the "public domain." This was especially true of gospel songs whose origins were uncertain. Since he recalled Patsy singing gospel tunes on broadcasts of Wally Fowler's *All-Night Sing*, he suggested a plan that would appease everyone involved. She could record a couple of gospel songs, McCall could extract his publishing money on the "musical arrangement," Patsy would get her $50 per song, and everyone would be happy. This seemed especially amenable to the Jordanaires, since they were known for their gospel harmonizing.

Recalls Bradley, "So I said, 'Why don't you do "A Closer Walk with Thee," and maybe he can claim [arrangers' rights to] that.' And she said, 'That'd be great.' She was for that. Well, you know, I told her when I was a kid up in the country they used to sing an old song, 'Life is Like a Mountain Railroad' ["Life's Railway to Heaven"]so we did those two songs. But, they [Decca] wouldn't release them. They left those 'in the can' and she got some little advance."

It is difficult to choose which of the two songs is the dreariest of the pair. Both "Life's Railway to Heaven" [46] and "Just a Closer Walk with Thee" [47] were joyless laments. There is nothing wrong per se with the vocal performances on either of these numbers, which can be descirbed as "somber". However, knowing how full of life Patsy truly was, these are clearly the product of a diva in depression. Aside from the money she received from the sessions, these songs epitomize how a songstress at the bottom of her emotional depths must try to pull it all together.

On July 20, Decca released Patsy's fifteenth single: "Gotta Lot of Rhythm in My Soul"/"I'm Blue Again." Again it failed to chart. By now the debit column of her 4 Star royalty account far outweighed any profits that her one hit single could ever offset.

In addition to her money problems and her dysfunctional marriage, it was becoming increasingly clear that living in Winchester, Virginia, was a hindrance to her career. Patsy was constantly traveling from there to Nashville for recording sessions and concert appearances. She was hundreds of miles away from the epi-center of the country music world. Throughout 1959, Patsy and Charlie continued to consider picking up and moving to Nashville. The only obstacle was money. Suddenly a solution presented itself.

Charlie recalls, "When I got out of the Army, Patsy was getting an allotment check of $137 a month. I got out a month early, and the first month after I got out, she still got the check. So, we didn't think nothing about it, thought when we first started getting it, it started a month late or whatever, so we spent it. But then a next check came, so we ended up, including the one we spent, we had seven checks. Well, after the first one, we didn't spend 'em, because we knew damn well that they weren't ours. And then, when we decided we was going to move to Nashville, we ran to the bank and cashed all of them at one time, and took off!"

It was toward the end of the summer of 1959 that Patsy and Charlie packed up and moved to Nashville. They found a house in the suburb of Madison, on Marthona Drive, and while they waited for their furniture to arrive, they stayed in a motel.

Utilizing his skills learned on *The Winchester Evening Star*, Charlie soon landed a job as a linotype operator. However, his job at Curley Printing Company only earned him $110 a week. For several months, Patsy and Charlie did without their own telephone, because they couldn't spare the $50 it would take for a deposit.

Not long after they had moved to town, Faron Young recalls Charlie coming over to see him, to ask if he could put Patsy on the bill for his touring concert shows. He told Charlie that he would be happy to, but confessed that he could only pay her $50 a night. Acting as her agent, Charlie was glad to accept those terms.

Depressed about her lack of funds, several of Patsy's cohorts recall that on occasion she would tend to drink before she went onstage. In order to conceal the fact that she was drinking liquor, she would put it in a Listerine mouthwash bottle. Increasingly unhappy with her marriage, and on the road away from Charlie, a couple of her co-stars recall their casual affairs with Patsy from this time. Both Faron Young and Porter Wagoner have spoken about their post-show liaisons with Patsy. In a cavalier fashion, Porter was later to say, "It made a few lonely nights out there bearable."

Things on the road weren't always smooth sailing. Country singer Roy Drusky tells of several nights where promoters tried to weasel their way out of paying the performers. According to him, "I vaguely remember a tour we worked, where suddenly the money wasn't there anymore, and we were all trying to figure out who was going to tell the people [in the audience] if we didn't get paid, we couldn't work. Patsy said, 'I'll tell them … I'll go tell them.' And she did." When a near riot took place, thanks to Patsy's pre-show speech, the promoter suddenly produced the money, and the show went on as scheduled.

Faron Young recalls Patsy's weight increasing and then dramatically decreasing with some instant diet she would go on. On one occasion when he noticed that she had put on a few pounds, he said to her, "Man, that ass of yours is getting wider and wider."

Not one to take unflattering criticism well, Patsy shot back at him, "You must like my ass, you little bastard—you keep looking at it and talking about it!"

June Carter, who was on several of the road shows with Patsy, recalls that it was Cline who first introduced her to diet pills. The two of them had attended a horse race in Mississippi. When one of the prize horses dropped dead with exhaustion, both Carter and Cline burst into tears. When Patsy gave her a green and white pill to take her out of her saddened mood, she explained that it was similar in effect to an aspirin. June recalls being buzzed on it for the next three days.

It was on this same tour that Patsy was involved in her first major car accident. One version of the story claims that although she was not seriously injured, she spent the night in a Mississippi hospital for observation. For whatever reason, she never detailed this accident to Charlie, but June Carter confirms that it did happen. Patsy was later to refer to this accident as the first in a series of near-fatal experiences she encountered.

Phil Whitney, who was WINC's station manager at the time, recalls, "Her mother called and said that Patsy was in a hospital somewhere down in Mississippi. She said she was in a terrible car accident. She said she was in bad shape and it could have killed her." (Was the reason why Patsy never divulged any of the details because she was in fact at fault?)

While touring with Ferlin Husky, Patsy was to meet one of the most important men in her career, Randy Hughes. At the time that they were introduced, he was the guitar player in Husky's touring band. He turned out to be a jack of all trades, and a master of them all. During the nine-to-five work week he was an investment banker. At night he was an accomplished stage musician. On the side he was an aspiring personal manager in the music business. On top of that, he was also an amateur airplane pilot.

When Patsy complained about her screwed-up recording deal with Bill McCall, Hughes looked her in the eye and told her, "What you need is a manager. One who knows how the hell this town operates. Someone who'll fight for you."

Besides being tall, handsome, and talented, he was also very well-connected within the Nashville circles. He had played guitar on the *Opry* since he was fifteen years old, and also toured with the Carter Family. At the time he was a guitar player for Lloyd "Cowboy" Copas ("Signed, Sealed and Delivered"). Randy fell in love with the boss's daughter, Kathy Copas, who also performed with her father. When she was expecting their first child, Kathy retired from the business. This was the accepted course of action in Nashville back then, and unsurprising, the exact opposite behavior of Patsy's.

Through his vast contacts, Hughes soon turned his interests toward management. When Randy offered to guide Patsy's floundering career, she discussed the matter with both Owen Bradley and Charlie. Broke and despondent about the stalemate in which she found herself, no one could figure out how a professional manager could possibly do any more damage than had already been done.

Patsy signed an agreement with Randy, and his first order of business was to get a complete accounting of McCall's dealings with Cline. McCall was not contractually obligated to turn over his books to Hughes, so he told him to take a flying leap. After investigating Patsy's soon-to-run-out contract with 4 Star, he had to recommend that she simply ride out the agreement. Then she'd be free to make some truly significant changes in late 1960.

In the latter part of 1959 and early 1960, it became Randy Hughes' objective to keep Patsy as busy as possible. This would keep her ahead of her bills, and out there in the public eye.

In spite of her string of failed singles, from the outside it looked like Patsy was in the middle of an active and lucrative career. She continued to be a popular guest on several nationally broadcast network television shows. On the November 7 episode of *Jubilee U.S.A.*, she sang her two trademark songs; "Walkin' after Midnight" and "Come on in (and Make Yourself at Home)." She and Slim Whitman also performed the song "Let's Go to Church" together. On December 12, she was back on the program, singing Christmas carols. She performed "Let It Snow, Let It Snow, Let It Snow" with Faron Young, and "Winter Wonderland" with Red Foley. On that same program she also sang her newly recorded song "Gotta Lot of Rhythm in My Soul," and a new number she was working on, "Lovesick Blues."

On December 21, 1959, Patsy appeared on the bill with Porter Wagoner and Roy Drusky at a charity event at the Tennessee Vocational School. It was a Christmas benefit that was sponsored by the local Elks club for underprivileged children. After they were finished singing, the stars came down from the stage and played Santa Claus. Cline scooped ice cream, served candy and cake to the kids, and helped to hand out crisp one dollar bills to the 750 children gathered there.

On January 9, 1960, Patsy was again appearing on the *Grand Ole*

Opry as a guest star. Ever since she was known as "Ginny Hensley" in Winchester, Virginia, her big goal was to be a bonafide "member" of the *Opry*. Tired of waiting for an official invitation, she finally took the bull by the horns. Ott Devine, the stage manager of the *Opry* remembers that evening very distinctly. "I was standing onstage watching one of the performers," he recalled, "and Patsy came up behind me and said, a bit hesitantly, 'Mr. Devine, do you think I could ever become a member of the *Grand Ole Opry*?' Of course, I knew of her talent. I had heard her sing. She had a beautiful voice. And so I replied, 'Patsy, if that's all you want, you are on the *Opry*.'" Among the *Opry* members at that time were Minnie Pearl, Grandpa Jones, Ernest Tubb, Roy Acuff, and Faron Young. "The Cline" was enthusiastically welcomed aboard.

Like joining a club with rules and regulations, membership to the *Opry* at the time meant that for twenty-six weeks out of the year she had to make herself available in Nashville for their weekly broadcasts. At an additional $25 per performance, she was happy to receive a steady paycheck. At long-last, Patsy Cline was a member of the *Grand Ole Opry*.

Weeks later, on January 27, Patsy was back in the recording studio, but this time without the Jordanaires. They didn't happen to be free, and she needed the money that the recording session could bring her. Somehow she managed to sneak a non-4-Star-owned song into the session. This four-song session was to be her final recording work under her 4 Star agreement, and so she more than likely talked Bill McCall into letting her "sneak one in."

The song was "Lovesick Blues" [48], recorded by Hank Williams, who had turned it into a million-selling hit in 1949. Patsy had been performing it in concert, and it always got her a great response. She also managed to put a bit of yodeling in the beginning of the song. This version features a nice rocking beat to it, but Patsy's vocal approach is 100 percent country. She sounds excellent on this cut, and the way her voice reaches for the stars on the end, you can hear her as a woman about to be released from a prison sentence of a recording deal.

The next three songs all carried the infamous "W. S. Stevenson" moniker tacked onto the other songwriters' names in the credits. "How Can I Face Tomorrow?" [49], which begins with the twanging of a steel guitar, harkens back in sound to her earlier pre-pop material. This is one of the first songs she recorded on which Patsy "overdubbed" her own voice on the tracks. Patti Paige had recently capitalized on that same gimmick. The effect is great on this song: after all—the only thing better than one Patsy Cline vocal is two!

"There He Goes" [50] is a pleasant country-blues ballad, which is actually one of her strongest cuts from this era. Thematically, Patsy sings about being caught cheating, then dumped by her lover. An excellent showcase for her voice, every breathy nuance of her stylish singing was shown off beautifully. This song had previously been a hit for June Carter's first husband, Carl Smith.

The final cut of the day was "Crazy Dreams" [51], with a tasty up-tempo shuffle beat to it. Again on this cut Patsy can be heard singing her own harmony vocals behind herself. This song was one that she performed several times throughout the coming year, and on it she sounded snappy and self-confident. She knew that this was the last song she owed Bill McCall, and she made every moment of it count.

Since beauty is in the eyes of the beholder, different people's opinions of Patsy's visual "look" differ. Although not classically gorgeous, some of her contemporaries have referred to her as "sexy" and "beautiful." Others found her "plain" and "hard" looking. Although her weight fluctuated a bit during this era, I personally find many of the photos of her very attractive. The sensuous lips and the mischievous expressions on her face betray her as a lively and exciting woman in her prime.

One of her acknowledged assets was her figure, and her ability to wear skintight outfits—tailor-made for her frame. *Opry* star Minnie Pearl remembers, "I think her wardrobe had a lot to do with her being known as a 'sex symbol.' She wore tight clothes—tight around her hips—flashy material. She went in for sequins and lamé—gold and silver lamé. And, she went in for a little shorter dresses than most of those girls were wearing at that point. Patsy stuck to shirtwaist type dresses, but very tight. And, she could wear 'em—she knew how to wear 'em, and high-heeled shoes. It kind of went with her. I mean, it was the package. She had a full figure. She was not overweight, I just think she was a big girl. She was a sexy girl. I would like to see her walk out and compete with some of these girls now. I've seen some television stuff that they've unearthed. It doesn't begin to do her justice."

Hilda continued to custom-make all of Patsy's stage costumes. She was one of the first country singers to have the nerve to wear pants onstage. There was one of her outfits that consisted of tight lamé pants and matching lamé vest, white cowgirl boots, a white long-sleeved blouse, a white scarf tied around her neck, topped off with a white cowgirl hat. Although the outfit revealed very little flesh—with the exception of the "v" neck of the shirt—she was forbidden by the *Opry* to wear the outfit onstage in 1960. Their reasoning was that "nice" girls wore dresses or skirts.

Patsy's individual style was part of what made her stubbornly original. Besides, she never wanted to be remembered as a "nice" girl. She just wanted to be remembered!

121

Chapter Nine

The Recipe for Success

hen Patsy appeared on the *Grand Ole Opry*'s "Prince Albert Show" on April 12, 1960, she sang her newest single, "Lovesick Blues," and received a huge round of applause. On April 29 she was back at the *Opry*, singing the single's "B" side, "How Can I Face Tomorrow?" Unfortunately, this promotional push did little toward creating a hit for her. Her career was still stuck in an unescapable rut.

~⁓~

In addition, Patsy complained bitterly to several of her friends about her relationship with Charlie. That spring, Ray Walker of the Jordanaires remembers her arriving at the recording studio visibly bruised. "One time she came in with a black eye," he explains. "She had sunglasses on. We didn't say anything about it because she'd always say something first, and she said 'I asked Charlie something and he answered me.'" That was her only reply.

Del Wood, a singer on the *Opry*, recalled Cline confiding in her about her troubled marriage, in the ladies room at the Ryman. She told Wood, "I got to be constantly reassured that somebody loves me. A lot of people say you've got all the loving in the world when you walk out onstage and you feel the beat of that applause. But, hell, that goddamn applause don't help you any when you're laying in that bed at night being totally ignored."

Several of Patsy's intimates also recall that Patsy was quite capable of holding her own in her domestic battles. Faron Young once beat Charlie at a game of pool, and Charlie paid off the debt with a $50 check—announcing that it couldn't be cashed just yet. Waving the freshly written check at Patsy, he complained that whenever he lost a pool game, he paid off his gambling debts in cash. Patsy grabbed the check out of his hand, tore it up, and reached into her purse to pay off the debt with cash. She then marched over to where Charlie was standing, whirled him around and lit into him on the spot. "If you want to bet on pool games," she shouted, "from now on bet with your own money! Now, you son-of-a-bitch, go across the street and get me a hamburger!" With his tail between his legs, he did exactly what he was told.

For better or worse, Charlie was her mate, and in spite of the storms they weathered together, they stayed married. This was something that amazed all of her friends. Several times in the middle of the night, Randy Hughes would receive phone calls from Patsy. She would be in tears, having just had a "knock down, drag out fight." This only caused further speculation that Patsy and Randy were having an affair on the side.

In spite of the bruises and battles, in the spring of 1960, Patsy announced to Charlie that she was again pregnant. She was not thrilled about her condition, and instead of slowing down, she pressed further on the accelerator of her career.

With Randy Hughes booking her for dates across the country, Patsy busied herself with concert and television appearances. Leaving Charlie and Julie in Nashville, Cline hit the road in May. Patsy was to spend a month and a half in California, and on June 4, she was in Springfield, Missouri, to make an appearance on the TV show *Jubilee U.S.A.* She performed the song "I'm Hog-Tied over You" with Cowboy Copas, and proudly dedicated the solo "Mother, Mother" to Hilda.

While in Nashville, and performing on the *Grand Ole Opry*, one of Patsy and Charlie's favorite nightspots was Tootsie's Orchid Lounge, located on the same block as the Ryman. There is an alley-way that separates the back door of Tootsie's from the side door of the Ryman, so it was the *Opry* stars' favorite watering hole. Several aspiring songwriters would also hang out there, hoping to make the right contacts to further their careers. It was at Tootsie's that Patsy and Charlie met Roger Miller.

Miller was later to recall, "She liked to come to Tootsie's with Charlie. We'd have a few beers, laugh, and play music. We usually ended up at somebody's house after Tootsie's closed. It would close around midnight. Then we'd go out to somebody's house and sing all night. We had some great times and made some good memories. She loved to laugh. She told a lot of dirty jokes. She liked to howl and laugh. She had a good soul and a good heart."

Recording another *Country Style U.S.A.* transcription disk for Army radio station broadcast, in June of 1960, Patsy performed Miller's "When Your House Is Not a Home," which had been previously recorded by her friend Little Jimmy Dickins. That September she recorded her version of the Connie Francis hit "Stupid Cupid" for another *Country Style U.S.A.* outing. (Both of these recordings were finally released to the public on the 1989 album, "Patsy Cline Live, Volume Two.")

On August 1, 1960, Decca released her seventeenth single, "Crazy Dreams"/"There He Goes." Still in search of a hit record, Patsy vigorously promoted both sides of the record. On August 12, she performed "Crazy Dreams" on the *Grand Ole Opry*, and on September 3, it was "There He Goes" that got a plug. That night at the *Opry*, it was singer Jim Reeves who introduced Cline.

Unfortunately, neither of the songs contained on the single ever charted. (Both of these well-received performances can be heard on the 1988 album, "Patsy Cline Live at the *Opry*.")

Finally, the day came that Patsy had waited so long for: the day her 4 Star contract finally lapsed. There was all kinds of talk about what recording label she would subsequently sign with. Chet Atkins, who at the time was the A&R Director at RCA Victor, had made overtures toward her joining his label. She surprised everyone by approaching Decca herself. She realized that her current troubles had to do with Bill McCall, and not the label that released her recordings.

At the time, Owen Bradley had an assistant by the name of Harry Silverstein. Bradley recalls, "Harry Silverstein came in to me and said, 'Owen, Patsy Cline called and said she would like to get a $1,000 advance and she would sign with us [Decca].' I said, 'Really?' because I thought she would try to go somewhere else. I figured Columbia or [RCA] Victor or somebody, because everybody liked her. They thought she was great, but she was sort of 'in the red.'"

With that, Bradley immediately phoned the label's New York office and was given "the green light" on both the $1,000 check for Patsy, and for a long-term recording contract. Free from Bill McCall and Paul Cohen, at long-last Owen Bradley was truly to be in control of Patsy's recorded destiny. All she needed now was the right song, and she'd truly be on her way!

One of Patsy's new songwriter friends at the time was a gentlemen by the name of Harlan Howard. He had just moved to Nashville from California, having hit the jackpot with his first compositions: "Mommy for a Day," which Kitty Wells recorded, and "Heartaches by the Number" which had been a country hit for Ray Price and a pop hit for Guy Mitchell. When he suddenly received $100,000 in songwriters' royalties, he bought himself a new Cadillac and drove to Nashville to cash in on his newfound success.

When another writer friend of his, Hank Cochran, came to him with a half-finished tune called "I Fall to Pieces," he asked Harlan if he could help him complete it. When he did, he was sure that they had a smash hit on their hands. Harlan asked his wife Jan to record a demo version of the song, which she gladly did. When Owen Bradley called Harlan one day in 1960, he asked what new tunes he had available. Harlan presented him with the demo for "I Fall to Pieces." Owen immediately loved it. Free of gender references, the way the song was written it could be sung by either a man or a woman. The first person he offered it to was Brenda Lee, but for some reason she didn't care for it. At the same time, Bradley was actively looking for a song to produce for Ray Drusky. He called Drusky into his office and played him the demo of Jan Howard singing "I Fall to Pieces."

Although Ray could appreciate the lyrics of the song, he whined, "You don't hear a man saying, 'I fall to pieces.'" Claiming that it was a woman's song, he refused to record it.

With Patsy's first Decca recording date coming up, Bradley decided that it would be perfect for her. Unfortunately, she hated it the minute she heard it. The other side of the publisher's demo record had a song on it called "Lovin' in Vain," written by Freddie Hart. That was the song she preferred. When she arrived at Bradley's studio on November 16, before the tape started rolling, Patsy and Owen got into a huge argument.

Although she agreed to record the song, Owen had a particular arrangement in mind for "I Fall to Pieces," which was unlike any of the songs he had ever produced for Patsy. Having just scored a huge hit for Brenda Lee on "I'm Sorry," he felt that a similar, lush, understated sound would be great on this song. Patsy was intimidated by this slower, stripped-down arrangement, and felt that her real strong point was her ability to give each number a real knock-out, vocally-acrobatic finale.

"She was nervous in the studio," recalls Owen of this session. He even had her new manager, Randy Hughes, playing acoustic guitar that day, to give her extra confidence. "We used the exact same studio players and equipment to make the bombs that we did to make the hits. But if you don't have a good song, then you don't get anything out. And it doesn't make any difference what kind of 'mike' you've got. That's all a myth, believe me."

Bradley was so confident that this new approach was just what Patsy needed, that he took her up to his second floor office for a one-on-one confrontation. When they emerged, and rejoined the musicians and the Jordanaires, Patsy was still skeptical, but agreed to sing the song again—against her will.

Ray Walker of the Jordanaires recalls that it took several takes before Patsy finally relaxed into the song. According to him, "Patsy was scared. She was quite an artist onstage, and she had done pretty well with the 'Western Swing' type up-tempo music. She had never sung a song like 'I Fall to Pieces' before, and she didn't consider herself that kind of singer. The first time she did the ending, she came up on the tag, went up an octave, and actually sang a little faster. It just floored me. I stopped right in the middle of the 'oohs' and 'aahs' or whatever we were doing, and she looked over and said, 'What's wrong Ray?' I said, 'Is that the way you're going to end the song?' She said, 'Well, Owen wanted me to end it by slowing down and taking the last line out, but I feel safer going up and really belting out the ending.' I said, 'Patsy, this is not a belt-out song. You had me practically in tears, and then all of a sudden the clowns walk in!' She said, 'Well, okay,' and went back, and things really smoothed out. She got lower and lower, and so gutsy. She had us spellbound."

What ended up happening was that Patsy recorded "I Fall to Pieces" Owen's way. "I Fall to Pieces" [52] is one of the finest songs Patsy ever recorded. With a simple shuffle beat moving it along, it is charged with understated emotion. Devoid of vocal tricks, or sweeping dramatics, it shows off every heartbroken nuance of Patsy's expressive voice. Little did she know at the time, but this song was going to change her from a "one hit wonder" into a star.

The next song she recorded that day was the nice but gimmicky Hank Cochran–Velma Smith tune called "Shoes" [53]. Amid the medium-paced country number, Patsy sings about putting aside an old love like a pair of shoes that no longer fit. A pleasant performance, it is light in content and pales in comparison to "I Fall to Pieces."

Freddie Hart's "Lovin' in Vain" [54] completed the session, and found Patsy back in her older, more comfortable approach to recording. A bit on the twangy side, this song reflected the way Patsy imagined herself: a country gal clinging to a love gone wrong. On the end of the song you can hear her swinging into the kind of finale treatment that Ray Walker had just talked her out of doing on "I Fall to Pieces."

According to Freddie Hart, the writer of "Lovin' In Vain," "I met Patsy while on tour. I remember so well her singing harmony with me on a great Harlan Howard song, 'The Key's in the Mailbox.' We didn't rehearse it. It was all a surprise to me and to the audience. She just walked out, put her arms around me and started singing. It was a blessing I will always cherish. Backstage I sang a few songs for her. She liked one called 'Lovin' In Vain' and recorded it. What can I say? I felt ten feet taller!"

They worked for a long time on "Lovin' in Vain," and originally Patsy was going to record a fourth song that day, a Hank Cochran song called "Perfect Example of a Fool." Cochran had been in the studio with them earlier that afternoon, but had stepped out for a while. When it came time to work on his composition, they found that Patsy had lost the demo for the song, and Hank was nowhere to be found.

According to Cochran, "When I got back, they said, 'We was looking all over for you. We couldn't get "Lovin' in Vain" to come off, really, and we was looking for you to get the other fourth song on, 'cause she misplaced the tape.' But they just went ahead and kept working on 'Lovin' in Vain,' and spent the whole time on that." Patsy never did get around to recording "Perfect Example of a Fool."

When the session was over, Patsy sat in the control room chain-smoking cigarettes and listening to the playback of the three songs. The song Patsy was the most proud of was "Lovin' in Vain," and the song she liked the least was "I Fall to Pieces." Owen insisted that "I Fall to Pieces" was a hit, but Patsy disagreed, favoring "Lovin' in Vain." As a bet to find out who was right and who was wrong, Owen promised to release a single with both songs on it, and then they would see who won. She was so confident that she was right that she continued to rehearse "Lovin' in Vain," and immediately added it to her stage act.

One of the first people Patsy telephoned after the session was her new friend Jan Howard, Harlan's wife. Jan had hoped that she would be able to record "I Fall to Pieces" for the small label she recorded for, Challenge Records. However, when she heard Patsy's restrained, yet emotion-charged version of the song, she knew right then and there that she had just heard the ultimate rendition.

129

When Jan and Harlan had moved to Nashville earlier that year, Jan's initial meeting with Patsy was less than cordial. Jan became a singer on the *Grand Ole Opry*, and that's where she first saw Cline perform. She stood enthralled in the wings watching Patsy, and then retreated to the ladies room, where all of the girls on the show changed clothes and did their make-up. Shy and unaggressive, Jan had been too timid to walk up to Patsy to introduce herself that night. After her set was over, Patsy came storming into the ladies room and immediately lit into Jan.

With her head cocked to one side, and a hand on one of her hips, Cline looked Jan right in the eye and said, "You're a conceited little son-of-a-bitch. You just waltz in here and do your bit and waltz out and you don't say 'hello' or 'kiss my ass' or nothin' else to no damn body!"

Not one to take such a statement lying down, Jan turned the tables and answered back, "Now wait just a damn minute. Where I'm from it's the people that live in town that make a newcomer feel welcome and ain't nobody made me feel welcome in this damn town!"

Exploding with laughter, Patsy was startled that someone that seemed so quiet and polite could turn around and throw it back at her. "You're alright honey," Patsy proclaimed. "Anybody that'll stand up to 'the Cline' is all right. We're going to be good friends." That's exactly what happened.

Although she was nine months pregnant when the new year began, on January 21, Patsy was still onstage singing at the *Opry*. As Charlie tells it, "Patsy was so determined to sing that she worked the *Opry* one night and gave birth to Randy the next." That was precisely what happened.

When Patsy returned from the *Opry*, Charlie stayed out all night, drinking and partying. According to him, "I go home—it might have been six o'clock—no big deal. And I went on in to bed. But then about seven o'clock—I'm not sure about the time—very shortly after I got to bed, Patsy went in and tried to wake me up. She said she had to go the hospital. Had labor pains. I said, 'Yeah, uh huh.' In my mind I was just thinking she was trying to get me up because she was mad because I'd been out all night." Charlie just continued to lie there and sleep.

In a pinch, Patsy called the next door neighbor, Joyce Blair, to drive her to St. Thomas Hospital. Patsy gave birth to Alan Randolph Dick on January 22, and from that point on, her son was known as "Randy." This is most ironic, because several people—including Mae Boren Axton—confirm that beginning in 1960, Patsy was actively having an affair with her new manager, Randy Hughes. It is not out of the realm of possibility for one to suspect that it was directly due to her love for Hughes that she middle-named her second child after him. The boy was always referred to as "Randy."

On January 30, 1961, Decca Records released Patsy's eighteenth single: "I Fall to Pieces"/"Lovin' in Vain." No one was sure how the song was going to fare, except for everyone who had heard the "A" side. Everyone but Patsy—that is. Immediately recognizing the song's potential, the publisher of "I Fall to Pieces"—Pamper Music—began promoting it with press releases and phone calls. It was a fledgling little publishing house at that time, and it had a lot to gain if the song became a hit.

With her career demanding her concentration, Patsy was back to work only two weeks after the birth of little Randy. She taped an episode of *Country Time U.S.A.* for Army base TV broadcast. Similar to a music video, Patsy's rendition of "Walkin' after Midnight" was staged, with props and costumes. Patsy performed the number as if she was working in the fabric department of a general store, while singing about her nocturnal lover.

Surrounded by several dozen bolts of fabric and lace, and wearing a gingham dress, they really played up the country gal image. Poking fun at her on the set, musician Lightnin' Chance nearly got smacked over the head with a bolt of fabric when he quipped, "Well, hello! You look like you just got back from town selling eggs and milk!"

Still feeling a bit of a cash crunch, Patsy got in contact with her old friend Jim McCoy from Winchester radio station WINC. She told him that she didn't have enough money to come home to spend some time with Hilda, and inquired as to whether he could book a local gig for her so she could pay for her trip. McCoy knew someone who owned two drive-in movie theaters in the area, and booked her for a special appearance between films, for $150. She was thrilled that he had not only pulled it off, but he had reunited his band, the Melody Playboys, especially for her.

McCoy took out a special display advertisement in The Winchester Evening Star which read,

Onstage—In Person
Winchester's Only
PATSY CLINE
Singing Her Latest Decca Hit Recording
"I Fall to Pieces"

Well, she drew a crowd alright. However, her reception was less than optimal. Standing on the roof of the concession stand during the intermission, Patsy sang her heart out, only to have several of the women in the audience honk their car horns and loudly "boo" her onstage. She may have been a big hit in Nashville, but her hometown would always think of her as the local tramp who destroyed Bill Peer's marriage and broke Gerald Cline's heart.

Afterward, in the trailer that the drive-in theater owner used as an office, Patsy broke down and cried. With tears streaming down her face, she looked Jim McCoy in the eye and sobbed, "Why do people in Winchester treat me like this?"

It was in April of 1961 that "I Fall to Pieces" finally hit the country charts and began its slow upward climb. Although it registered more sales than radio airplay at first, once it hit the airwaves, things really began to heat up.

As her first single on Decca, with a clean royalty sheet under her new deal, it hit *Billboard's* country chart and it became clear there would be money coming to Patsy. Banking on Decca's confidence in the song, she secured an advance from her projected earnings that month, and suddenly she felt like a million bucks. With money-hungry creditors wanting to repossess her household appliances, she was anxious to get her hands on some cash.

Running into the Jordanaires one day at Owen's Quonset Hut studio, she was absolutely beaming. "Boys," she proudly announced, "those bastards can't take my refrigerator now. They'll never get my car now. I paid cash for 'em and they're mine, and I'm a keepin' 'em!" When Ray Walker asked her where she got the cash, she answered, "Owen gave it to me, 'cause baby, they tell me I got one hell of a hit record!"

Concert dates were booked in California, where she flew in mid-April. On her plane ride home, on Delta Airlines letterhead stationery, Patsy penned her own will, and had one of the other passengers sign it as witness. When she had visited with her friend Don Hecht in Los Angeles, she told him that she had a premonition that she was going to be involved in an accident and she didn't want to leave anything to chance.

In the will, dated April 22, 1961, Patsy was very specific about her wishes to have her children raised by Hilda, not by Charlie. In the instance that Hilda passed away, she wanted them to go to her sister Sylvia.

To her children she left her 5 percent royalty earnings from her new record deal, to be used for their education. Hilda inherited all of her clothes; her Kenmore stove, washer, and refrigerator; plus all of her dishes and kitchenware.

133

She specified that Charlie was to receive, "my western-designed den furniture, a hi-fi stereo record player and radio, records and albums and tape recorder and blond floor model television set." She also left him her car.

This was the only will she was to ever make. It even included her funeral request. She stated, "I wish to be put away in a western dress I designed, with my daughter's little gold cross necklace and my son's small white testament in my hands, and to be buried in the resting place of my husband's choice, and my wedding band on."

Almost immediately, as soon as "I Fall to Pieces" started to pick up airplay, Patsy's concert dates were now commanding a steeper asking price. Only months ago she was happy to receive the same $50 per night she had received from the beginning as a featured performer. Now she was suddenly garnering $350 a night for club dates.

It was during that same year that Patsy met two of her best girlfriends, and most famous protegées: Dottie West and Loretta Lynn. Dottie was married to steel guitar player Bill West, whom Patsy occasionally used as a touring musician. Dottie had come up to her after a show, introduced herself, and explained that she was a big fan of Patsy's. Immediately, they hit it off and became close comrades.

When the money started to roll in, one of the first things that Patsy did was purchase a giant white Cadillac. Dottie West was later to recall, "We'd go from date to date in this big Cadillac. Sometimes, when he could, Charlie would go with us and drive. But, oh boy, could that Patsy drive that car. I remember on one tour, Roy Orbison was holding on for dear life in the back seat. Patsy was a daredevil behind the wheel!"

Suddenly unsaddled from money worries, Patsy often enjoyed being the ringleader of her own clique of Nashville girlfriends. She'd have Jan Howard, Dottie West, and Brenda Lee over to her house to eat, hang out, and share the latest gossip. "We had our little hen parties while the men gabbed and drank beer," Dottie was to recall.

It wasn't long before Patsy was known in Nashville circles as a big-hearted gal, who was also one of the boys. Roger Miller once recalled, "A bunch of guys went into Juarez [Mexico] after a date in El Paso. Over there they bought a little grass and started to worry about how to get it back across the border. Patsy was too much. I don't think anything scared her. She said, 'What the hell y'all worried about when you got Patsy here? Give me that stuff. I'll take care of it.' And she did. She grabbed it and stuffed it down her bra as a favor—she was one of us!"

Patsy was always the life of the party after the *Grand Ole Opry*, when "the clique"—as they called themselves—converged on Tootsie's Orchid Lounge. Tootsie herself, the proprietor, would keep running tabs for all of the musicians and singers who came in for burgers, chili, and beer. Anyone who came in looking to find Patsy could track her down in the crowd by her hearty, rowdy laugh, which often punctuated the smoke-filled beer joint.

In May of 1961, "I Fall to Pieces" was the number one pop hit on Nashville's local chart. "The Cline" toured relentlessly, fanning the flames of the hottest song of her career. With a dozen failed single releases since "Walkin' after Midnight," it suddenly felt fabulous to have a hit on both the country and pop charts.

Always a champion of her songwriter buddies, in May of 1961, Patsy surprised Hank Cochran and Harlan Howard. She walked into the offices of Pamper Music Publishing, where they worked, and presented them both with gifts of gratitude. For Cochran she bought a black onyx and sterling silver ring, and a money clip which was engraved with the words, "To Hank for 'I Fall to Pieces.' Love, Patsy." She presented Howard with a sterling silver I.D. bracelet, engraved with the message, "Harlan, thanks for the hit. Patsy."

Overcome with gratitude, Patsy took out an ad in *The Music Reporter* to thank all of the disk jockeys and radio stations for helping to make her latest recording a hit. Such acts of gratitude are very rare indeed. According to Harlan Howard, he has never received such a gift of thanks from another singer.

Also in May, riding high with "I Fall to Pieces," Patsy played a date in Houston, Texas, and became chummy with a woman close to her age by the name of Louise Seger. She was divorced, and worked as an electronics technician. A dyed-in-the-wool Patsy Cline fan, Seger introduced herself to Patsy when she came to perform at a local club.

Seger and Cline had a lot in common, both being women with two children, and having experienced rocky marriages. Seger listened intently as Patsy told her about several of her disappointments with Charlie. According to Louise, Patsy told her of her domestic battles, claiming, "Charlie and I ain't getting along too well at all right now.... Lots of times he bruised me up so bad I've had to work with my face—or a black eye—all covered up with make-up. I get so mad at him, I'd like to throw a skillet at him."

Since she was performing with the club's house band and knew no one in town, Patsy palled around with Seger that evening between sets. After the show they went to Louise's for breakfast, and then Seger arranged for Patsy to be a surprise guest on the local morning "drive time" country radio station. Louise was to become a pen pal and confidante throughout their friendship. The very first time Patsy wrote to Seger, it was a breezy note to thank her for her hospitality in Houston. The subsequent letters Patsy wrote to Seger throughout the next two years have since become legendary. In the 1990s they have become the basis for a narrative stage play about this era of Cline's life. Years before *People* magazine, or TV's "Entertainment Tonight," there were very few recorded or written personal statements from stars like Patsy Cline. These letters to Louise express what was really going on in Patsy's mind at the time. Because Seger was totally uninvolved in the world of show business,

Patsy was comfortable occasionally exposing her private thoughts, along with some chatty news.

In the thank-you letter to Louise, which she wrote on May 29, Patsy proclaimed, "Well, I'm nearly up on the moon and didn't need a rocket. My record sold 10,000 in Detroit last week alone and is hitting all pop charts. It's number one on both pop stations here in Nashville and is the number one best-seller at Decca and is already being put in three [compilation] albums right away of different artists. I go to the 5 *Star Jubilee* [TV show] on July 7th, and it's in color. Swingin' huh? I think I told you I'm getting things in shape for the Dick Clark [*American Bandstand* TV show] but don't know the date yet. But I'll let you know."

In early June, Patsy returned to Winchester to attend the high school graduation of her younger sister Sylvia. Since Sylvia was the first member of the family to graduate from high school, Patsy wanted to throw a party in her sister's honor. While in town, she ran into and old neighborhood friend, Patsy Lillis. Lillis was a clerk at the local McCrory's Five and Dime store, and she distinctly remembers Patsy sweeping into the store with curlers in her hair, scarlet lipstick accentuating her full lips, and a flame red scarf tied about her head. "The Cline" was wearing form-fitting Capri pants, a pair of chic shades, and glowing about receiving her first Decca royalty check. When Lillis inquired how she was going to spend it, she exclaimed, "I'm gonna buy my mom a new stove and refrigerator!"

After the party, Patsy returned to Nashville, driving with her mother, younger brother Sam and Sylvia. The next day, back in Nashville, June 14, 1961, Patsy and Sam headed out in the car to buy sewing supplies. She needed buttons, ribbons, and thread so that Hilda could repair some of her stage costumes.

A sudden rainstorm blew in, about 4:30 in the afternoon, and Patsy and Sam decided to immediately head for home, with Sam behind the wheel. Descending across the bridge, down Halls Lane, two cars were coming toward them, when suddenly the second car attempted to pass the front car. Accelerating at full speed, the passing car bolted across the double-yellow median line, and was suddenly coming right toward Sam and Patsy. With split seconds to make a decision, Sam laid on the horn: there was nowhere for him to turn, as the car rushed head on toward them.

Patsy was later to recount, "I was just a-yelling, but she gunned her car and tried to get around, then ran smack dab into us. No way at all of getting out of it for us. I went through the windshield and flipped back over the car."

The passenger of the passing car, a thirty-two-year-old woman, was pronounced dead on arrival at the hospital, and her six-year-old son was in critical condition. The driver, twenty-two-year-old Mrs. Harold Clark, walked away with minor cuts and bruises.

Patsy was not as fortunate. Covered in blood, she had a huge gash that ran across her forehead from eyebrow-to-eyebrow, a dislocated hip, and several fractures. Her brother Sam suffered from a three-inch-deep puncture wound through the breast bone, and had several cracked ribs.

When the ambulances arrived, radio reports of Patsy being involved in a near-fatal accident immediately hit the airwaves. Dottie West heard the news, and as she didn't live far from the scene of the accident, rushed over immediately. When Dottie arrived there, she found Patsy sitting by the side of the road. She was horrified by what she saw, and impressed beyond belief at how Patsy was insisting that the other victims be treated before her.

Dottie rode in the ambulance with Patsy, picking bits of broken glass from Cline's bloody hair during the drive to Madison Hospital.

Dr. Hollis Evans, the attending physician at Madison Hospital, recalls, "It was a gory mess—bleeding and crush injuries that looked hopeless at first glance.

Patsy was later to write, "I never lost consciousness from the time it happened, through the sewing up of my head (saw the other lady die) and until they gave me gas to set my hip. I cut an artery and I lost lots of blood. They thought I was gone twice during the sewing up and had to give me three pints of blood. I don't think I'll ever be able to ride in a car again. I just thank God above that I can see *perfect* and my *babies* weren't with me." Patsy was listed as being in "critical condition" for two days, and then her status was upgraded to "fair."

The hospital switchboard lit up with all of the phone calls from well-wishers. Fields of flowers arrived at Patsy's room from all of her country music friends, a virtual "who's who" in Nashville, including Brenda Lee, Webb Pierce, Tex Ritter, Ralph Emery, Faron Young,

Harlan and Jan Howard, and Roy Acuff. Mountains of mail arrived at her room, both from people known and unknown to her. With her head still wrapped in bandages, she passed the time by personally answering each of her fan letters.

She wrote her new friend Louise Seger, "I didn't know there was so many people in this world that knew of me. But it sure gives me faith and a wonderful feeling to know how many fans and friends are wanting me well again."

One of her biggest surprises came the first Saturday night she was in the hospital. She had a radio next to her bed, and she listened to the broadcast of the *Grand Ole Opry*. After it was over, she kept the radio station on WSM, and stayed tuned to hear Ernest Tubb's *Mid-Nite Jamboree*.

There was a new singer in town, a twenty-six-year-old girl by the name of Loretta Lynn. She was scheduled to appear on Tubb's radio show that night. When she got up to the microphone, she started talking about her idol, Patsy Cline, and announced, "Patsy has the number one record, 'I Fall to Pieces,' and she's in the hospital…. So I want to dedicate this song to her. Patsy, if you're a'listening, this song is for you, 'I Fall to Pieces.' I hope you get well real soon." When she was finished with her introduction, she proceeded to sing her version of Patsy's hit record. Loretta didn't even know the lyrics to the song, so her husband, Doolittle, had to hold up the latest issue of *Country Song Roundup* magazine, so that she could read the lyrics.

Sitting in her hospital bed, Patsy was genuinely touched by Loretta's sweet sentiment. She said to Charlie, "Well, I'll be damned! That was pretty nice of that gal. Charlie, go down to the record store and thank her for me, and tell her I want to meet her."

Charlie ran down to Ernest Tubb's record store, and walked up to a skinny young girl dressed in a western-style outfit. When he introduced himself as Patsy's husband to Loretta, she threw her arms around him. When he delivered Patsy's sincere "thank you's" she turned to Doolittle and exclaimed, "I just can't believe it. Patsy heard me and now she wants to meet me!"

Charlie made plans for Loretta and Doolittle to come and visit Patsy the following afternoon. When Loretta walked into Patsy's room, she recalls being overcome by the sight of all of the flowers.

Patsy still had her head wrapped up in bandages, she had two black eyes, and her right arm was in a splint. She was in traction, and her leg was hoisted up so that her hip could heal. Loretta could tell that is was painful for Patsy to even talk, but talk she did. She was fascinated to hear all of the details about Loretta's life and career. She was so flattered by Lynn's kindness, and they immediately hit it off as instant best friends.

According to Loretta, Patsy was just beaming over her success with "I Fall to Pieces" and its hit status. Says Loretta, "She told me, 'I finally did it, hoss. I got me a number one!' She said 'Oh, I never want to record again! I just want to enjoy this one song forever!'"

Even broken up and bruised, Patsy retained her sense of humor. Since Madison was a Seventh Day Adventists hospital, she complained bitterly that they didn't serve meat. Her sister Sylvia covertly smuggled hamburgers and fries into the room of the bashed up Cline. A few weeks later, in the July 1961 edition of her fan club newsletter, Patsy poked fun at her appearance by writing, "I'm having surgery today to have my face cleaned up. But it will take some fancy stitching to make me all beautiful again!"

However, after the accident, Patsy's attitude towards several things changed drastically. Suddenly, her life seemed even more precious to her. Patsy had several long conversations with Pentecostal Reverend Jay Alford. They discussed life, death, and the hereafter. When her neighbor Joyce Blair came to visit, she noticed that there was a spiritual awakening in Patsy. She said to her, "Blair, Jesus has been in my room. He has taken my hand and told me that: 'No. Not now. I have other things for you to do.'"

She was genuinely relieved to have had this "visitation," and the reassurance that "her time" had not yet come. However, Patsy began to have feelings of impending doom.

On July 7, 1961, Patsy was heard on the radio broadcast of the *Grand Ole Opry*, since the program had been pre-recorded prior to her accident. That evening millions of listeners heard Hank Snow announce, "Let's hear the perfect combination when it comes to singing: a good voice, and a great song—as Miss Patsy Cline lets us hear her great Decca record which is a way up the charts, both country and pop—'I Fall to Pieces.'" She also sang the other side of her new single—"Lovin' in Vain."

She was home ten days later, and extensive facial plastic surgery was scheduled for three months down the road. Although she was confined to a wheelchair, she was absolutely itching to get back to work.

Only days out of the hospital, Patsy made her triumphant return to the *Grand Ole Opry* on July 22. Grant Turner, an announcer who worked at the *Opry*, recalled, "They wheeled her out and the crowd went absolutely wild."

Met with a thunderous round of applause and a standing ovation, from her wheelchair at centerstage at the Ryman, Patsy announced, "Thank you so much, you're wonderful. I'll tell you something, the greatest gift that I think you folks could have given me was the encouragement that you gave me. At the very time that I needed you the most, you came through with the flyingest colors, and I just want to say that: you'll just never know how happy you made this ole country gal!"

On July 29 and 30, she was back on the concert trail. Playing dates in Tulsa and Enid, Oklahoma, Patsy used crutches to get up onstage, and stood there singing her heart out. The huge red scar that ran across her forehead was filled in with several layers of make-up. She wore a wig with bangs to cover and diffuse the scar. Only Patsy could turn a disaster into an opportunity for a new look!

"I Fall to Pieces" finally peaked at number one on the *Billboard* magazine country singles chart on August 7, 1961. The week of September 12, it was number twelve on the pop chart. She continued to make jokes about how her near-fatal car accident was one hell of a way to launch a hit single!

On August 13, Patsy performed two songs on another *Country Time U.S.A.* Army transcription disk. She announced on it, "Well, I guess we might as well move along and do one that we're gonna put in the album before too long—a new album that's comin' out called, of course, 'I Fall to Pieces,' and it's called 'Side by Side.'" With that, she launched into her country/swing version of the song which had been a big hit for Kay Starr in 1953. (For some reason she never did get around to doing a studio version of this song.) For another song, she said, "For our closing song, I'd like to do a fine old favorite of everyone's, that's always been real close to me, called

'Just a Closer Walk with Thee." This touchingly reflected her thankful-to-be-alive frame of mind.

Almost immediately after her release from the hospital, Patsy and Owen Bradley began planning for her next Decca recording sessions. Now that they knew what direction Patsy's records should have, they began to prepare fourteen new cuts to select tunes from for Patsy's second record album. With a number one hit single on the charts, there was an immediate demand to come up with an album package to feature "I Fall to Pieces."

Up until this point, Patsy didn't fully realize what her real strengths were. "I Fall to Pieces" changed that. Now she was more trusting of Owen's musical concept and Randy's image of her as a sophisticated pop singer with a country flavor. That wasn't to say that she didn't still clash with her producers.

Owen Bradley recalls, "Right away we started having good luck because we started recording songs that we both liked instead of trying to please a third party. We just tried to do songs that fit her. And we also had the first big hit. It makes a lot of difference when you've got a hit. Then we had a clue. When you don't have one, why you're just floundering around."

Although she had a number one hit on her hands, she still had very definite ideas about how her records should sound. During the four sessions that she did in August of 1961, she continued to argue with Owen Bradley. First of all, there was this song that everyone was trying to talk her into singing. It was written by this Nashville newcomer who sang on his demo like he was drunk and just talking his way through the number. She hated it the minute she heard it. First the songwriter gave a copy of the demo to Charlie, and he came home and played it to death on the stereo. Finally she hollered at him to turn that awful song off. Then, her friend Billy Walker gave her another demo copy of the same song, and she still hated it. She was absolutely dead set against having anything to do with performing that strange Willie Nelson song "Crazy," and that was that! Finally Owen Bradley had to talk her into it.

Gordon Stoker of the Jordanaires recalls, "She argued with Owen almost any time when he would start playing the piano and we'd start running something down. She would have something about the song that she didn't like that Owen was doing. Maybe she had been listening to the demo at home, and she had in her mind, maybe, how she wanted to record it. And, of course when you go in the studio and you sit down with the A&R man in the studio, most of the time it comes off different from how you thought it was gonna come off. My point: she was very headstrong, extremely headstrong."

Patsy's first post-accident session was set for August 17, from 2:00 P.M. to 6:00 P.M. Not only did Owen book the same musicians he had used for "I Fall to Pieces" and the Jordanaires, but he also did something that was unprecedented for a "Patsy Cline session"—he booked a string section of three violins, a viola, and a cello. Patsy wasn't just a country recording star anymore; she was a pop star as well, competing for a spot on that chart with the likes of Roy Orbison, Connie Francis, and Pat Boone.

The first song she recorded that day was the Cole Porter classic, "True Love" [55]. A beautiful, string-laden ballad, this rendition of the 1927 chestnut is flawless. It found Patsy at her most focused, and most confidently relaxed. Never before had she sounded so lush and so refined. This is one of the finest cuts of her entire recording career.

Next they picked up the pace a bit, to tackle the Bob Wills' country hit, "San Antonio Rose" [56]. Floyd Cramer concurrently had a hit with it on the country and pop charts, and it was a perfect "cowgirl style" showcase for "the Cline." Swinging, mid-tempo and upbeat, it heavily features Walter Haynes' steel guitar twangings and conjures up vivid images of a Hollywood western, as if Patsy was singing it while riding into town on horseback.

Patsy had been in love with the song "The Wayward Wind" [57] ever since Gogi Grant took it to number one on the pop charts in 1955. Strong, pensive, and in excellent voice, on this recording Patsy again showed off her newly centered approach to singing. With beautiful vocal dexterity, Patsy took each note an caressed it like never before. When it came time to give the ending a note-holding punch, she didn't try and take the roof off of Bradley's Quonset Hut studio. Instead, she held it in a way that is emotional and gives you goose bumps to listen to it.

The fourth song of the day was a fresh approach to one of her favorite songs from the 4 Star era, "A Poor Man's Riches (or a Rich Man's Gold)" [58]. This new reading of the former rocker repositions it as a lush string-laden pop ballad, with the Jordanaires nicely improvising a sweeping vocal background. Listening to both of Patsy's versions of this song back-to-back brilliantly shows off her vocal development. Her phrasing and her vocal control had grown so dramatically, this second version witnesses a chanteuse in her prime.

On the night of August 20, Patsy was at home in a complete dilemma. Owen had let her record two of her favorite songs—"True Love" and "The Wayward Wind." Now he was *insisting* that she record Willie Nelson's "Crazy." Listening to the dreadful demo recording over and over again, she complained how she hated talking the lyrics, like the unconventional songwriter interpreted the song. Finally, sick of hearing her bitch about it, Charlie said to her, "Well, honey, if you don't like talking it, why the hell don't you just sing it all the way through?" She liked that idea, but the problems were far from over.

How was it that Patsy consistently hated the majority of her greatest hits before she recorded them? It's almost as if her fame happened while she was trying to do something else.

When she arrived for the 7:15 P.M. session on August 21, they spent the entire four-hour session just trying to get one satisfactory take with "Crazy" [59]. On every one of Patsy's previous recordings, she recorded her vocals right along with the musicians. Finally, after nearly four hours, Bradley suggested that they just lay down the vocal and background tracks, and Patsy could simply come in a couple of days later to do the vocal track over again.

She came back to the studio on August 24, and in one "take" nailed "Crazy." She had finally found a melodic way of singing the lamentful ballad—in her own trademark style. During the next four hours, she knocked out five additional songs as well. With the pensive "Crazy" masterfully out of the way, she leapt into the peppy country number "Who Can I Count On?" [60], and the rocking "Seven Lonely Days" [61]. For "I Love You So Much It Hurts Me" [62], she was back in serious ballad mode. With the sparse organ work of Floyd Cramer and the Jordanaires behind her, this chilling heartbreaker is emotionally devastating the way Patsy performs it, especially the mid-finale pause she makes and takes an audible breath as though she is overcome with pain.

Patsy has wicked fun on "Foolin' Around" [63], which was written by Harlan Howard and Buck Owens. Sassy and full of life, you can tell that she is having a good time on this mambo-flavored number. She even finished off the track with a playful Cajun-style accent on the last chorus lines, just for fun.

She closed the successful session with the country shuffle of "Have You Ever Been Lonely (Have You Ever Been Blue)" [64], which had been a 1960 hit for Theresa Brewer. This song benefitted from a great synthesis of country and pop. Pianist Floyd Cramer, who was the piano player on several of Elvis Presley's greatest hits—including "Money Honey" and "Heartbreak Hotel"—helped make this one a true Cline classic.

The following day, on August 25, they tackled four more songs. Continuing on her western theme, Patsy and the Jordanaires spiced things up with the cowboy-flavored "South of the Border (Down Mexico Way)" [65]. With maracas and Mexican musical touches behind her, Patsy weaves a spell of intrigue with this exotic musical ode. Next, she updated for stereo her classic "Walkin' after Midnight" [66]. This time around, Patsy breathed new life into the song. She had sung it in concert hundreds of times by now, and on this "take" she added several new nuances to it. On the first version of the song her vocal delivery had sounded more matter-of-factish. On this new rendition, she gives her phrasing more heartbroken emphasis, and the addition of the Jordanaires also gives it a new, fuller dimension.

The Mel Tillis/Fred Burch song "Strange" [67] was tailor-made for Patsy's new simmering singing style. Song by song she was becoming a masterful storyteller with her songs of love-lost and love-found. She rounded out the session with Hank Cochran and Jimmy Key's "You're Stronger than Me" [68]. Beginning with very country-sounding guitars, and smoothed out with the Jordanaires' mellow vocal "ooh's" and "ahh's," Patsy glides her way through this beautiful ballad. Both of these songs were compositions of the new batch of songwriters she was becoming close with, and they each fit beautifully with Patsy's new vocal persona.

After these sessions were completed, when the musicians and singers had left the studio, Owen and Patsy sat listening to the playback. She turned to him and said, "Well, we finally did it!" When Bradley asked her what she meant, she further explained, "I think

I've found out who I am and what we've been looking for. We don't have to search for my identity anymore. This is it—we're doing it!"

By the second half of the year, Patsy Cline was very much in vogue. *Country Song Roundup* magazine oozed with personal details and fashion tips from the glamorous "I Fall to Pieces" singing star. In one issue they glowed, "The ensembles she wears onstage depend on the occasion and location. She has something in her wardrobe to answer every requirement—fringed costumes, full-skirted dresses with tight bodices, formal-type wear, and skirts and blouses. Slacks and blouses answer most of her at-home requirements, and one of her major concerns always is that everything must have that 'just pressed' look."

Regarding her accessories, it further pointed out, "As one of her hobbies, she collects earrings, then goes out of her way to find bracelets to match them, and exactly opposite from the rich simple lines of her dresses, her jewelry is of the 'sparkly' type, but again, in excellent taste because she doesn't 'overdress' with it, usually wearing only the bracelet and earrings."

Another of Patsy's hobbies was collecting unique salt and pepper shakers during her tours. However, with the emotion-packed songs she was now recording, her career was suddenly becoming far spicier than either salt or pepper could provide.

On October 16, 1961, Decca released her next single "Crazy"/ "Who Can I Count On?" It was an instant smash hit. Patsy and her expressive voice were now firmly planted in the American consciousness, riding a crest of popularity that cemented her as the top female in the country music world. Only six months ago, her biggest concern was saving her Kenmore stove, washer, and refrigerator from being repossessed by Sears! Now she suddenly had to deal with the pressures of stardom. With an exciting musical direction clearly defined for her, she was about to hit a new zenith.

Chapter Ten

THE DREAM
HOUSE

The fall of 1961 was a time of healing and reflection for Patsy. Unfortunately, she didn't have much time to sit and contemplate her life—she was too busy living it. She had prayed for a career that was both demanding and rewarding, and now that she had it, she scarcely had time to enjoy it.

During this period she went through a couple of scar-reducing plastic surgery sessions, and still there was work to be done on the jagged gash across her forehead. For Patsy, the operations were worse to go through than the extra time that it took applying additional layers of pancake make-up to hide the scars. Vain as she was, one might guess that Patsy would jump at the opportunity to do away with the scars as soon as possible. She came to rely on wigs in varying shades of brown and auburn to provide her with thick bangs of hair to comb over the scar. She also began penciling in dark, arching eyebrows to diffuse attention. Occasionally she would wear a cloth headband across her forehead while her latest facial work healed.

Fortunately, she was busier and more in demand than ever. Because of this, she didn't have a lot of time to concentrate on feeling sorry for herself, or centering her thoughts on the effects of the post-accident trauma that were building up inside of her.

One night at the *Grand Ole Opry*, with the assistance of crutches, Patsy made her way to the backstage area, having just received a huge standing ovation. Typical of their bantering and humor-filled relationship, Faron Young announced to the triumphant Cline, "Some people will do anything to get applause!"

Cocky as ever, Patsy spewed back at him, "No, Sheriff, it's talent and guts they're applauding!"

"Well, who wouldn't?" he complained. "They can't help it when you go out there with those 'sympathy sticks'!"

"Why you jealous little son-of-a-bitch!" she said in retaliation. "You take 'em, and you go out there with 'em."

Faron laughingly proclaimed "Oh no honey, I wouldn't want to deprive you. Hark! Your public is demanding you!"

It wasn't long afterward that Patsy abandoned the crutches as well. No freak car accident was going to keep her from doing the job that she so intensely loved. To maintain her sanity while her body repaired itself, she took up embroidery, which she would work on while traveling from one concert date to another.

After all those years of struggling, Patsy was at long-last in the winner's circle. Now that she was "in the chips" she didn't hesitate to share her newfound prosperity with her friends and running mates. Sitting at one of the checkered cloth-covered tables at Tootsie's, with a group of her musician and songwriter buddies, she delighted in being able to pick up the tab from a post-*Opry* cocktail session. Grabbing the check and pulling out her cash, she would always announce, "I can't take it with me."

Loretta Lynn and Dottie West were both feeling the financial pinch of launching a singing career in Nashville. Patsy saw herself in both of them, and—although far from rich—she would bestow them with little gifts and cash, to help them survive.

Loretta was becoming popular on the *Opry*, but without a solid hit record of her own, she and her husband were still "dirt poor." When Patsy got wind of the fact that Loretta had hardly a stitch of clothing to call her own, Patsy dragged her over to the house and gave her several of the cowgirl outfits she had abandoned since she started dressing like the sophisticated contemporary pop star she had suddenly become.

On several occasions, Patsy would return from a shopping expedition having purchased something for herself, and would pick up a similar item for Loretta as well. When Cline presented her with an outfit decorated with rhinestones, unschooled Loretta just assumed they were real diamonds, having scarcely laid eyes upon a genuine diamond. With regard to Patsy's generosity, Loretta recalled, "She gave me one pair of panties I wore for three years! They were holier than I am."

"She enjoyed playing mother hen," Dottie West recalls. "Patsy loved people and having them around her."

She also began to enjoy her own two children. Her daughter Julie remembers her mother "always having time for us. She would sit for hours and color in coloring books with me. That's what's important to a child—those special little moments."

With the fresh new sound that Patsy was now recording, she was clearly on a hot streak. The night she introduced her new single, "Crazy," at the *Grand Ole Opry*, she received an overwhelming trio of standing ovations. As she came sweeping backstage, she announced to her friends, "I guess that's gonna be my song!" Indeed, it was, and still is.

She had fun introducing the song onstage. Quippingly she would announce, "I recorded a song called 'I Fall to Pieces,' and I was in a car wreck. Now I'm worried because I have a brand-new record, and it's called 'Crazy'!"

"Crazy" indeed became Patsy's biggest smash recording yet. By the first week in December of 1961, it was number nine on the country charts, and in January it peaked at number two on the pop charts. Suddenly she found herself hotter than ever before, with her world beginning to spin faster and faster.

By 1961, WSM's annual November Country Disk Jockey Convention had changed titles to become "The WSM Country Music Festival." On November 2 of that year, Patsy received the award as the "Favorite Female Artist." Long recognized by her peers as a phenomenal talent, she was finally getting the kind of public adulation that she so clearly deserved.

Her sudden acquisition of "the Midas touch" was to rub off on her friends and comrades as well. Owen Bradley was named the "Country Western Man of the Year" for producing hit records not only for Patsy, but also for Roy Drusky ("Three Hearts in a Tangle"), Brenda Lee ("Dum Dum"), Kitty Wells ("Heartbreak, U.S.A."), and others. Harlan Howard took the "Favorite Songwriter" award, and Loretta Lynn was named "Most Promising Female Artist."

In addition to those awards from WSM, Patsy was also given the "Favorite Female Artist" honor from *Billboard* magazine. *Music Vendor* magazine named her the jukebox world's "Female Vocalist of the Year."

Loretta distinctly remembers the evening of the awards ceremony, and what a proud event it was for Patsy. "She had this little lace suit on that somebody [Hilda] had made for her. It was the same material as the curtains she had made for my house. It was aqua blue. She already had two operations on her face and had more to go, 'cause her face was [scarred] so bad. When it was all over she come back and she cried and hugged me and said, 'Now, little gal, next year you're goin' to get this!'"

On November 27, Patsy's second record album, "Patsy Cline Showcase," was released. The twelve cuts on it were chosen from the seventeen tracks that had been recorded in the past twelve months. The repertoire included: "I Fall to Pieces," "True Love," "San Antonio Rose," "The Wayward Wind," "Crazy," "Seven Lonely Days," "I Love You So Much It Hurts Me," "Foolin' Around," "Have You Ever Been Lonely (Have You Ever Been Blue)," "South of the Border (Down

Mexico Way)," and the new versions of "A Poor Man Riches (or a Rich Man's Gold)" and "Walkin' after Midnight"—just for good measure.

Amid all of this excitement, the true highlight of the month was Patsy's performance at Carnegie Hall. If ever there was a concert appearance that should have been recorded for posterity, it was that night. Unfortunately it was not.

Carnegie Hall has hosted a wide variety of musical styles, from opera singers to jazz, to symphonies, to pop, and on rare occasions— country. The evening Patsy Cline performed, she was one of several of the stars of the *Grand Ole Opry* to headline a special evening of country entertainment, for a benefit to raise money for the Musicians' Aid Society. Among other things, the funds were going toward supporting retired musicians.

Along with Patsy, the other *Opry* performers booked to stand under the proscenium arch of Carnegie Hall that evening were Minnie Pearl, Marty Robbins, Jim Reeves, Faron Young, the Jordanaires, Bill Monroe and His Bluegrass Boys, star fiddler Tommy Jackson, country dance troupe the Stony Mountain Cloggers, banjo-playing comedian "Grandpa" Jones, and the radio program's master of ceremonies T. Tommy Cutrer. What resulted was a variety show in which all of the headliners had their own spot in the show to shine.

The idea of juxtaposing the crème of country stars with the virtual palace of classical music was a difficult event for many Manhattan journalists to resist poking fun at. The most famous bit of New York snobbery came from one of the top syndicated gossip columnists, Dorothy Kilgallen, who wrote for *The New York Journal American* newspaper. Although the debut of TV's "Beverly Hillbillies" was a full year away, Kilgallen wittily referred to the upcoming date that would feature Cline and company as the invasion of the "Carnegie Hillbillies."

When she got wind of the attack from the gossip columnist, Patsy was up in arms. People across the country knew Dorothy Kilgallen from network television, as she was one of the four celebrity contestants on the popular TV game show "What's My Line?" Onstage during a Saturday night concert in Winston-Salem, North Carolina, on November 25, Patsy let her feelings be known about

Dorothy Kilgallen's snide comments. "Miss Dorothy, the Wicked Witch of the East," is how she referred to her, announcing, "We're gonna be in 'high cotton' next week—Carnegie Hall in New York City! That old Dorothy Kilgallen in The *New York Times* [sic] wrote 'everybody should get out of town because 'the hillbillies' are coming!' Well, at least, we ain't standin' on New York street corners with itty-bitty cans in our hands collecting coins to keep up the opera and symphonies. Miss Dorothy called us Nashville performers 'the gang' from the *Grand Ole Opry*—'hicks from the sticks.' And if I have the pleasure of seeing that wicked witch, I'll tell her how proud I am to be a 'hick from the sticks!' "

At first, the advance tickets for the Carnegie Hall event sold very slowly. The staff members of the *Grand Ole Opry* were quite worried that they had made a huge mistake by setting up this date. With just a little over a week to go before the concert, the head of WSM's public relations department, Trudy Stamper, came up with a brainstorm. Through her contacts, she was able to get in touch with Jack Benny. Known for his running gag with a violin, Benny agreed to pose for press photographers as he purchased a ticket for the *Opry* event at the Carnegie hall box office. While the flashbulbs popped, in his trademark penny-pinching deadpan style, Jack Benny moaned, "I should be buying a plane ticket to Nashville. I'm paying $7.50 here for what would cost me $1.50 there!" It was a clever twist on the fact that there would be some violin playing of a different variety at Carnegie Hall that night. The next day, the switchboard at the Carnegie Hall box office lit up. The day before the event, nearly all of the 2,700 seats were pre-sold.

Patsy and the majority of the stars flew to New York on a chartered TWA craft with the words *"Grand Ole Opry* Liner" painted on the door of it. In addition, Patsy also brought along Charlie, Randy Hughes, and Hilda. She had truly come a long way from that night she slept on a cement picnic table bench outside of Nashville, and she wanted to make sure that her mother witnessed this historic event.

At another publicity opportunity, Patsy Cline, Grandpa Jones, Minnie Pearl, Faron Young, and Bill Monroe were presented with a golden "Key to the City of New York" at a ceremony held on the steps of City Hall. While photographers clicked away, the quintet of *Opry* stars posed for pictures with Robert W. Watt, the city's

Director of Commerce. He was presiding over the ceremony on behalf of the mayor, Robert Wagner.

The afternoon before the Wednesday night concert, the stars got to mingle with the press at a gala cocktail party, held in the bar at Carnegie Hall. It was a mob scene, as record company representatives, writers, photographers, and interviewers clambered for the attention of the stars. Patsy was particularly in demand, since she was riding the crest of her biggest top ten smash pop hit yet.

Backed into a corner with Randy Hughes by her side, Patsy grabbed one of her co-stars. "Hey Sheriff, loan me one of your guns. The blasting kind!" Patsy exclaimed to Faron Young, in hopes of diminishing the crowds around her.

"Well, honey, I got three like that!" he recalls zinging right back at her.

"No, you don't!" she laughingly argued. "You got two. The one between your legs don't count!" You could take Patsy out of the country, but you couldn't take the "country" out of Patsy!

153

Even in Carnegie Hall, with her friends Patsy acted and spoke as brassy and bawdy as ever. However, that night onstage, in her lace dress and orchid corsage, she was the picture of poise and sophistication.

In the next morning's *New York Times*, Robert Shelton wrote up the event with a glowing review. According to him,

> *An unusual sort of opera was staged last night at Carnegie Hall. Its musical score was very much in the American idiom; its libretto was casual and folksy. Most of the recitatives were delivered by a radio announcer and there wasn't a coloratura or a basso in the house ... Nashville has a button-busting pride about the Opry and the huge music industry it helped spawn ... This program was representative of the two chief currents in country music, the traditional and the popular, although there is considerable overlapping ... Faron Young and His Country Deputies sang several of the more popular songs in the Nashville vein competently. The Jordanaires, a polished vocal quartet, were pleasing and spiritual, and Patsy Cline, a mod-*

ern popular singer, had a convincing way with "heart songs," the country cousin of the torch song.

In the Nashville *Tennessean*, reporter Phil Sullivan wrote,

> *For one who knew Carnegie Hall only through reading of the great princely affairs that have gone on there, it was novel to see tattooed snakes moving down the halls on bare arms. It was that kind of crowd. Leather jackets mingle with mink stoles and clerical vestments. The* Opry *show, generally, was well-received courteously by the critics when it was noted at all. After indirectly twitting the show in advance, Dorothy Kilgallen in* The Journal American, *subsequently ignored the performance. On Wednesday she had taken a poke at the show by writing and commenting on a letter from a country music fan protesting her previously expressed attitude toward hillbillies.*

154

When she found out later that Dorothy Kilgallen in fact had not attended the show, Patsy blasted, "She was chicken to show her face!" Without a doubt, "the Cline" would have relished the opportunity to have personally given Kilgallen a piece of her mind!

After the concert, the *Opry* troupe headed over to the Barbizon Hotel on Central Park West for a private celebration. Very early the following morning they headed for LaGuardia Airport, where everyone broke out their bottles and had a swingin' party in the air—all the way back to Nashville.

When she got back to Nashville, she recounted her thoughts back to Dottie West. According to West, Patsy told her, "As I walked from the dressing room to the stage up this flight of stairs all I could think of when I touched the railing was of all the famous, fantastic people—singers and musicians of all kinds—who had walked up those stairs to the stage. I got a rush as I walked onstage and heard this mob cheering. I could feel the good vibes as I moved up to the microphone. You really don't need a mike in that place! The acoustics are so good, you can just stand there and be heard even by the people sitting way up in the Gods—the last row of the uppermost balcony."

On the following Saturday night, Patsy guest starred on TV's *Dixie Jubilee* which was broadcast live, and performed before three hundred studio audience members. That night she sang several of the same songs she had sung only three nights before in Carnegie Hall, including "Bill Bailey, Won't You Please Come Home," "A Poor Man's Riches (or a Rich Man's Gold)," and "Come on in (and Make Yourself at Home)."

Addressing the audience as if they were intimate friends, Patsy related some of her feelings and experiences to her adoring public. "This ain't like New York, but it's uptown," she announced. "Oh, doggies, you talk about a hen out of a coop. I really felt like one up there. I'm telling you. But you know what? We made 'em show their true colors. We brought that country out of 'em if anybody did. They were sitting up there stomping their feet and yelling just like a bunch of hillbillies—just like we do. I was real surprised! Carnegie Hall was real fabulous, but you know, it ain't as big as the Grand Ole Opry. You couldn't get 'em in there. We were awfully proud of having the opportunity to go that 'fur' up in high cotton. Well, I guess, I'd have to say that's the cream of the crop. And, believe you me, it really did my ole heart good, because little did I know who was sitting in the audience a-watching me, 'cause if I had a wouldn'ta been able to went on, I guarantee you. They had Jimmy Dean sitting in the audience and Jack Benny. I guess he come to see Tommy Jackson play the fiddle! He was there. Anyway, above all, and the most inspiring thing of the whole thing that excited me the most was Princess Menassia, who is the sister of the King of Persia! The Princess of Persia was there in the first box on my right. And after the show was over, she came to the fella who was in charge of all the doings, Dr. Brooks of the Musicians' Union there in New York, and she told him—and I haven't gotten over it yet—she said, 'The girl that knocked me out—the whole acts were tremendous—but the most tremendous thing on the show, as far as I'm concerned, was 'the Cline girl!'"

Composing herself, Patsy continued, "Talk about it! Well, I was all shook up. They couldn't hold me! I said, 'Well, why didn't you tell me?' We had WSM's photographer there, and I'd a took a picture of me and her and hung it on the wall!"

155

It was now the beginning of December of 1961, and one of Cline's songwriter buddies, Hank Cochran, knew that Patsy was getting ready to record songs to be considered for the third single of her Decca Records deal. He was determined to come up with a song that was so perfectly tailor-made for Patsy, that it would leave no doubt that this should be her next hit. Working in the little garage outside of the house where Pamper Music was based, Cochran recalls, "Willie [Nelson] and Harlan [Howard] and all of us wrote out there. And after everybody had left work, I was sitting out there by myself, and come up with the idea and just wrote it within ten or fifteen minutes, and called Patsy and said, 'I've got it!' And she said, 'Well, bring it over here!' I said, 'I will, right now!' And she said, 'Well, on your way, stop and get us a bottle.' I had to go all the way to Nashville and bought us a pint of whiskey."

When he arrived at Patsy's house, he found Dottie West over there, helping Cline get dinner ready. Patsy poured each of them a drink, and then Hank proceeded to sing his new song, "She's Got You," for them. Patsy loved the song the minute she heard it. It fit right into the new mode of her recording songs of heartbreak, and this was the heartbreak song to end them all.

"She poured us another drink and said, 'Sing it again!'" he recalls. "I did. Then she poured us another and said, 'Hoss, sing it for me again.' And I sat there and sang it over an over until we drank that pint of whiskey. Then I did it some more. She wanted me to, so she could learn it—and she did!"

Patsy then proceeded to dial her manager, Randy Hughes, on the phone, and she sang it to him. He too was convinced that it was a hit, exclaiming, "Go with it, gal!" The following day Patsy and Hank Cochran went into Owen Bradley's studio and performed the song for him and he immediately scheduled a recording date for December 17.

This was to be Patsy's second one-song recording session of the year. This time around, the problem wasn't like in August when she couldn't get the right sound with the phrasing of the song—like "Crazy." This time it was because she was so emotionally involved with the lyrics of "She's Got You" that she kept breaking down and sobbing in the middle of it.

"She's Got You"[69] is truly one of the most beloved songs of

Patsy's entire recording career. Beginning with a long harmonizing sigh from the Jordanaires, Patsy sings about the fact that while she possesses the class ring, the records, the photos, the mementos, and the memories of her beloved: "She's Got You." Slow and emotionally wrenching, "the Cline" really put her heart into this song so deeply that she even startled her studio musicians with this masterpiece of recording.

The day after she recorded "She's Got You," Patsy was emotionally drained. The whirlwind of the past year—hitting number one on the charts with "I Fall to Pieces," the car accident, her "instant" financial success, a second baby, fighting with Charlie, her twenty-ninth birthday, the triumph of Carnegie Hall, and the unexpected pressures of suddenly becoming a star after so long a struggle—finally got to her. On December 18, 1961, Patsy was diagnosed as having a "nervous breakdown." Suddenly she was medically commanded to spend the next two weeks at home in bed.

On January 10 of the new year, Decca released her next hit single: "She's Got You," backed with "Strange," and she immediately hit the road to promote it. Again it was enthusiastically received, and it immediately went into "heavy rotation" on both country and pop radio stations. The two-week January tour was headlined by Johnny Cash, and also included George Jones, Carl Perkins, Johnny Western, June Carter, and Gordon Terry. The two-week tour took them in a big circle of eastern North America, encompassing Canada, South Dakota, Indiana, Iowa, Illinois, and Missouri. Another attraction on the tour was a little girl who played multiple instruments and performed like a seasoned trouper.

In a January 22, 1962, letter written to Louise Seger, Patsy claimed, "Got a twelve-year-old girl who plays steel guitar out of this world. My ole ears have never heard anything like it. She also plays a sax and sings. Looks like a blonde doll. And, boy, what a showman. She's great. Her name is Barbara Mandrell. Wish you could hear her."

That January jaunt is something that Barbara Mandrell would never forget. Although she was just a child, her parents trusted Johnny Cash to make certain that nothing was going to happen to her on the road. After all, he had children of his own, and he knew what a child should or shouldn't do. However, when Patsy came aboard the tour, she saw some of the wild parties that the musicians were throwing, and was appalled that little Barbara would be exposed to this at such an early age. When she found out that Barbara was staying in a room by herself, she put her foot down and insisted that she was going to be her roommate and chaperon for the entire two-week tour.

On the first night, Patsy's room had only one double bed, so she took Barbara in hand and told her which side of the bed was hers. In the middle of the night, Mandrell recalls being awakened by Cline gently shaking and saying, "Barbara, could you please move back to your side?" According to Mandrell, she had unconsciously sprawled herself all over the bed. After that, Patsy saw to it that they shared a room with twin beds.

Patsy took Barbara on a surprise shopping spree, and Cline had her hair done. When they returned to the hotel, Patsy hated the way the hairdo looked. Barbara volunteered to comb it out and re-style it for her. From that day on, Barbara was Patsy's personal hairdresser for the rest of the tour.

Mandrell also recalls one icy day in Des Moines, Iowa. The two of them were walking back to the car, when Patsy asked Barbara if she could hold onto her to help her get across the parking lot safely. According to Mandrell, she'll never forget the impression it left on her. Tough as nails, Patsy was terrified of slipping on the ice and falling, and the young girl was thrilled to be able to turn the tables, and look out for her for a change.

Barbara Mandrell recalls, "You couldn't tell Patsy had been injured, if you didn't know. But I remember feeling the tension in her hand as she leaned her big frame against me on that icy sidewalk in Des Moines. She was looking after me on that trip, but in a way, she needed me to look after her, too. She was a grown woman, in the prime of her life, and she was fearful."

On this particular tour, Patsy would generally open the second act of the show, being the second-biggest star on the bill next to Johnny Cash. People who saw her on the bill with Johnny Cash that year recall the chilling effect she would have on an audience. Long gone were her days of cowgirl fringe and boots. She wore her tightly-fitting shirtwaist dresses or long gowns, appeared in a solo spotlight, and wove a mesmerizing spell of heartache and unrequited love. She had a nice string of hits to draw from, and she was enthusiastically welcomed wherever she appeared.

On February 12, she was back in the recording studio, cutting four tracks for her next album. First she reached back to the beginning of the century for "You Made Me Love You (I Didn't Want to Do It)" [70]. It had become one of Al Jolson's trademark songs when he recorded it in 1913, then teenage Judy Garland made it popular again as she serenaded Clark Gable's photo with it in *Broadway Melody of 1938*. With the Jordanaires stylizing a barbershop quartet background section, Patsy gave the ending of her version a real Broadway showtune feel.

"You Belong to Me" [71] had been a hit for Jo Stafford in 1952. In the lyrics, Patsy sings about a lover who roams to the pyramids, a tropical island, a market place in Algiers, and the jungle, but she convincingly begs him to come home to her on this medium-tempo ballad. On "Heartaches" [72], Patsy tackled a big band standard from the 1940s that was a wartime favorite, recorded by everyone from Guy Lombardo to Harry James. "The Cline" did a nice updating of this chestnut.

"Your Cheatin' Heart" [73] brought her back across the fence to the country side of things. The trademark song of Hank Williams, this slowed down pop-oriented version gave Patsy the space to really open up on the ending, and concentrate on every vindictive note.

The following day, she came back to the studio and spent three and a half hours working on two more songs. "That's My Desire" [74] had been a hit in 1947 for Frankie Laine, and a jazz/R&B hit for Hadda Brooks. A slow, thoughtful ballad, Patsy caressed the lyrics, and made the song all her own. She is especially convincing as she sings about meeting her lover in their favorite rendezvous. Similarly paced "Half as Much" [75] had been a hit four different times in four different genres: Hank Williams/country, Dinah Shore/jazz, Rosemary Clooney/pop, and Ray Charles/R&B. With a harmonica leading her into it, Patsy took a pop-western direction with this number.

After giving herself Valentine's Day off, she returned to the studio on February 15. This time around, Owen Bradley brought in another string section. From this session on—there would always be strings present for all of Patsy's recordings.

According to Owen Bradley, "We were just crossing our fingers and holding our breath. You'll notice in the original albums, probably at least half of the songs would not have strings on them, which probably just shows how chicken I was, how safe we were trying to be with it." He didn't want Patsy to lose her country fans or her pop fans, so they walked on a taut tightrope between both musical styles. As it was, they were managing to make Patsy's recordings a hit in both arenas, and they were careful to make it continue.

They started this session out with another winsome and somber harmonica-led western number, "Lonely Street" [76], with which Don Gibson had just scored a 1960 hit. Picking up the pace a bit, they next swung into Eddy Arnold's 1948 hit "Anytime" [77]. On this number, the Jordanaires held back until the bridge of this peppy middle-of-the-road standard. "You Were Only Fooling (While I Was Falling in Love)" [78] got a straight pop rendition, very similar to the original Kay Starr version from 1948. The session finished up with Patsy's interpretation of Hank Williams' "I Can't Help It (If I'm Still in Love with You)" [79]. Another song featuring the harmonica of Charlie McCoy, Cline's recording again conjures up visions of the Old West.

On February 22, 1962, Patsy finally made her long-awaited debut on Dick Clark's afternoon network television show, *American Bandstand*. She had written to Louise Seger the previous May that she was about to appear on the show singing "I Fall to Pieces." Then came her accident. She performed her latest hit, "She's Got You," which was excellently received. Patsy had a very strong teenage following, and *American Bandstand* was the perfect vehicle to reach them. The song went on to become a huge number one country hit for her, and by March it peaked at number fourteen on the pop charts. The flip side, "Strange," also made a dent in the pop chart as well at number ninety-seven.

On February 28, Patsy was in the studio again. "You're Stronger than Me" [80] is a re-recording of the song she originally sang the previous August. Her original version had a shuffling beat to it, while this new rendition is slower, and closer in approach to "She's Got You." Written by Hank Cochran and Jimmy Key, this "second take" put more emphasis on Patsy's heartbroken, inflection-filled voice.

Harlan Howard's "When I Get through with You (You'll Love Me Too) [81], is a rock-flavored number that sounds like the "answer song" to Dion and the Belmonts' "Runaround Sue." This pure-pop bopper finds Patsy proclaiming that when she's finished with the "him" he is sure to love her and "not Sue!" According to Harlan, "She was selling kids, so I wrote her something to sell to kids." This was a perfect pop foray for Patsy.

"Imagine That"[82] found her back in a pensive mode. Written by Ernest Tubb's son, Justin, Patsy gave it an expressive, bluesy reading. Especially fun is the hearty laugh Cline added to the end of the song. She finished off the session with "So Wrong" [83], a similar-paced ballad about awakening to a surprising love. Patsy finished the song off with a bang, singing several of the last lines a capella. She had discovered the song by Carl Perkins while she was on tour with him in January, and insisted that she be given the first opportunity to record it. He knew better than to say "no" to "the Cline!"

Justin Tubb recalls distinctly the evolution of Patsy's version of "Imagine That." According to him, "On an October night in 1961 during what was then known as 'The D.J. Convention,' I was driving down Broad Street—on my way to Tootsie's, I believe. I met Patsy and Charlie coming the other way. We recognized each other and stopped right in the middle of the street. Patsy got out and hollered to me over the top of the car to follow them to their hotel room. And Charlie told me they were having a few people by, and Patsy wanted to hear 'that song.' I had mentioned 'Imagine That' to her before, and sang a line or two. She had told me she really wanted to hear it. I don't know how many times I sang it to her that night, but I'll never forget her reaction. Patsy was a 'writer's singer!' She got so excited when she liked a song or when a song touched her, and you just knew she felt about it like you did when you wrote it. It was kinda like giving up a baby for adoption. You knew she loved it, and would take good care of it … and that your song was in good hands!"

Carl Perkins still tells the evolution of how Patsy ended up with the song "So Wrong." According to him, "I first met Patsy Cline on tour in the early 1960s. I remember I was in a dressing room in Omaha, Nebraska. I was writing a song called 'So Wrong.' Patsy

161

heard me singing the song and she asked, 'Perkins, whose song is that?' I said, 'It's mine. I'm just writing it.' She said, 'No, it's mine, I'm recording it.' And record it she did. I think she did a wonderful job on the song as well as on anything she ever recorded. Patsy Cline was truly one of those rare people in our profession. Patsy copied no one, but many have borrowed from her magical style."

All of Patsy's music industry friends recall this as being the lowest point in her relationship with Charlie. He had quit his job so that he could take of the children in Patsy's absence, and if they weren't fighting about their relationship, they were fighting about money. When Patsy was on the road, the fights didn't stop. She and Charlie simply resumed their battles long distance on the phone.

Dottie West remembers, "Patsy could really hold her own. She was strong and that was sometimes rough on a tough guy like Charlie. Maybe Charlie turned to drinking because of her assertiveness. In the early sixties very few women were as opinionated or commanded as much respect as Patsy."

According to Jimmy Dean, "Patsy and Charlie used to fight—I mean *fight!*—with an exclamation point! She'd call up and have the cops grab him," he recalls. "She'd keep saying, 'I'm leaving that damn son-of-a-bitch, that no good bastard!' But she didn't. She never left."

While most of Patsy's friends confirm that Charlie was an abusive husband, several of them also confirm that Patsy could also pound on him from time to time. There was one reported occasion, where Patsy literally threw Charlie out of her car. Singer Pearl Butler, who was one of Patsy's Nashville friends, recalls, "Now, Charlie may have been the strongest man in the world, but I imagine if he ever took a notion to hit Patsy, he lived to regret it. She could hold her own with anyone, I'll tell you!"

Likewise, Dottie West recalls, "Charlie would go to hit Patsy and she'd pick something up and throw it at him. I think she was always careful not to throw something she really liked or could not replace. Patsy could kick back. Charlie knew that if he hit or kicked her, he'd get one, too."

Looking at Patsy's rough and tumble life, it is easy to see how naturally she took to songs about disappointment and heartbreak. They were a mirror reflection of her life. This was also true of some of her up-tempo songs as well. All of her friends knew that it was common knowledge that Charlie was fooling around on the side. After all that she had been through in the past several months, she was really craving some genuine affection and companionship of her own, and Charlie was not providing it. Perhaps that's why the song "Foolin' Around" from her then-concurrent album is such a fun—and an oddly coincidental—cut to listen to, especially since Patsy also had several casual affairs of her own during this era. Mae Boren Axton claims that Patsy's rumored affair with Randy Hughes was quite real. "Randy, he was kind of a cute guy," she recalls.

"Foolin' Around" had been written by Harlan Howard and Buck Owens. Before she recorded it, Buck had turned his version of the tune into a big country hit. Although it was a little suggestive, it was a fun song, and it surely couldn't hurt Patsy to record her own rendition of it. However, when she recorded the song, she started laughing when she and Owen and Harlan were listening to the playbacks in Bradley's office.

"Harlan, you are a slut!" she exclaimed. "That's a dirty song!"

"It's not dirty, it's a fun song," he argued.

"It's talking about getting laid!" Patsy laughed back at him. That was part of the reason why she liked it so much!

In March of 1962, Patsy was in the middle of a concert tour of the American Northeast and southeastern Canada, and she was in a lusty mood. She was with two of her singing buddies from the past: Jimmy Dean and George Hamilton IV. Both long-free from their business ties to Connie Gay, Patsy and Jimmy had finally patched up their friendship.

It is Jimmy Dean who has recounted the now-famous "Patsy and the Mountie" story. According to him, this was a period where Patsy was determined to get back at Charlie for cheating on her—by cheating on him.

Recounted Dean, "I'm not that easily shocked, but one time we were working a date somewhere in Canada and were checking into the hotel. Patsy and I were together and she looked around and saw this big guy—a Canadian Mountie. Right out loud she said, 'He's a big good-looking son-of-a-bitch! I want him! I'm screwing the boots off him tonight.' And, she took off across that lobby for him, made contact, and did what she was going to do!"

In addition to snagging a Mountie in Canada, she also purchased a gorgeous silver fox wrap that she was most excited about owning. She certainly wasn't going to sit around and wait for Charlie to present her with the luxuries she craved, so she bought them for herself. She was country music's reigning diva, and she was playing the part to the hilt!

On tour with Jimmy Dean, he and Patsy swung into Peoria, Illinois, as co-stars for a concert appearance. In an interview with a local school newspaper, *The Limelight*, Patsy made the statement, "I have gotten more than I asked for. All that I ever wanted was to hear my voice on record and have a song among the top twenty.

On May 7, Patsy's latest single, "When I Get through with You (You'll Love Me Too)"/"Imagine That" was released. The "A" side peaked at number ten on the country chart, and number fifty-three pop. "Imagine That" also charted, hitting number twenty-one country, and number ninety pop.

Although she did have several of the things that she had longed for, she still dreamed of a huge house she could call her own. Randy Hughes was the one who first located the home that filled the bill.

It was absolutely perfect when Patsy and Charlie first laid eyes on the red-brick house. Located fifteen miles out of Nashville, situated on tree-lined Nella Drive, in the suburb of Goodlettsville, it was exactly what she desired. With three stories, there was room for a den downstairs, and enough bedrooms for each member of the family upstairs. Priced at $30,000, Patsy's logic was that she was just going to have to hike her asking price to $1,000 as her new bottomline minimum asking price per gig. With that, she put a downpayment on the house, and threw herself into decorating it just the way she wanted it.

Charlie thought she was crazy when she insisted on certain touches—like putting an artificial magnolia tree in the living room, but it was her dream house and she was going to have it just so. Another of her requirements was to have a bathroom with gold foil in the countertops and the linoleum. In her mind, that was luxury! When Dottie West came over to visit this new work in progress, Patsy enthusiastically glowed, "I just love this house, hoss. I waited so damn long. Now I have something that's made the waiting worth it. This is my blood, sweat, and tears!"

On June 15, 1962, along with the Johnny Cash troupe, Patsy performed her next prestigious gig at the famed Hollywood Bowl. The show was billed as the "Shower of Stars," headlined by Cash and his band the Tennessee Three, Don Gibson ("Oh Lonesome Me"), Leroy Van Dyke ("Walk on By"), George Jones ("White Lightning"), and Patsy as the main stars. The show was rounded out by Mother Maybelle and the Carter Family (including June Carter), Johnny Western, Gordon Terry, and Georgie Riddle.

They were also booked for subsequent dates in Arizona, New Mexico, and Texas. When the "Shower of Stars" package tour rolled into Tucson the next week, the show was held at the outdoor base-ball stadium, Hi Corbett Field. On that day, June 17, 1962, you could see all those stars for the astonishing price of $1.75 if you bought advance tickets, or $2.50 at the door!

Days later, in Albuquerque, New Mexico, Johnny Western recalls Patsy going toward the motel swimming pool looking as smashing as Miss America in a brand-new silver lamé one-piece bathing suit. Patsy was feeling sexy and lonely that afternoon. She was setting the scene to make a play for Johnny Western.

After the show that evening, they both went back to Patsy's room to talk. He distinctly recalls her seductively saying to him, "I need somebody real bad. I think it could be you." He could tell by the look in her eyes exactly what she meant.

Startled, he replied, "Well, Patsy, I'm going through a really, real-ly bad thing, as you know, my marriage is dissolving. Probably the last person in the world you need is me."

Patsy thought for a moment, sighed, and said, "It's probably a good thing, because I'm right in the middle of my [menstrual] cycle and now is the time when I get pregnant, just as fast as Saturday is to Sunday. It's already happened once, and I had to do something about it." With that the subject was dropped.

In July of 1962 came Patsy's next foray into a movie career. Along with Dottie West, Sonny James, and Webb Pierce, Patsy was flown down to Deland, Florida, to appear in a country music ver-sion of a rock and roll film. It promised to feature everyone with a solo number, strung together with a light story. Several reels were shot—then suddenly production came to a halt. Dottie later explained, "It was fun. We had expenses picked up and had several days to relax on the beach. In the end, it was one of those stories you used to hear about a lot in country. The producer ran off with the money, we were never paid, and the movie, or what was made of it, never saw the light of day."

Dottie was also present for the aftermath of one of Patsy's and Charlie's biggest battles yet. It was in the summer of 1962, and Dottie got a late night phone call from Patsy. She was on the line, sobbing about how she and Charlie had a huge argument, and that he had smacked her in the head and broke open the scar that ran across her forehead. Patsy explained how she ran to the phone, called the police, and had Charlie arrested. Dottie immediately raced over to the new house to comfort Patsy.

While Charlie sobered up in a jail cell, Dottie spent the night with Patsy, talking heart-to-heart with each other about their lives. After a couple of drinks, Patsy went and got the scrapbook that she had been keeping on her career. Together the two girls perused it, and Patsy told Dottie things about her life, her feelings, and several of her deepest secrets.

Flipping through the pages of the scrapbook, they came to a photo of Patsy with Elvis Presley. It had been taken at a charity event held at St. Jude's Hospital in Memphis. Also present at the event were Ann Margaret and Danny Thomas. Patsy told Dottie, "Of all of 'em this is my favorite picture—the time I got to meet Elvis was one of the greatest moments of my life!" Imagine "the Cline" and "the King" in the same room!

She came to a photo of her with Jimmy Dean, from her days on *Town and Country Jamboree*. There was also the nearly full-page ad for her disastrous drive-in appearance in Winchester the year before. After they were finished looking through it, Patsy turned and stared out of the window into the darkness. She was in an oddly pensive frame of mind. When she turned around, she picked up the scrapbook, presented it to Dottie and said, "I want you to have it and keep it for me."

Dottie protested, "I can't do that. You should save this and give it to your grandchildren someday."

"You gonna argue with 'the Cline?'" she railed. "I want you to have it. Anyway, it ain't gonna do me no good 'cause I'll never live to see thirty."

In shock, Dottie tried to talk her out of saying such things, and she claimed that Patsy insisted, "Well, it's the truth. I'll never live to see thirty."

When West returned home at the crack of dawn, she leafed through the scrapbook and discovered a folded piece of stationary. Wrapped in it was a check of $75, and on the piece of paper was a note which read, "I know you're having it hard and that you're not working. You can use this to pay the rent. Love, Patsy."

On July 16, Decca released Patsy's next single, "So Wrong"/"You're Stronger than Me." On August 6, "Sentimentally Yours," Patsy's third record album was released. The cover shot evokes her inner battle with the blues. She is lying on a stack of pillows in one of her many blue lace dresses, with a reflective look on her face. She is still wearing a wig hairsprayed into a coiffed and curled helmet. She has several curls combed down to diffuse the forehead scar. On the original version of the LP, the scar is faintly visible under Patsy's make-up.

Aptly titled, "Sentimentally Yours," the selections included on it were in a decidedly sentimental mood. They included: "She's Got You," "Heartaches," "That's My Desire," "Your Cheatin' Heart," "Anytime," "You Made Me Love You (I Didn't Want to Do It)," "Strange," "You Belong to Me," "You Were Only Fooling (While I Was Falling in Love)," "Half as Much," "I Can't Help It (If I'm Still in Love with You)," and "Lonely Street." The back of the original album read, "Sometimes a photograph can do it, but nothing erases time and distance and brings fond memories into life-clear focus as well as a familiar song. For those who aren't ashamed of being a little sentimental; for those who now and then enjoy the warm experience of nostalgia, there's nothing quite like listening to the songs that bring back the special, magic moments in your life. Here, in this exciting new album, you'll find a collection of some of the most beautiful and everlastingly popular songs of our time ... performed in the distinctively warm and irresistibly charming vocal style of Patsy Cline."

She had come a long way from being that yodeling honky tonk gal in gingham and fringe. Patsy Cline was not only a country legend; now she was an immensely successful pop diva!

While Patsy was celebrating her newfound winning streak with a new house, her manager, Randy Hughes was celebrating in another way. He had just passed all the necessary tests it took to get his pilot's license. With his money from guiding Patsy's career, he purchased himself an airplane—a Piper Comanche 250. According to Roy Drusky, "I flew Randy to St. Louis to get it. It was a green and white airplane. The number of the airplane was 7000 PAPA, and I said, 'Randy, boy that's a lucky number!'"

On September 5, Patsy, Owen, and company reconvened at Bradley's studio. The first number they tackled in this afternoon recording session was the incomparable effective ballad "Why Can't He Be You?" [84], which Hank Cochran wrote. It is one of the most masterful songs of the entire Patsy Cline songbook. A powerhouse ballad about dissatisfaction with one's seemingly perfect lover, Patsy makes you believe every mournful word of the song.

Picking up the pace a bit for Roy Drusky's composition "Your Kinda Love" [85], Patsy put a bit more country twang on this song which questions the double standards of a love affair. It sounds like Drusky had Patsy—and Charlie—in mind when he wrote this one.

Hank Cochran's "When You Need a Laugh" [86] is tailor-made for Patsy's forlorned-lover-blues stance. Slow paced and mournful, Cline brilliantly interpreted this moody cut. Likewise, Webb Pierce's "Leavin' on Your Mind" [87] finds Patsy at her sad and dejected best. In it, "the Cline" makes it clear to her lover that if he is going to leave—go ahead and get it over with!

Roy Drusky remembers being at the recording session which yielded "Why Can't He Be You." According to him "After the session, Hubert Long and I went over to Owen's office, along with Hank Cochran, and Owen played the session back. When he played that song, Hank Cochran was sitting there with tears coming down his face. That really impressed me. I thought, 'Wow! It was really a tremendous record: "Why Can't He Be You."' I had never seen a writer that excited and emotionally spent by hearing a song he'd written being recorded."

When September 8 rolled around, Dottie West was relieved beyond belief. Patsy had indeed reached her thirtieth birthday, and now she could finally abandon this silly talk about death.

Patsy threw a huge party to celebrate the event. It was a combination fête, for not only was it her birthday, but it was also her official housewarming party. She had finally gotten the colonial/

western/modern decor just the way she envisioned it, and she wanted all of her friends to get a look at it. Among the seventy-five guests were Loretta and Doolittle Lynn, Dottie and Bill West, Faron Young, Randy and Kathy Hughes, Jan and Harlan Howard, and the rest of her Nashville buddies.

On September 10, it was back in front of the microphones for Patsy. In a 2:00 P.M. session, she tackled three more songs. Starting off with "Back in Baby's Arms" [88], Patsy is found in an "up" and optimistic mood amid this peppy ballad. Continuing in the same energetic mode came the whimsical "Tra Le La Le La Triangle" [89]. Although uplifting in presentation, the song aptly found Patsy singing about having her personal life in a crazy "tangle." She finished off the session with the light, Harlan Howard composition, "That's How a Heartache Begins" [90], a ballad in which Patsy philosophizes about the disappointment that comes with the erosion of a love affair. It was a subject she could write volumes about.

A couple of days after her birthday, Patsy phoned Dottie West and asked her to come over. She wanted to talk about something. When she got there, Patsy told Dottie that she had been hiding large amounts of cash behind a brick in the fireplace "for a rainy day." Dottie thought it odd at the time that Patsy was concerned that West knew where it was, in case anything happened to Cline. Again, Dottie just took Patsy's fatalistic tone in her stride.

During this era, Patsy said something to her frequent tour musician, bass fiddle player Lightnin' Chance, that he has always recalled. She looked him in the eye and proclaimed, "I've become a captive of my own ambitions." Perhaps that was true. As her career kept her busier and busier, everything was moving at an increasingly swift pace. In spite of her impending sense of doom, she didn't choose to slow down; she only moved forward faster. In her mind, time was running out, and she was in a hurry to fit everything into her life that she could.

Chapter Eleven

Queen of Country Music

Sailing through 1962 on a triumphantly navigated course, Patsy tallied one career victory after another. Not only was she a huge pop and country star in the United States, but she was also cracking the music charts in Europe as well. "She's Got You" had become her first British hit, and there were plans for her first European trek that spring.

"We talked about Europe," Brenda Lee recalls. Brenda, who was now seventeen, had first crossed the Atlantic when her song "I'm Sorry" had become an international hit. Conquering Europe with her music was very much on Patsy's mind, and she asked Brenda several questions about her experiences over there: "How was it? Did people recognize your songs? How different was it from here?"

Any thoughts of traveling to Europe were a ways down the road. As it was, Patsy was booked solid for the next several months. The second half of September was relegated to a five-week engagement at a club called Dan's Bar in Rapid City, South Dakota, plus a gig at the Frontier Hotel in Cheyenne, Wyoming.

Several of Patsy's traveling musicians confirm that Dan, the owner of Dan's Bar, was one of Cline's secret admirers. On special occasions—like the evening at Carnegie Hall—it was Dan who sent her exotic orchid corsages as a token of his love for her. Like the lyrics of her newly recorded song "Why Can't He Be You," Patsy would stop to wonder why Charlie wasn't capable of such thoughtful extravagances. Was it Dan who could fill this void in her life?

Dan was a wealthy rancher who could afford to lavish extravagances upon his friends, and his bar was just one of his investments. According to Johnny Western, who met Dan in Lincoln, Nebraska, "It was very obvious from the minute he walked in backstage that they knew each other better than nightclub owner/singer. Then she told me about him. She said, 'I only see him a couple of two, three times a year, but he's really good to me and he really likes me.' She kind of left it like that, but it was very, very obvious. She just flat out told me she had a fling with him every time she went up there."

Pumping out one hit after another, on October 8, her latest single, "Heartaches"/"Why Can't He Be You" was released. This was her first single release to become a hit on the pop chart and not even show up on the country chart in Billboard magazine. The fact of the matter was that Patsy's music appealed to virtually everybody, and she was becoming increasingly difficult to categorize. She was simply a huge star whose appeal was so great that she was impossible to tag with any one label.

According to Mary Wilson of the Supremes, "I loved Patsy Cline's music, and she was very big on the charts in Detroit. She wasn't *just* a country star, we all knew who she was, because her music touched everyone's hearts. She sang songs that everyone could identify with."

November 9 and 10 marked the next Country Music Festival in Nashville. In the ballroom of the Andrew Jackson Hotel, wearing a gown of gold brocade, an expertly coiffed wig, and gold spike heels, Patsy virtually swept through the awards, collecting one honor after another. *Billboard* magazine named her again as the year's "Favorite Female Artist," *Cashbox* heralded her as "Most Programmed Country and Western Female," and "Sentimentally Yours" the "Most Programmed Album of the Year." *Music Vendor* crowned her "Female Vocalist of the Year," and *Music Reporter* touted her as its "Female Vocalist of the Year" for the singles "She's Got You" and "Crazy." Patsy told the press, "It's so unbelievable! My new house is gonna have wall-to-wall awards! It's wonderful, but what am I going to do next year?!"

Reporting the weekend-long awards celebration, the local Nashville newspaper, *The Tennessean*, gleamed with accolades for "the Cline." The November 11 issue reported, "Singer Patsy Cline, the spunky girl with a golden voice, is 1962s queen of the country music field with sweepstakes awards from leading musical publications and official title of 'Star Performer of the Year.'" Chic and exciting, Patsy Cline was absolutely fabulous, and now the whole world knew it too.

Aside from all of the honors and glory that were bestowed on Patsy at the Country Disk Jockey Convention, there was also one unfortunate incident. Patsy had a brand-new coat that she was very proud of, complete with fur trim, which was stolen that weekend. Angered beyond belief, Patsy vented her frustration in a letter to one of her fans. According to Cline, "The jewel of all—some son-of-a-bitch stole my beautiful black fox fur-trimmed collar and cuffs coat that I paid $350 for last year, and there isn't another one of its kind. They stole it at the damn convention off the coat rack, while I was just inside the door of the Decca cocktail party. Whoever it was, I hope it chokes 'em to death before sun-up! I put two private dicks—and my Mr. Dick—on it, and they looked and watched all night, but still no coat. If I see anybody with it on, I'm gonna take blood, ass, and all!"

Heeding the lines of that old show business adage, "it's lonely at the top," Patsy wanted to make sure that she opened the door of opportunity for her friends Loretta Lynn and Dottie West. She was pleased when Loretta was ranked fourth in the "Favorite Female Artist" that weekend, and Dottie was in fifth place in the "Most Promising Female Artist" honors.

Dottie West always remembered the advice that Patsy gave her. Giving her pointers about her career, Cline proclaimed, "Hoss, if you can't do it with feeling—don't!" For Dottie, Patsy's parable became career-long "words to live by."

Loretta confirms, "She taught June Carter, Dottie West, and me so much. She taught us everything about singin', about how to act onstage, how to stagger the numbers, how to dress."

Married at the age of thirteen, and pregnant at fourteen, Loretta was the most sheltered of Patsy's singing buddies. In order to help her, Cline would spend hours teaching her how to walk in high-heeled shoes, and how to behave in front of an audience. According to Loretta, "She told me how to dress. She said, 'Now Loretta, when you go out onstage don't wear anything too low-cut. Leave something to the imagination. Not a lot, but some. Don't go out flauntin' things—it makes you look cheap. When you're walkin' onstage, let 'em know you're in charge. And always leave 'em wantin' more—don't ever do an encore.'"

Patsy also liked to tease Loretta from time to time. On one such occasion, Patsy had invited Loretta and her husband over to the house for dinner, and wanted to surprise her. "Patsy got her a blond wig one time and she called me. This was before wigs was 'in,' but Patsy was always twenty years ahead of her time," Lynn recalls. "She just had her new home built. She had her 'rec room' down in, well, kind of like in the basement. And there was two big glass slidin' doors there, you know. *Beautiful* home. And instead of goin' to the glass slidin' doors, I had went to the front door and down the stairs. And, there sat this blond girl. She was embroiderin' a tablecloth. And I was always so bashful and timid, you know, so I didn't look at her very good. So, I walked into the 'rec room,' and Charlie Dick, her husband, was behind the bar. And I said, 'Where's Patsy?' He kind of grinned and looked over at the blond, and I looked back over at the blond and she kept embroiderin'. And finally she looked up at me and grinned, and I said 'No! What did you do? Get your hair dyed?'

That was so funny! We had a big laugh about that, and we had many laughs together."

As a tough gal who could hold her own in the music business, Patsy not only appealed to the "straight" men and women in her audiences, she also had several gay and lesbian fans who adored her. Instead of being put off or narrow-minded about such matters, she had a big "hoot" out of their alternate lifestyles.

Patsy telephoned Loretta one day and announced, "Hey gal, come on over. I got something for you to see."

When she arrived, Patsy brought her in the house and said, "I have a friend here."

"A friend?" Loretta asked.

"Yeah," said Patsy, "but this is a *different* kind of friend, and she's at my house today, and I just wanted to tell you." With that, she introduced Loretta to one of her lesbian fans who had a "crush" on Patsy. This really threw unworldly Lynn for a loop.

According to Loretta, "I think she wanted to teach me: see, this girl was in love with her! I said, 'But *she's a girl!*'—not really understandin'. But, she told me. She took care of things like that."

Totally perplexed by this whole situation, Loretta asked Patsy, "Well, what are you goin' to do about it?"

Patsy just laughed and said, "Oh, Charlie, he's makin' a big deal about it. He's teasin' me, and her too, and gettin' a big bang out of it, but she's lovin' every minute of it!"

In the fall of 1962, Patsy had another new stretch of stateside territory to concentrate on: her upcoming Las Vegas debut. For country performers at the time, landing a gig in the lucrative casinos of Vegas was about as easy as being booked in the Emerald City of Oz. Continuing her list of new conquests, Patsy became the first major female country star to become a headliner in Las Vegas—at the casino "The Mint."

This gig was a special challenge for Patsy. Not only was there a unique glitzy mystique to playing "Vegas," but this engagement called for performing every day for thirty-five straight days, four shows a night, the last one ending at 3:00 in the morning.

This was going to be work, but Patsy was up to the challenge. She complained at the time, "Four shows a night, forty-five minutes each, and seven nights a week for five weeks—this cat's ass will be draggin' the bottom of the desert!"

Patsy and Randy assembled a band, and immediately began to stage rehearsals for her Vegas debut. The band was to consist of steel guitar player Sonny Geno, drummer Don Light, and guitarist Joey Lemon. The musicians were part of Roy Orbison's band, and they were on hiatus because Orbison's wife was expecting a baby and he was taking a break from touring. There was a male trio who performed under the name of the Glaser Brothers. They would be Patsy's opening act, and then when Cline made her entrance, they would sing background vocals for her.

Las Vegas was the height of sophistication in the show business realm, so Patsy decided to revamp everything in preparation. All totalled, she spent $5,000 getting ready for this upcoming gig.

Patsy immediately set Hilda to working on two glamorous new gowns especially for the glitz of Las Vegas. One was a floor-length black sequinned number with a tastefully low neckline, and three-quarter-length sleeves. She wore it with black and gold dangling earrings, and a large black onyx and gold bracelet on her right arm, and a pair of gold open-toed high heels. She also had Hilda make a similar gown with snowy white sequins as well.

She had ten days to get ready for Las Vegas, and she immediately went on a crash diet. Elvis Presley had just broken through with a Vegas act, and she was not about to be outdone by him. To add extra polish to her stage routines, she went and hired choreographer Gene Nash. Patsy harbored visions of descending a grand staircase to the stage, like she had seen in the movies. She and Nash devised a stunning stage entrance for her with a drumroll, and grandiose movements.

Holding rehearsals in her own house, she was a bit on edge when things began to progress less-than-perfectly. When snare drummer Don Light proved inept at playing a drumroll, Patsy broke into tears and bolted upstairs.

According to Tompall Glaser, "Charlie had to go up and get her to come back down and finish rehearsal. But that's what she wanted, that big entrance and a drumroll, so I had to let Don go then. He'd quit another job, so I had to pay him to stay home, and that's when I got Dewey Martin."

The casino that Patsy was booked to perform at was "The Mint," right on "the strip" in Las Vegas, and the room she was set to headline in was called the Merri-Mint Theater. "The Mint" itself was a casino only—no hotel. Its entrance was a sea of blinking lights and neon, but inside the casino and showrooms were of modest dimensions. Owned by Del Webb—who also owned the Sahara—this gig was an important engagement that could lead to bigger and more elaborate bookings for Patsy in Vegas. Unfortunately, the setup was something less than Cline had envisioned. First of all, there was no sweeping staircase, only two steps down to the floor of the stage. And the stage itself was about the size of a postage stamp. However, at $1,000 per night, this was a deal that was too good to miss. After it was over she would fondly refer to her home as "the house that Vegas built!"

Tompall recalls, "We really thought we were going to Las Vegas, you know? And it was going to be this big beautiful place to work. And instead it was *six* forty-five-minute shows a night and a dressing room that was a closet.... It was not glamorous."

Although Patsy herself was glamorous in Vegas, this gig turned out to be work! The real reward was the fact that all of her friends showed up to witness this milestone in Patsy's career. She even flew Charlie and Hilda out for opening night, Friday, November 23, 1962. Hilda bleached her hair blonde especially for the occasion.

Opening night was almost a disaster in itself. Besides being frazzled by the whole event and the rehearsals, when she arrived in Las Vegas Patsy developed what is known in the business as "Vegas throat." She wasn't just hoarse from the arid desert air—she totally lost her voice. To even get through the opening night's six shows, they had to play Patsy's record album's backstage while she lip-synched to her songs.

According to Charlie, "I think she was scared.... She got there the first night, she just started crying. She wanted to go home. She didn't want to stay at all. I don't know whether she thought she wasn't prepared, or she'd heard so much about Vegas and all the big names out there. She wasn't ready for it for some reason."

Tompall Glaser also remembers her being very emotional during the engagement. Being presented with bouquets of flowers from fans while onstage would bring a flood of tears. Says Glaser, "She would cry a lot, her and Charlie fought a lot."

To inject some more recognizable pop music into the set, Patsy added her versions of Connie Francis' "Stupid Cupid," Elvis Presley's "Shake, Rattle and Roll," and Theresa Brewer's "Ricochet." In spite of losing her voice, and her disappointment over the miniature stage and dressing room, "the Cline" triumphed. Her star stature had nothing to do with staircases or drumrolls or any stage gimmicks—it was her stage presence and her glorious voice that made her a star.

When her Las Vegas act was reviewed by the local newspaper, *The Sun*, they glowed in their November 27, 1962, issue:

> *Patsy Cline made her local debut before a SRO throng and delivered the goodies! She's described as a "switch hitter" since topping both popular and country ballad balloting by* Music Vendor, Music Reporter, Billboard, *and* Cashbox *magazines. The crowd enthusiastically applauded for "more!" at the conclusion of a solid session which included songbird Patsy's interpretations, including "I Fall to Pieces," "Heartaches," "Crazy," "(I Don't Want a) Ricochet (Romance)," "I Am a Fool." ... Miss Cline's accompanists did a whale of a job too, as the singer moved efficiently from one ditty to another. "This is the song Connie Francis made famous," she said, introducing "Stupid Cupid," and credited "the late Hank Williams" as she dipped into "Your Cheatin' Heart."*

Vegas had never seen a country performer like "the Cline" before. Its image was more out of the Frank Sinatra/Rat Pack mode at this point. When Elvis played Vegas for the first time in 1956, the casinos began to consider other performers with pop-rock appeal.

While Charlie was in town, they fought constantly. Fortunately, several of her friends came to visit, and it made her feel better. Don Hecht stopped in one night. From the stage, Patsy introduced him to the audience as "a fine country writer who's played an important role in my career." Patsy was always thankful for his song "Walkin' after Midnight" having launched her recording stardom, and they discussed the possibility of doing a whole album together. "I owe

Having shed her cowgirl image, Patsy became the height of Nashville sex
appeal and sophistication. Here she is wearing her first fur—the stole that
Bill Peer gave her—and her see-through high heels. (Photo: Country Music
Foundation)

LEFT: As her hit "I Fall to Pieces" climbed the charts, Patsy looked and felt great about herself and her career. This photograph was taken in May 1961, the month before her near-fatal automobile accident. (Photo: Globe Photos)

ABOVE: Patsy sustained extensive facial scarring as she was thrown through the windshield of her car. Heavy make-up, a soft focus, and strategically placed curls of hair are used to hide the scars on her forehead just a few months later. (Photo: MJB Photo Archives)

LEFT: After sweeping the charts in 1961 with "I Fall to Pieces" and "Crazy," Patsy Cline was truly the queen of country music, and she had the tiara to prove it! (Photo: Pickwick Records)

ABOVE: Patsy with Jim Reeves (left) and Grandpa Jones. All three performers were on hand to bring Country Music to Carnegie Hall later in November 1961. (Photo: Country Music Foundation)

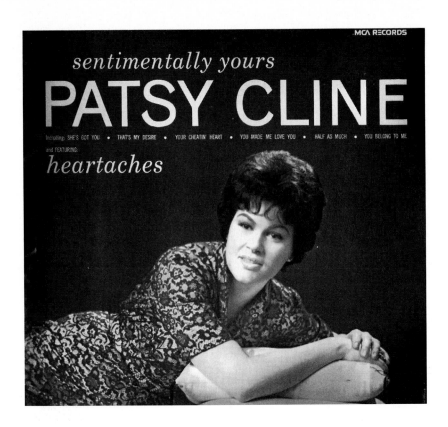

ABOVE: Patsy's 1962 album, *Sentimentally Yours* found Patsy at the pinnacle of her fame. (Photo: MCA Records)

RIGHT: In spite of her rocky marriage to Charlie Dick, Cline enjoyed her home life. She especially liked to entertain her friends, hostessing many a post-*Grand Ole Opry* gathering. (Photo: Country Music Foundation)

LEFT: From the Tucson newspaper, the *Arizona Daily Star*, June 17, 1962, an ad for the "Shower of Stars." That afternoon you could see Patsy Cline, Johnny Cash, George Jones, Don Gibson, and the Carter Family for $1.75 in advance, $2.25 at the gate! (*Arizona Daily Star* courtesy of Tucson Public Library)

ABOVE: After losing weight and scoring a solid string of top ten hits, Patsy began to look and feel great. She was in the midst of her greatest success when these television performances took place in 1962. (Photos: MJB Photo Archives)

Patsy at WSM's TV stu-
dios for an *Opry* event.
Patsy was perfectly happy
hanging out with the guys
in the band, and they all
loved working with her.
(Photo: Country Music
Foundation)

ABOVE: In early 1963, Patsy began to tell her close friends that she was going to meet a tragic ending soon. (Photo: MJB Photo Archives)

RIGHT *(top)*: Patsy's *Greatest Hits* album is still the biggest selling female country album ever released. This is the original album cover. (Photo: MCA/Decca Records)

RIGHT *(bottom)*: This cover photo was meant for Patsy's fourth album, to be entitled *Faded Love*. Instead it became the cover of her posthumous anthology, *The Patsy Cline Story*. (Photo: MCA Records)

.MCA RECORDS

PATSY CLINE'S
GREATEST HITS

CRAZY

Back In Baby's Arms

Faded Love

YOU'RE STRONGER THAN ME

Sweet Dreams

Walking After Midnight

STRANGE

I FALL TO PIECES

So Wrong

Leavin' On Your Mind

She's Got You

WHY CAN'T HE BE YOU

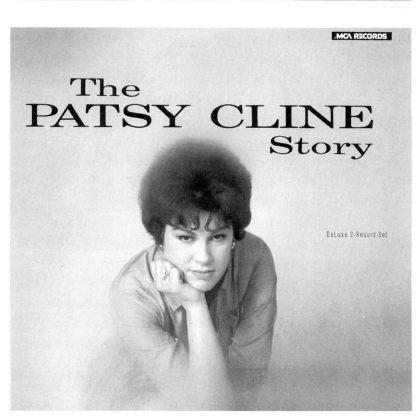

.MCA RECORDS

The
PATSY CLINE
Story

DeLuxe 2-Record Set

Nashville Banner.

Nashville's Oldest Newspaper

LONG MAY OUR LAND BE BRIGHT WITH FREEDOM'S HOLY LIGHT; PROTECT US BY THY MIGHT, GREAT GOD, OUR KING

Founded April 10, 1876

VOL. LXXXVI, NO. 283   NASHVILLE, TENN., WED. AFTERNOON, MAR. 6, 1963   40 PAGES   PRICE: TEN CENTS

4 OPRY STARS DIE IN CRASH

Plane Debris Yields Bodies At Camden

By LARRY BRINTON and CLAY HARGIS

Camden—The remains of four country music personalities, including three nationally-known Grand Ole Opry stars, were found this morning in the scattered bits of a private plane which crashed in rugged woodlands near here.

The victims were Patsy Cline, Cowboy Copas, Hawkshaw Hawkins and Randy Hughes, believed pilot of the ill-fated aircraft.

The wreckage was discovered about 6 a.m. after a night-long search by highway patrol, Civil Defense and local officers.

Parts of the yellow plane and bits of human flesh were scattered over a 60-yard area a mile off Highway 70 about three miles west of Camden. The wreckage was between the highway and a ranger tower, which had served as a base of operations for searchers.

Civil Defense official Dean Brewer, asked whether all four bodies had been located, replied: "There's not enough to count . . . They're all in small pieces."

The plane left Dyersburg about 6 p.m. Tuesday for a flight to Nashville. The entertainers had been in Kansas City, Kan., for a benefit performance for the late Cactus Jack Call, a disc jockey.

Sam Webb, whose farm is near the dense woodland, said he saw a plane circling his home about 7 p.m. and that it was "revving up its motor . . . going fast and then slow, like it was a tempting to climb."

Webb said the plane left his sight and then he heard something "like it struck the top of some trees.

The weather in this area at the time of the accident was termed "extremely turbulent."

Investigators of the Civil Aeronautics Board were enroute to the crash scene to make a detailed probe of the wreckage in an effort to learn the cause of the smashup.

Meantime, in another phase of the investigation, Dr. J. B. Butterworth, C&B medical examiner, and Dr. A. T. Mitchell, Benton County medical examiner, were examining the remains of the four victims.

The wreckage was located by searchers using field glasses in the fire tower and almost simultaneously by ground crewmen led by Chief Deputy Lewis and Chief Bradford, bushmen, who farm near the scene, and W. J. Hollingsworth of Sandy River Road.

The plane apparently struck a large tree before hitting the ground. Pieces of the aircraft

The Tennessee House of Representatives stood for a moment of silent tribute today to the four Grand Ole Opry stars killed Tuesday night in a plane crash near Camden.

were hanging in the tree and a three-foot hole marked the spot where the main part of the fuselage struck the ground.

The tornado in the area is so rugged that some searchers on horseback during the night were covered with bruises, scratches and blood soil, according to one observer, "looked like they had been in a battle fight."

The wreck scene is about five miles west of the Tennessee River.

After the wreckage was located, about 100 cars lined Old Stage Road, about 100 yards from the scene.

Benton County Sheriff Lon Ford described the area as "full of woods, hills, hollows and swamps."

(Turn to Page 2, Column 8)

POLICE OFFICERS and funeral home attendants comb wreckage of a plane which crashed near Camden for parts of the bodies of four Grand Ole Opry personalities. The wreckage was strewn over an area of about 60 yards. Pieces of the single-engine plane hung in trees, along with some clothing.

★ ★ ★

Three Were Headliners

Opry Hit Hardest By Fatal Air Crash

By RED O'DONNELL
Television and Radio Editor

country music industry

Television and Radio Editor

four victims of the plane crash Tuesday night near Camden represented a multi-million dollars worth of show business talent.

Patsy Cline, 28, has been described as one of the finest girl singers in the world.

Cowboy Copas, 49, was a long-established country and western star, one of the most popular performers in the field.

Hawkshaw Hawkins, 41, either a long, hard persevering struggle, was putting into his own career—personal appearances and television work.

Randy Hughes, 35, was known—for his versatility. He functioned as a manager of talent (one of his clients was Patsy Cline). He was a musician and member of the Grand Ole Opry. He was one of the entertainment world's finest brokerage firms.

"With the deaths of Patsy Cline, Cowboy Copas, Hawkshaw Hawkins and Randy Hughes the entertainment world suffers a great professional loss and Tennessee suffers a great personal loss.

They were typical of the unconfounded, hard-working and generous people dedicated to the country music industry.

No Space On Plane

'God On My Side,' Says Billy Walker

"God was on my side," Billy Walker said today.

"Else how can you explain my being on the road when Patsy and Randy and Cowboy and Hawk, Copas and Randy Hughes—all were killed in the horrible tragedy that took Patsy Cline and Cowboy Copas and Randy Walker, who lives at 1003 Jesperson Dr. Madison.

Cuba Caves Said Hideout For Soviets

Other Cuba Stories Pages 2 and 5

By FRANK VAN DER LINDEN
Chief of The Banner's Washington Bureau

Senate Delays On Truck Weights Bill

By NEIL CUNNINGHAM
Chief of The Banner's Washington Bureau

The controversial bill to increase the maximum weight for trucks from 55,560 to 73,280 pounds ran into trouble in the State Senate today.

Woman Burned On Burial Pyre In Ancient Rite

'Round The Clock

WITH RED O'DONNELL

Cold Front May Mean Snow On Way

Don't Dare Miss Comics Showing

DO YOU HEAR ME?

CITY NEWS ROUNDUP

FEATURE INDEX   Page 12

Three Cigarettes in an Ashtray: Remembering Patsy Cline. Three decades since her fatal plane crash, "the Cline" is hotter than ever. In 1991, the boxed CD set *The Patsy Cline Collection* was released. In 1994, Patsy was honored with her own U.S. postage stamp, and in 1995 she received a Grammy Award for Lifetime Achievement. (Photo: Mark Bego)

you, hoss!" she exclaimed to him. She also got to bitch to him about "that snake" Bill McCall. She was still verbally upset that he had buried her recording of Hecht's song "Cry Not for Me" on the "B" side of a single. Still on her fatalistic bent she announced to Don, "When I'm gone, that's the way I'd like to have people think about me—'cry not for me'!"

Amid his visit, Hecht observed in Vegas, "Perhaps Patsy and Randy were more than client/manager, and things had not been going well in their [Patsy and Charlie's] marriage."

Mae Boren Axton, who had given her the song "Pick Me Up (on Your Way Down)," maintained an apartment in Las Vegas, and one day Patsy and Charlie stopped by to see her. Mae recalls that Patsy had a velvety full-length sheared-fur coat that she had paid an astonishing $2,500 for. Patsy startled Axton when she said to her "Now, if anything happens to me, I want you to have this coat! Charlie, I want you to remember that."

179

Several other friends of Patsy's migrated to Vegas to witness her ground-breaking act. They included Willie Nelson, music publisher Al Gallico, and Mae's songwriter son—Hoyt Axton ("Joy to the World").

Patsy even worked on Christmas. Although she paid to fly Hilda, Charlie, and her kids—now ages one and three—out for the holidays, she was still upset about spending December 25 working in a Vegas casino. That day she broke down and cried during one of the sets, sobbing to the audience, "No matter what, I will never do this again! This is the time to be with your family, not away from them."

Although she was now $35,000 richer, she was happy when Friday, December 28—the last day at "The Mint"—finally rolled around. She immediately hightailed it back to Nashville.

Little did Patsy know that Randy Hughes had already committed her for a return engagement at the Mint. With five top ten hits, and two number one smashes to her credit, everyone knew who Patsy Cline was, and the club was happy to meet—and exceed—her $1,000 a day minimum.

According to Charlie, "Randy rebooked it for a little more money, but we never told Patsy. We figured we'd let her get home and rest a little bit.

Although Patsy was relieved that her Las Vegas debut had gone so successfully, she wasn't about to rest. On January 7, 1963, Decca released her latest single, "Leavin' on Your Mind"/"Tra Le La Le La Triangle." The "A" side was destined to become her next top ten country hit.

On Tuesday, January 15, she recorded her next Armed Forces live-in-the-studio transcription disk. That day she plugged "Leavin' on Your Mind" and did her version of Patti Paige's "Tennessee Waltz." She had several more tour dates booked during that month as well. With Charlie driving her back from one of them, Patsy was in the backseat asleep. According to Charlie, "Jackie De Shannon came on the radio singing 'Faded Love,' the Bob Wills song. I thought Patsy was in the backseat asleep, but she popped up, scaring the devil out of me, saying, 'Everybody's modulating down these days. I wonder why Jackie did it?' I told her, 'Probably the song is not in her key. If it's too high for her it would have been hard to do without bringing it down.' Patsy replied, 'No it wouldn't! I can do it!'" She made up her mind right then and there that "Faded Love" was going to be the next song she was going to record.

In late January, Patsy and Charlie flew out to Los Angeles. She was scheduled to make a television appearance at local station KCOP, and she and June Carter were booked at a couple of small California nightclubs. Johnny Western was at the TV studio when Charlie Dick—looking very L.A.—started instructing the lighting director exactly how he wanted Patsy's spotlight placed. Patsy flew into a rage over the fact that he was suddenly playing Cecil B. De Mille, telling a veteran lighting man how to do his job.

As the ultimate put down, Patsy would refer to Charlie as "Mr. Cline," knowing full-well that it was *she* who wore the pants in the family. Johnny Western's jaw dropped open when—with fire in her eyes—Patsy blasted out, "'Mr. Cline' doesn't even know it, but his ass is grass, because he's just minutes away from having papers served on him, because I am divorcing his ass!" Again, this was just another case of Patsy letting off steam. She constantly claimed she was going to divorce Charlie, but she never acted on these threats.

Later that week, Patsy and June Carter rented a car and went to perform a couple of nightclub gigs together. As they were getting into the car, ready to leave Oxnard, Patsy insisted on getting behind the wheel. According to June, Patsy said to her, "Please, June, would you let me drive. There's something I've got to tell you." Carter complied, wondering what on earth Patsy could be talking about.

She was stunned when Cline launched into another one of her premonitions about dying young. As she drove, Patsy insisted, "I want you to write all this down, because I'm 'going out' soon, and I'm really going out fast, and it's going to be tragic. I want you to tell my mother and Charlie, after I'm gone, what I want done. I want you to write it all down so that they'll know I'm not making all this up."

Patsy sounded so serious that June didn't dare argue back. June searched for a pen, and using a cigarette lighter as a writing light, she took dictation as Patsy said to her, "I want my mother to raise my daughter and I want Charlie to raise the boy. I want to make sure that they bring my body home to my house. Just tell Charlie I want him to bring me home, and I want him to raise my son, and my mother to raise my daughter." Swears Carter, "That is what she told me."

Patsy Cline's career was hotter than ever, and in February she began working on songs for her projected next album. On February 4, 5, 6, and 7, she was in Owen Bradley's studio with the Jordanaires, the usual band—with Randy Hughes on acoustic guitar, and a nine-piece string section. The first song they tackled that day was "Faded Love" [91]. It has been acknowledged as one of the most chillingly effective songs of her recording career. Beginning with the string section, and the Jordanaires providing an ethereal chorus, Patsy literally threw herself into this ultimate ode of love gone bad. The way she soars on the high notes, and sighs between choruses, she elicits shivers of emotion from every heartbreaking note. As she comes to the last two words of the song, she sings "faded," then pauses for a split second, takes an audibly deep on-the-verge-of-tears breath, and sings "love."

Who was it Patsy was thinking about as she sang that song in that evening's recording session? Was it Charlie? Was it Dan? Was it Bill Peer? Was it Randy Hughes?

Charlie, who had returned to his printing job on a part-time basis, recalls, "I worked right around the corner from [Owen's recording studio] at the printing plant, and I went down one evening on my dinner break. And, at the old studio, if you walked in, the control room was looking out on the studio. And the singer's back was to the control room. So I came in and Owen motioned me into the control room, and he said, 'I want you outta here!' And I said, 'I just walked in, what did I do? What's the matter?' And he said, 'You and Patsy have a fight or something?' And I said, 'No.' He said, 'Well, she's cried on every song she sings. I don't want to break the mood. I don't want her to see you. Get outta here.' So I went back out there, and that was when she did 'Faded Love.'"

Equally emotional came the next song, "Someday (You'll Want Me to Want You)" [92]. Originally a hit in 1946 for Gene Autry, Patsy again soared on this brilliantly heartbreaking ballad. With equal sentimentality and feeling came the similarly paced "Love Letters in the Sand" [93]. Although the song dated back to 1931, Pat Boone had turned it into a hit in 1957, and Patsy claimed it for her own with this effective slow and string-laden version.

The following day, things lightened up for Patsy's recording of Bill Monroe's "Blue Moon of Kentucky" [94]. Sung in a lilting breezy fashion—without the strings—she got a chance to growl a bit on this country classic. The next song they came to was one of Patsy's greatest masterpieces: Don Gibson's "Sweet Dreams" [95]. It is a slow, expressive song that will forever be associated with Patsy. Lush and sentimental, again, "the Cline" sounds as if she is going to break into tears with every shattering line of it. That day's session ended with the Irving Berlin hallmark, "Always" [96]. Patsy's singing was crystal clear, as she caresses every note of the song and makes you believe every single lyric. Finishing off with just Patsy's voice and Floyd Cramer's piano, puts the focus brilliantly on the heartwrenching singer's voice, and it creates an indelible effect.

The following day, February 6, she worked on just two songs. The first one, "Does Your Heart Beat for Me" [97], continues on the sentimental mode, with the Jordanaires more prominently featured. The second song of the day was a new arrangement of the blues-oriented showstopper, "Bill Bailey, Won't You Please Come Home" [98]. She had such fun singing it onstage that she longed to record it. It was Owen Bradley who had suggested that she start the beginning slow and understated, and then wind up to a double-time fast finale. In the beginning half of the song, there is one point where Patsy improvises an "aah" that is so pensive it draws you right into her blue mood. Suddenly the song kicks into high gear for the second half. Rousing and exciting, Patsy put her personal stamp on this old chestnut.

Her next session was set for 7:00 P.M. the following night, and for some reason she wanted some company with her. During the day of February 7, Patsy spoke to Jan Howard on the phone, and she invited her to come down to the studio to sit in. After all, she was getting ready to cut two of her husband Harlan's songs that day: "He Called Me Baby" and "You Took Him off My Hands."

"I don't want to bug you when you're working," Jan argued, not wanting to be in the way.

"Aw shit! Bug me!" Patsy proclaimed.

"Are you sure?" Jan Asked.

And Patsy replied, "Oh, my God, Yes! I'd kind of like to have you there."

With that, Jan agreed to show up for the session. Along with Randy, who had played guitar on every one of her straight-to-Decca sessions, Charlie, and Dottie West, it became more of a celebration than a session.

During this studio party, Patsy produced four songs. The first one was Harlan's new composition, "He Called Me Baby" [99], which was composed with Patsy in mind. Slow and passionate, Cline again emoted on every single lyric of this beautiful love song. The next cut was a remake of "Crazy Arms" [100], which was a favorite tune she had originally done during her tenure at 4 Star. This new bossa-nova-and-strings version is by far the superior and more effective rendition.

Harlan Howard's "You Took Him off My Hands" [101] was another emotional high-water mark for Patsy. Pensive and brilliantly written, Patsy soared on this lovely ballad of love lost. Another chilling performance from "the Cline."

With regard to "You Took Him Off My Hands," Harlan Howard recalls, "Wynn Stewart, Skeets McDonald and I wrote this song in 1956, and Wynn recorded it first. Ray Price recorded it in 1961, and had a hit with it. And one night just before Patsy recorded what was to be her last album, I sang this song to her and she loved it, as you can tell by listening. Patsy was unique in the respect that she had no fear of recording songs that had just been hits, as she knew she was going to have to make them her own anyhow."

Ironically, the last song of the day, "I'll Sail My Ship Alone" [102], was the last song Patsy Cline ever recorded. Wistful and prophetic, in it she sings about traveling on a trip alone—destination unknown. Lighter and less somber in feeling than the three songs that preceded it, in retrospect it was an odd choice on which to finish up. In the context of the song, Patsy sings about how—when her ship sinks—she is going to blame the one who broke her heart.

Even more ironic was the fact that "I'll Sail My Ship Alone" was the fifty-first song she recorded directly for Decca. That meant that she had recorded exactly the same number for 4 Star, leaving her studio-produced catalog with precisely 102 songs. Perhaps, Patsy herself knew that there was a significance to this numbers game she was playing.

After the session was over, Dottie West recalled breaking open bottles of champagne and listening to the playbacks. Even more eerily, Jan Howard remembers Patsy going off into Harry Silverstein's office, and returning with a single record in her hands.

"Well, here it is," Patsy said in an odd sort of way, waving a 45 r.p.m. single in one hand.

"What are you talking about?" Jan asked her.

"The record."

"What record?"

"Here's 'A Church, a Courtroom, and Then Goodbye.' It's the first and," motioning at the tape machine before them, "the last."

"Don't say that!" Jan exclaimed.

"Oh, hoss, I just meant here's the first record that came out and here we are listening to the last one."

It was such a bizarre and eerie thing to say, that Jan just let it go.

Chapter Twelve

Reaching for the Stars

Patsy's fourth album was all set to be entitled "Faded Love," and it was scheduled for release at the end of March 1963. She had already posed for the album cover, wearing a tightly tailored gold-colored dress with a misty looking gold background. In the photo she again utilized the bangs of her brunette wig to masquerade the scar that still faintly crossed her forehead.

There were already plans for her to record Roger Miller's newly-written song "Lock, Stock and Teardrops." Owen and Patsy had also discussed the possibility of her doing an album completely comprised of Broadway showtunes. She had already picked out Jerome Kern's "Can't Help Lovin' Dat Man of Mine" from *Show Boat* to include in the album.

That Saturday night, February 9, Patsy appeared on the *Grand Ole Opry*. On the broadcast she performed her new arrangement of "Bill Bailey, Won't You Please Come Home," with the Jordanaires singing the backup vocals, just as they had done in the studio, days before. Thanks to her insurance claim, she had just replaced her expensive black fox fur-trimmed coat with an exact replica of the one that had been stolen in November. According to Ray Walker of the Jordanaires, "It had the beautiful, kind of bouffant laid-back collar. When I say full-length, I mean *full-length*—it wasn't to the knees. It was a beautiful coat. So that night she was tickled to death."

Ray helped her into her coat, and when it was securely on her shoulders, she flipped up the collar, and spun around to say "good-bye." As she turned, Ray said to her, "Patsy, honey, you be careful. We love you, we love you a lot."

Referring to her two previous automobile accidents, Patsy flashed her eyes at him and said, "Honey, I've had two bad ones. The third one will be a charm, or it'll kill me!"

June Carter, Dottie West, the Jordanaires, Jan Howard, and just about everyone who was close to her all remember in great detail the chilling clairvoyance with which Patsy foretold her own demise. They all claim that she predicted her own death and insisted that it would be swift, tragic, and soon. According to Brenda Lee, "I've always felt that Patsy had a premonition that she didn't have a whole lot of time here to do what she had set out to do, and that accounted for her amazing drive."

Patsy was suddenly weeding out her belongings. On Monday, February 11, singer Pearl Butler came over to borrow several of Patsy's old fringed cowgirl costumes. Pearl had a West Coast tour coming up, and needed several changes of stage outfits. After they were done going through Patsy's closets, Butler profusely thanked her for her generosity. Cline said to her, "I'm glad I can do something for you. You can have 'em all—boots and everything."

On Wednesday night, Patsy made a surprise visit to the WSM studios. Ralph Emery had the late night radio show on the station, and a number of times before, Patsy had shown up with an entourage and there was always quite a commotion. That particular evening, it was just Patsy, and Ralph recalls how candid and focused she was. She was relaxed and entertaining, and the interview Emery conducted, he claims, was the best he had ever heard her give. He claims that he has always regretted not taping that evening's insightful interview.

Saturday night, Patsy and Charlie had some people over at their house. Music publisher Al Gallico, who had given her the song "A Poor Man's Riches (or a Rich Man's Gold)," recalls having a long conversation with Randy Hughes. According to Gallico, he tried to talk Randy out of flying around in that little mosquito of an airplane. Randy argued back to him, claiming, "I don't take chances—it's a good plane."

The next week, Patsy spoke to her former neighbor, Joyce Blair, who had been helpful driving her to the hospital when little Randy was born. Joyce was startled when Patsy—very seriously—said to her, "Promise me you'll take care of my babies if anything happens to me." Stunned by the statement, she naturally promised to comply exactly with her wishes.

When Patsy wasn't bending someone's ear about her premonitions, she was alternately making plans for the future. She called her cousin, Punk Longley, in Elkton to talk to him about getting all of her taxes and paperwork together—with some sense of urgency. He swears that her reasoning had to do with the fact that she was planning to divorce Charlie and wanted her finances in order. She especially wanted to make certain that both of her children had trust funds set up for their education and future.

On Friday, February 22, Patsy was one of several acts booked on a show in Lima, Ohio. One of her co-stars that night was Billy Walker ("Forever"). Walker recalls, "Charlie and Randy were with us, but that Charlie seemed to have gotten uncontrollable. He'd get drunk and be very abusive around Patsy. It was embarrassing and a shame."

The following night, Patsy was booked to perform in Toledo. It wasn't until she was in Lima though, that she discovered that she was scheduled to be the only performer on the Toledo show. She invited Walker to join her in Toledo, so that she wouldn't have to do the entire two-hour show alone. He agreed to be her opening act, performing for an hour, and then Patsy was able to do a solid hour-and-a-half set after the intermission.

Walker recalls how gracious and beautiful Patsy was toward everyone. After her performances were over, she would spend all the time that was necessary to accommodate any of her fans who stood in line to get her autograph.

Back in Nashville the following week, Patsy surprised financially-strapped Loretta Lynn with some new draperies for her living room. That evening, she invited Loretta and Doolittle Lynn over to her house to listen to some of her latest songs, including "Sweet Dreams." She quizzed Loretta and her husband about the string-laden stylings of the tunes, fearing that she might lose her country fans if she strayed too much farther from her winning formula. Loretta loved what she heard, and assured her that her fans were going to love the new music she heard that night.

That same afternoon, Patsy got a phone call from Randy, asking her if she minded appearing at a benefit the following Sunday. A well-known D.J. who went by the name of "Cactus Jack" Call had been killed in a car accident on January 25, and several country artists were going to do a benefit in Kansas City, to raise money for his widow and two small children. "Cactus Jack" had passed away without any life insurance and several members of Nashville royalty had volunteered to lend their time. Still traumatized by her own most recent automobile accident, Patsy immediately agreed to be there as well.

Patsy had two performances on Saturday, March 2, in two different cities: New Orleans, Louisiana, and Birmingham, Alabama. That night, when Loretta was over at the house, Patsy offered her $50 if she would join her for the weekend in Kansas City. Loretta told her that she'd have to decline her offer, because she had a $70 offer for Saturday and she had to keep that commitment.

That evening, as Loretta and Doolittle were preparing to leave, Patsy gave Loretta a big box of clothes, knowing how few outfits Lynn owned. As she turned to leave with the box of clothes, Loretta suddenly said to her husband, "I forgot to say goodbye to Patsy."

Loretta set the box on Patsy's Cadillac, and ran back to the house. According to Loretta, "I hugged her and kissed her, and as I went back out the door, Patsy hauled off and hit me a little bit. She said, 'We're gonna stick together, aren't we little gal?'"

Patsy left the next day for the two dates in Louisiana and Alabama. The New Orleans show was performed late Friday night— actually early Saturday morning, and Saturday night was the Birmingham show. In Birmingham, Tex Ritter, Charlie Rich, Jerry Lee Lewis, and Lester Flatt and Earl Scruggs were all on the bill. Patsy was the headliner, and she closed the show. Randy flew his plane, with Patsy and Charlie, to both dates. On Sunday morning, March 3, Randy navigated the plane back to Nashville, and at 8:00 A.M., he dropped Charlie off. With two seats now available, Hawkshaw Hawkins, and Randy's father-in-law, Cowboy Copas, got into the plane, and left for the benefit.

Landing immediately in Kansas City, Kansas, they were joined by the other acts also on the bill that night, including Dottie West, Wilma Lee, George Jones, and Billy Walker. There were two sold-out shows that day at the Memorial Building in Kansas City, and the crowds were so big that there was a demand for a third show. Once all the acts' expenses were paid, only the small sum of $3,000 went to "Cactus Jack's" widow, Ann, and the two children. That was nowhere near the kind of money they had expected to raise.

Patsy looked absolutely gorgeous that evening. She wore a white gown that was mid-calf length, and white high heels. All of the acts spent the night at the Town House Motor Hotel, where there was a little reception afterwards. The event and the concerts had been put together by promoter Hap Peebles. He had been a longtime friend of all of the acts. Even though she was fighting off the flu, Patsy was in great spirits that night.

The plan the next morning was for Randy to fly back to Nashville with Patsy, Cowboy Copas, and Billy Walker. However, with wind, rain, and fog dominating the skies overhead, all of the flight plans for Randy's plane had to be cancelled. On Monday morning, Walker received the bad news that his father had unexpectedly suffered a heart attack. Graciously, Hawkshaw Hawkins went to Walker's room and gave him his commercial plane ticket, which would get him home sooner. Hawkshaw would simply fly back with Randy and Patsy.

On Monday morning, the whole gang met in the coffee shop at the Town House. Patsy wasn't going to leave her room, but Dottie talked her into joining them by underscoring the fact that breakfast was going to be Hap Peebles' treat. Sweeping into the coffee shop, Patsy announced, "Hap, now don't expect me to be cheery—I'm as sick as a dog! But, well, when I heard you was buying, I just couldn't resist! I got out of a *sick bed!*"

Dottie and her husband, Bill West, were preparing their car that morning to return to Nashville. They had made the drive in sixteen hours. Patsy was on her third cup of coffee when Dottie invited Patsy to join them in their car. After all, the rain showed no signs of letting up.

"All right!" said Patsy, "I will 'cause I got things to do at home. Let me go upstairs and finish packing. I won't be long."

However, when she met Dottie in the lobby of the hotel, she announced that she had changed her mind. "I'm not gonna ride home in the car. I'll wait for Randy. I think I'll get home quicker," she claimed.

Dottie was to remember saying to Patsy, "I'm just gonna be worried about y'all. I don't want y'all riding in that small plane. It might crash in this weather. Please don't let Randy take off if it's bad."

According to Dottie, Patsy said to her, "Don't worry about me hoss, when it's my time to go, it's my time!"

Although Randy had his license to fly his plane, he was not "instrument trained," and could only navigate by sight. The storm continued unabated. Committed to stay and fly back with Randy, Hawkshaw, Patsy, and Cowboy Copas ended up spending another night in Kansas City, as the Fairfax Municipal Airport was still fogged in. They all called home that night to let their families know that they were safe, and would return to Nashville a day late.

The following day, the fog finally subsided enough to allow them to schedule a take off at 1:30 on the afternoon of March 5. Before they left the ground, Patsy called Charlie, then Hilda. According to Hilda, Patsy announced, "Hi! Here I am still fogbound in Kansas City. It seems that every time I stick my neck out, I get my foot into something else." After talking about the concert, the flight plans, and the children—who were at home with Charlie—they said goodbye. Not long afterward they boarded the plane.

Following the path of the clearing storm, they flew north to Arkansas, and landed until it cleared some more. Finally at 5:20 that evening, the plane landed in Tennessee, at the small town of Dyersburg, about 140 miles west of Nashville. According to the airport manager, Bill Braese, "Hughes told me he had followed a storm all day and that they had to land three or four times to let the front pass."

They refueled in Dyersburg, and Patsy, Hawkshaw, and Cowboy Copas signed autographs for some of the locals who were there in the tiny coffee shop of the airport. Still fighting the flu, Patsy couldn't wait to get home to her own bed. After the refueling was over, Randy rejoined his three *Opry* star passengers in the coffee shop. There, they weighed out all of their options. Braese recalls Patsy inquiring how long it would take to drive to Nashville by car. Randy decided that he would call his wife and see what the conditions looked like in Nashville. On the phone, Kathy told him that it had momentarily stopped raining. He took that as a sign that they could still make it, and he instructed her to go to the Cordelia Fort Airfield and make sure that they turned on the runway lights.

191

When he returned to his friends, Bill Braese tried to talk him out of getting back in the plane. Braese claimed that Kathy must have seen the eye of the storm, and that in Nashville it was nowhere near over.

"Why don't you spend the night?" the airport manager implored of them.

Randy thought for a moment and said, "I've already come this far. We'll be there before you know it."

With that, Patsy and her flying buddies all loaded into the plane. Although the conditions were described by the FAA as "extremely turbulent," the plane taxied down the runway at 6:07 P.M.

Braese was so certain that they were going to return, that he went ahead and booked them all rooms at a local hotel.

The rainstorm that was sweeping the eastern United States was far from over. When Patsy, Randy, and company took off, they ran smack dab into the middle of the worst of it. When the tiny plane began to shake and pitch, even fearless Patsy was worried. Judging by the density of the clouds, rain, and storm that they encountered, their tiny plane must have been tossed and turned quite a bit.

In less than fifteen minutes, Randy knew they were in trouble. In dense clouds, and unable to judge the terrain below, he was already searching for an emergency landing spot.

At 6:22 P.M., he attempted an "SOS" call over the radio. The next half hour was one of sheer terror for Hughes and his passengers, as they tried to survey the hilly, tree-lined terrain below in search of a place to land.

Emergency radio reports quoted Randy as saying, "Maybe I should fly low and follow a road, any road!" It was followed by, "No, that's bad to do. It's better that I gain altitude!" Unfortunately, tossed into a blanket of clouds, fog, and rain, he had begun to misjudge which way was "up" and which way was "down."

The last words heard over the static-filled radio may have been from Patsy herself, as they were reported as being "My god Randy— we're flying *upside down! RANDY!*"

Sam Wood, who has a farm near the thick woods where the plane's remains were discovered, reported that he had seen a small plane circling around near 7:00 P.M. According to him, it was "revving up its motor ... going fast and then slow like it was attempting to climb." Not long afterward he heard sounds "like it struck the tops of some trees."

About the same time, a resident of Camden, Tennessee, by the name of Mossie Miller reported that he heard a very loud "pop" in the thicket of wilderness near his home on Route 1 in Camden. His wife described it as a loud roaring sound, and then a popping sound, then silence.

Working backwards from the evidence, and judging by the remains of the tiny plane and the way it was discovered, what happened after Dyersburg is only theory. The most likely explanation is that, unable to see outside through the fog and unable to read the gauges and dials before him, Randy must have gotten vertigo, and when he thought he was accelerating to gain altitude, he was in fact heading at 120 miles per hour straight for the ground.

Patsy's songwriter friend Roger Miller left Nashville when he heard reports that the plane was missing. He drove to Camden and arrived shortly after 6:00 A.M. He was the first person at the site. He was horrified by what he saw. "It was ghastly," he later claimed. "That's the only was to describe it. The plane had crashed nose down."

Witnesses to what was discovered reported that they were sickened by what they found. The wreck was discovered in a crater formed by the tiny plane's impact, and later what was left of the bodies had to be pieced together.

A photo of men looking at some debris in a thicket of trees appeared on the cover of the Wednesday, March 6, edition of *The Nashville Banner*. The caption read, "Police officers and funeral home attendants comb wreckage of a plane which crashed near Camden for parts of the bodies of four *Grand Ole Opry* personalities. The wreckage was strewn over an area of about sixty yards. Pieces of the single-engine plane hung in trees, along with some clothing." The headline read, "4 OPRY STARS DIE IN CRASH" and a sub-headline read, "Plane Debris Yields Bodies at Camden."

Patsy had a little pair of gold lamé booties that she liked to wear around the house. She had reportedly worn those when she deplaned at Dyersburg. One of them was located at the crash site, along with her hairbrush with several of her hairs in it, and her favorite cigarette lighter—with the word "Dixie" on it. Patsy's red slip was tangled in the trees waving in the breeze when the search party located the wreckage after that somber dawn Wednesday morning. The bodies of the men were so dismembered that their still-intact wallets had to be used for identification. Patsy's remains were identified by the largest section found—the back of her head, shoulders, and right arm. Among the debris was a white tooled leather belt with the name "Patsy Cline" pressed into it.

For Patsy Cline's millions of fans, March 5, 1963, was the day the music died.

Chapter Thirteen

SINCERELY YOURS, PATSY CLINE

The shock and tears that reverberated through Nashville were felt far and wide. Patsy's death, along with Hawkshaw, Copas, and Randy, left people stunned. It had been exactly two years since "I Fall to Pieces" first started making noise on the airwaves, and now suddenly, she was gone.

Kathy Hughes had stood at the Cordelia Fort Airfield waiting for a plane that never arrived. Charlie was at the house telling the children that their mommy would be home soon. And Loretta Lynn was expecting to wake up Wednesday morning for a shopping expedition with Patsy. None of this was to be.

The coroners did what they could to reconstruct enough of the country music legends to give them all a decent burial. According to Patsy's wishes, her remains were placed in her casket, and she was sent to her dream house on Nella Drive.

Patsy's mother, brother, and sister came immediately to Nashville in shock. June Carter, who was out on the road, immediately raced back as well, and took Patsy's children over to her house. When Patsy's bronze casket arrived at the house, it sat in the living room, near the artificial magnolia tree. Atop the coffin was a photograph of Patsy in a beautiful frame. For one last night she was able to rest in the house that she so dearly loved.

Dottie and Bill West, Loretta and Doolittle Lynn, Harlan and Jan Howard, Owen Bradley, and all of Patsy's intimate friends came to comfort Hilda and Charlie. However, without Patsy, none of their lives would ever be the same.

On Thursday afternoon, at Phillips-Robinson Funeral Home in the heart of Nashville, a prayer service was conducted. Her casket was then sent on to Winchester, where it remained for another night at Jones Funeral Home. Winchester, Virginia, which had been so unforgiving, suddenly turned into a three-ring circus.

Patsy Cline was buried that Sunday at Shenandoah Memorial Park and the crowd of mourners, well-wishers, and fans who gathered there was estimated at twenty-five thousand.

Typical of celebrity funerals, people toted cameras along with them, hoping to get a glimpse of a star. At the cemetery, a fan grabbed at one of the dozens of flower arrangements and snatched a blossom. Suddenly, there was a locust-like frenzy. Souvenir-seeking fans who knew of Patsy only from what they had heard of her songs on the radio, suddenly descended and picked all of the flower arrangements bare.

Later, a small gravestone was added to her cemetery plot. It read quite simply, "VIRGINIA DICK 1932–1963." Patsy's story might have ended right then and there. But it didn't.

At the time of her tragic death, only twenty-four of the fifty-one recordings she made as part of her new deal with Decca Records had been released. Plans for the "Faded Love" album were scrapped, but her new single came out as scheduled on April 15. It consisted of "Sweet Dreams"/"Back in Baby's Arms." Partially due to interest generated by her loss, and partially by the sheer mastery of her performance—"Sweet Dreams" became her fifth country top ten hit (number five country, number forty-four pop).

On June 17, the two-record album, "The Patsy Cline Story" was released, and it too became a huge country and pop hit. It was issued with the misty golden album cover photo that had been shot for the abandoned "Faded Love" project.

Charlie was shattered. Hilda took the tragedy very badly. Loretta Lynn claimed that Patsy's loss left a hole in her life, that only Patsy's love and spirit could fill. She was determined to keep her promise to "the Cline"—when she agreed they would always be together as friends—to the end.

According to Loretta, she was devastated for months: "When I heard that morning that Patsy was gone, I said out loud, 'What am I going to do?' It was like a rug had been pulled out from under me. She was my friend, my mentor, my strength." Loretta was pregnant when Cline passed away, and in her honor, she named one of her twins "Patsy."

In August of that year, Decca released Patsy's final top ten hit of the 1960s, "Faded Love." In October, "When You Need a Laugh" was released and peaked at number forty-seven on the country chart, and the following September, "He Called Me Baby" was released and made it to number twenty-three. Eerily, Patsy's record career continued, even in death. Decca continued to bring out new Patsy Cline singles every remaining year of the 1960s, but after that only her version of "Anytime" appeared on the country charts (number seventy-three, 1968).

As per her will, the majority of her belongings went to either her mother or into a trust fund for her children. Speaking of Patsy's strained relationship with Charlie, her cousin, Punk Longley, confirmed, "When she got killed, the only thing he really got was the Cadillac."

Charlie couldn't seem to pull himself together for nearly a year after Patsy's tragic plane crash. "We were getting royalties from

Patsy's records, so money wasn't a problem," he claimed. Lost at sea without Patsy around, Charlie threw himself into taking care of his two children. In spite of Patsy's worries, Charlie became the kind of father that would have made her proud.

In late 1964, Charlie had a memorial entrance way added to the cemetery where Patsy was buried. On the granite wall of Shenandoah Memorial Park is a plaque which reads, "This entrance way is dedicated in remembrance of Patsy Cline, one of America's best beloved singers by her husband Charles Dick, and their children Julie and Randy."

Later, Charlie decided to go into the talent promotion business. It was through his business that he met and married a singer named Jamie Ryan. At first they continued to live in Patsy's dream house on Nella Drive, but her memory haunted every room of it, and they eventually moved.

Charlie was later to say, "Jamie was bothered by living in Patsy's house. It prompted a lot of talk about Patsy. That bothered Jamie because, well, you just can't compete with Patsy—alive or not." Together, Charlie and Jamie had a son named Chip, and in 1972 they were divorced.

On March 13, 1967, Decca released "Patsy Cline's Greatest Hits." A twelve-song compilation, it went on to become the first "Gold" album ever recorded by a female country artist.

In 1973, ten years after her death, Patsy Cline became the first solo female performer to be inducted into the Country Music Hall of Fame. Even in death, Patsy continued to break records and set standards in country music.

Inspired by Patsy, Loretta Lynn went on to become the kind of star that Patsy was. In 1976 she penned her own autobiography (with George Vecsey), entitled *Coal Miner's Daughter*, which included several Patsy Cline stories in it. It became such a popular bestseller, that it was made into a hugely successful movie, starring Sissy Spacek, released in 1980 and produced by Bernard Schwartz. Beverly D'Angelo masterfully played the part of Patsy in the film. Suddenly, a whole new generation of fans were introduced to the legend and the music of Cline.

That next year, Beverly D'Angelo received an Academy Award nomination for her portrayal of Patsy. Almost immediately, ideas began to be bantered around for the production of a whole film on the life of Cline.

Piecing together his own vision of a Cline film, Bernard Schwartz utilized the remembrances of both Charlie and Hilda, and decided to concentrate on Patsy's six years with Charlie—the last six years of her life. It yielded the very successful 1985 box-office hit film, *Sweet Dreams*. In it, Jessica Lange brilliantly portrayed Patsy, and Ed Harris convincingly brought Charlie Dick to the screen.

On camera, Ed Harris was very graphic about portraying Charlie's physically abusive side. "They changed a lot of things to sell tickets. If my kids were younger, I'd be pissed off," Charlie was later to complain, yet he found that Harris did "a helluva job playing old Charlie Dick." Julie Dick Connor Fudge recalled, "I know my parents fought. Sometimes they fought hard. But my father never hit my mother *in front of me!*"

In 1973 Decca Records had been purchased by MCA Records, and in 1980, two Cline singles were re-released. "Always" made it to number eighteen on the country chart in *Billboard* and "I Fall to Pieces" peaked at number sixty-one. The following year a unique single was released, featuring the posthumously edited together duet version of the song "Have You Ever Been Lonely (Have You Ever Been Blue)" by Patsy Cline and Jim Reeves, and it hit number five.

With the renewed interest in the life and times of Patsy Cline, none of the people from Patsy's past were amazed by her lasting appeal. According to Dottie West, "Patsy is still around because she is what we all want to be—a real star. And, people can't get enough of a *real star!*"

Owen Bradley recalls that when it came time to select songs to be included on Patsy's "Showcase" album, there was a definite plan. According to him, "I was talking to the people from New York, following orders. They said when you make an album try to make it so it will last at least ten years. Okay, if you do that, you can't just do a few of the pop songs of the moment. Many of them won't last three weeks. So we were trying to get good strong material. We were doing twelve songs [per album]. Out of twelve, we would have three or four sort of new songs that we felt would last. Then we put in some that were a little more country, but it was really a general mixture."

Well, "mission: accomplished!" Not only did the songs included on the "Patsy Cline Showcase" album last for ten years—the material on it has lasted over thirty years—and counting! Little did they realize at the time that they weren't just preparing an album for the moment; they were cementing the legend of brassy Patsy Cline in the annals of musical history.

Due to the success of the movie, all of Patsy's recordings were suddenly selling better than ever. Suddenly, even new compilations of the unique and variable 4 Star material began to appear on the market.

In the mid-70s, Loretta released her Cline tribute album, "I Remember Patsy." Although she had discussed the project for several years, Lynn finally got to the point where she could sing Cline's tunes without breaking down and crying mid-song.

In 1987, a unique country performer from Canada, k. d. lang, released her album "Angel with a Lariat," which included her forceful rendition of "Three Cigarettes in an Ashtray." Her delivery—especially on that song—was so dynamic, that it came to the attention of Owen Bradley, who was in semi-retirement. In several interviews, lang glowed about what Patsy Cline meant to her, and how much she loved her. The following year, lang coaxed Bradley out of retirement to create the excellent "Shadowland" album. On it, as another tribute to Cline, lang recorded "Lock, Stock and Teardrops," which Patsy would have sung on her next recording session—which never occurred.

That same year, quick to jump on the CD craze that was sweeping the market, MCA released three new Patsy packages: "The Last Sessions," "Patsy Cline, Live at the *Opry*," and the two disk "Patsy Cline Commemorative Collection" in compact disc format. In 1989 came "Patsy Cline: Live, Volume Two." Rhino Records, the premiere music repackaging label, in 1989 released three single disc Patsy Cline compilations from the 4 Star material. The cleverest one is "Patsy Cline—The Rockin' Side, 'Her First Recordings,' Volume 3." It was the first Patsy package that didn't mix the gospel tunes in with the rock material, and the first disk that truly acknowledged Patsy's role as a competent 1950's rock and roll singer.

A critically acclaimed four CD boxed set "The Patsy Cline Collection" was released by MCA in 1991. It presented the most complete package of Patsy performances ever released, from her first radio transcription performances to her final session with Owen Bradley. Although some of the 4 Star tracks have been omitted to make room for some newly discovered live cuts, it includes all fifty-one of her direct-to-Decca masterpieces, and it is a brilliantly devised package that really does Cline justice.

There have also been two very good video cassette packages produced by Mark and Greg Hall at Nashville's Hallway Productions. In 1989, they released "The Real Patsy Cline," which contained several interviews and performance footage of Patsy. It sold so well that in 1994 they released "Remembering Patsy Cline," which is a classier presentation, featuring more rare glimpses of Patsy—from "Arthur Godfrey's Talent Scouts" to never-before-seen home movie footage from Charlie Dick's private collection.

Just when it seemed that all of the sources for new Patsy Cline musical material was exhausted, the refreshingly different compact disc "Patsy Cline: Discovery!" was released in 1994. It is comprised of seventeen of Patsy's performances on Arthur Godfrey's various television and radio programs in 1957 and 1958. It kicks off with Patsy's first prize–winning performance of "Walkin' after Midnight," complete with dialogue from Arthur Godfrey and Patsy Cline. Especially touching to hear is the milestone moment when Patsy is declared the winner of that episode of "Arthur Godfrey's Talent Scouts." Her excitement is unforgettable.

"Patsy Cline: Discovery!" was released by the British label Lost Gold Records. What is unique about these seventeen cohesive performances is that they were recorded with a full TV studio orchestra behind Cline. The effect is like "Big Band Patsy!" Steel guitars are totally absent, as Patsy is heard for the first time in four decades with the scatting lilt of an oboe, or warbling with a full set of punctuating trombones. Patsy's singing sounds fantastic and clear on these just recently discovered tracks. They came from professionally produced acetate recordings and reveal a side of Cline rarely heard. This disc displays how Patsy might have sounded on record if she had submitted to Godfrey's many offers to manage her career, and turn her into a fully orchestrated pop singer.

It is likely only a matter of time before someone's long-lost recording of "Pasty Cline at Carnegie Hall" or "Patsy Cline in Las

Vegas" surfaces and makes its debut on disc. The voracious appetite for more of Patsy Cline continues to grow with time.

What has happened to all of the significant people in Patsy's roller coaster life? Most of them are still around, and active in their careers as of this writing.

Charlie is close to both of his and Patsy's children. Julie and her uncle, Mel Dick, operate one of several Patsy Cline fan clubs that continue to exist.

Loretta Lynn claims that the spirit of Patsy watches over her, and that she has conversations with Cline. She was undaunted when in the 1980s the tabloid newspapers got hold of this story. With the accuracy with which Patsy predicted her own death, who is to say that Patsy isn't Loretta's guardian angel? Loretta never got a chance to record a duet with Patsy during her life. However, in 1993, when she recorded the "Honky Tonk Angels" album with Dolly Parton and Tammy Wynette, Patsy's voice was edited into one of the songs, "Lovesick Blues," to make it a quartet.

Patsy's other protégé, Dottie West, also followed Cline's example and became a hugely successful country star. Dottie was in a tragic car accident in 1991, and passed away in the hospital several days later. She had been in a hurry to get to a scheduled performance at the *Grand Ole Opry* when her car broke down. She was offered a ride by an elderly man who was driving by and recognized her. Unfortunately, he lost control of his car as it was coming off the freeway, and it ultimately cost Dottie her life.

June Carter married Johnny Cash and they recorded several duet albums together. June performs with her sisters as the Carter Family from time to time. Brenda Lee still records, and performs for both country and rock and roll audiences. Owen Bradley produces records occasionally, and the Jordanaires perform, and continue to lend their distinctive background vocals to other people's albums. (Since that time, Hoyt Hawkins was replaced by Duane West. The Jordanaires—Stoker, Matthews, Walker, and West—are still active in the recording business, and can be heard in the 1990s on several albums—including Billy Ray Cyrus' "It Won't Be the Last." Jan and Harlan Howard live in the Nashville vicinity, and speak with great fondness about their dear friend Patsy.

Hilda Hensley is still alive, and in her living room hangs a portrait of her beloved Patsy. She still has several of her daughter's stage outfits. According to Julie, "Grandma loved my mother so much, that it is still hard for her to talk about her."

Several of Patsy's personal items are now on display at the Country Music Museum in Nashville. In Patsy's display is her "Dixie" cigarette lighter, one of her wigs, which was left at her hairstylist's shop at the time of her death, and one of the costumes that Pearl Butler had borrowed and then donated to the museum.

In the 1990s a whole new wave of country music talent has come to prominence. With country's nineties renaissance, female singers were suddenly emulating the simple sound of the 1950s and 1960s, when country relied on beautiful melodies and not merely bouffant hair. Several members of this breed of country gals have proclaimed that it was Patsy Cline and her unforgettable music that inspired them.

According to Reba McEntire, Patsy was one of the reasons she wanted to get into the music business to begin with. She claims, "The people I listened to for emotion were Dolly Parton and Patsy Cline … on 'Crazy' you can almost hear her cry from her guts, you know. That's the kind of stuff I wanted to do!"

A total Patsy Cline junkie, k. d. lang says, "Listening to her sing, and the production was Owen Bradley, you know, she had a type of soul that is hard to find in a singer."

Country music's number one 90's ballader, Vince Gill claims that Cline's vocal magic has made her a unique legend in the music business. According to him, "The greatest thing for me about Patsy Cline records is they still sound better than anything else on the radio today, and this is 35 years ago. Obviously a lot of it has to do with her voice, but it's the way her voice went to tape, it's one of those things that happens very few times in a lifetime."

Other stars admire her spirit. Lorrie Morgan points out, "I think Patsy was probably the first strong-headed woman in country music. It was like: She is not gonna take nothin' off of nobody. And I think we all admire that in Patsy. But there was a soft side to Patsy too, that came out in the ballads. Which I think we all like people to read in us, I think we all read in Patsy."

Trisha Yearwood is another of today's top stars who deeply identifies with Cline. According to her, "There's this emotion where you believe every word, it holds up, you know, after all these years. And on some of the songs you hear the catch in her voice, you hear her breathe, and you feel like she's in the room with you, singing. And there's just not very many artists that can leave that kind of impression and make you really feel something, and she's definitely one of the few."

Yearwood further illuminates the fact that "People talk about this big explosion in country music, and how women are now starting to sing about things that they wouldn't sing about twenty years ago, and have headlines and sell records. But Patsy Cline was singing about things that, you know, other women wouldn't sing about then, and she seemed to be the first real woman who didn't seem to really care what anybody said. She did whatever she wanted to, and it comes through in the music. And she definitely broke some rules, and I think it would be a lot harder, somebody had to do it, she was the one that did it."

According to country hunk Tracy Lawrence, "Wherever I travel, people are always aware of Patsy Cline and her music. I feel that both pop and country music owe her a great debt for all that she has contributed to both genres. Speaking for myself, I know what an impact Patsy Cline and her music have had on my career. Patsy Cline is still a creative force in music today, and I know that she will continue to influence many generations to come."

What is it about Patsy Cline that has made her a big—if not bigger—star in the 1990s than she was at the height of her career? What is it that makes her recordings sound as fresh, alive, and emotion-filled as they did when they were originally recorded? It has to do with the unmistakable magic of Patsy herself. It isn't just her voice, or her lyrics, it's her attitude, her phrasing, and her soul that comes through her recordings. It makes everyone who hears them think that she is singing to them alone. Her recordings today are just as vibrant and passionate as Patsy herself.

To date, Patsy's "Greatest Hits" album is still ranked as number one most weeks of the year on *Billboard* magazines' country catalog chart. It has been certified "Quadruple Platinum," for over four million copies sold, and is on the verge of going "Quintuple Platinum."

It is the best-selling solo female country greatest hits album in recorded history.

In 1994, to acknowledge her unsurpassed artistry, the U.S. Post Office issued a Patsy Cline postage stamp. Again, she was the first solo female country star to have such a distinction. She is now officially acknowledged as a "national treasure," a true musical legend.

On March 1, 1995, Patsy Cline received a "Lifetime Achievement Award" from the Academy of Recording Arts and Sciences, alongside Peggy Lee and Barbra Streisand. All three female superstars were honored as record-breaking women whose lives and careers have shaped the face and the sound of musical history. At long-last—thirty-two years after her death—Patsy is a Grammy Award winner!

In life, Patsy was driven, against sometimes insurmountable odds, to accomplish her goals. She was the designer of her own career destiny, and she made her own rules. She did this in an era when women in the music business were mere pawns in the hands of decision-making men.

Happiness came into her life in brief spurts, yet she never lost sight of her dreams. Along the way, she recorded several of the most significant and beloved songs of the twentieth century. The songs "Sweet Dreams," "Crazy," "She's Got You," "Walkin' after Midnight," and "I Fall to Pieces" will always be remembered as Patsy Cline songs. For all of these reasons, the world will never forget the girl who called herself "the Cline."

DISCOGRAPHY AND RECORDING HISTORY

*D*uring Patsy's Cline's lifetime, only three twelve-inch vinyl albums were released of her music ("Patsy Cline" 1957, "Patsy Cline Showcase" 1961, and "Sentimentally Yours" 1962). During her eight years as a recording artist, she made exactly 102 studio recordings—fifty-one fulfilled her 4 Star Record deal, and fifty-one directly for Decca Records. On the list that follows, all 102 of Patsy's "studio" recordings are listed in chronological order. On a couple of occasions, Patsy would re-record one of her previous recordings (i.e., "Walkin' after Midnight"). In those instances, both versions are listed with their own numbers and recording information. (Part of the reason was to upgrade some of the early songs to stereo.)

～～／～～

After viewing the dozens of Patsy Cline albums, compact discs, cassettes, and eight-track recordings in an overlapping assortment of compilations, I was in a quandary as to how to list the contents of these albums. What I chose to do was to list the packages that are available in the 1990s on compact disc. That way, you will be able to locate any of these recordings and easily acquire them for your collection.

I found that the majority of Patsy's material is available on the 104-song, four-CD/four-cassette boxed set "The Patsy Cline Collection" (1991). Although all of Cline's fifty-one Decca Recordings are included, several of her early 4 Star songs were left out to make room for some of the "live" and "radio transcript" rarities. Of the several "early Patsy" reissues, I found that three separate compilations on LaserLight CDs (1991), and three separate compilations on Rhino Records (1989) provided great overviews of her 4 Star years. For separate "best of" packages of Patsy's superior Decca recordings, I prefer the single disc, twenty-four-song "The Pasty Cline Story" over the twelve-song "Patsy Cline's Greatest Hits."

Since the rekindled interest in the music of Patsy Cline in the 1980s, there have also been thirty-three different "live" and "radio transcript" recordings that have been discovered and released. They are available on three different albums: "Patsy Cline: Live at the Opry" (1988), "Patsy Cline: Live, Volume Two" (1989), and the boxed set "The Patsy Cline Collection" (1991). These "live" recordings are listed in the order they were released on these three albums. Also included is "Patsy Cline: Discovery!" (1994), which comprises seventeen newly discovered recordings of Patsy on Arthur Godfrey's radio and TV programs.

The following abbreviations will help you locate songs on these currently available compact discs:

PCC = "The Patsy Cline Collection" (MCA Records/1991)
PCS = "The Patsy Cline Story" (MCA Records/orig. 1963)
GH = "Patsy Cline's Greatest Hits" (MCA Records/orig. 1967)
RR1 = "Patsy Cline, Her First Recordings, Volume 1" (Rhino Records/1989)
RR2 = "Patsy Cline, Her First Recordings, Volume 2" (Rhino Records/1989)
RR3 = "Patsy Cline, Her First Recordings, Volume 3" (Rhino Records/1989)
LL1 = "Patsy Cline Volume 1" (LaserLight/1991)
LL2 = "Patsy Cline Volume 2" (LaserLight/1991)
LL3 = "Patsy Cline Volume 3" (LaserLight/1991)
1PC = "Patsy Cline" (Decca-MCA/orig. 1957)
2PC = "Patsy Cline Showcase" (Decca-MCA/orig. 1961)
3PC = "Sentimentally Yours" (Decca-MCA/orig. 1962)

PASTY CLINE'S 102 "STUDIO" RECORDINGS

Note: These listings are chronological by recording date and running order. Recording personnel is listed whenever possible. In some instances, the words *"most likely"* precede the band members' names, as these have been reconstructed from the memories of several of the original musicians. All of these recordings were produced by Owen Bradley, with the exception of those songs recorded in New York City on April 24, 1957, and April 25, 1957, which were presumably produced by Paul Cohen, with Bill McCall overseeing the session. The exact time of the recording session is provided only when known.

June 1, 1955—Recording session: Nashville (4 Star)
Patsy Cline—lead vocal; *most likely*: Harold Bradley—acoustic guitar, Owen Bradley—piano, Farris Coursey—drums, Don Helms—steel guitar, Tommy Jackson—fiddle, Grady Martin—electric guitar/fiddle, Bob Moore—acoustic bass.

(1) "Hidin' Out"
     [Eddie Miller, W. S. Stevenson]
     RR1, LL3

(2) "Turn the Cards Slowly"
     [Sammy Masters]
     PCC, RR3, LL3

(3) "A Church, a Courtroom, and Then Goodbye"
     [Eddie Miller, W. S. Stevenson]
     PCC, RR1, LL2

(4) "Honky Tonk Merry-Go-Round"
     [Frank Simon, Stan Gardner]
     PCC, RR1

January 5, 1956—Recording session: Nashville (4 Star)
Patsy Cline—lead vocal; *most likely*: Harold Bradley—acoustic guitar, Owen Bradley—piano, Farris Coursey—drums, Don Helms—steel guitar, Tommy Jackson—fiddle, Grady Martin—electric guitar/fiddle, Bob Moore—acoustic bass.

(5) "I Love You Honey"
     [Eddie Miller]
     PCC, RR3

(6) "Come on in (and Make Yourself at Home)"
     [V. F. Stewart]
     PCC, LL1

(7) "I Cried All the Way to the Altar"
     [Bobby Flournoy]
     RR1, LL2

(8) "I Don't Wanna"
     (See no. 29 for alternate version)
     [Eddie Miller, W. S. Stevenson, Durwood Haddock]
     PCC

April 22, 1956—Recording session: Nashville (4 Star)
Patsy Cline—lead vocal; *most likely*: Harold Bradley—acoustic guitar, Owen Bradley—piano, Farris Coursey—drums, Don Helms—steel guitar, Tommy Jackson—fiddle, Grady Martin—electric guitar/fiddle, Bob Moore—acoustic bass.

(9) "Stop, Look and Listen"
[George London, W. S. Stevenson]
RR3, LL2

(10) "I've Loved and Lost Again"
[Eddie Miller]
PCC, RR1, LL1

(11) "Dear God"
[V. F. Stewart]
RR1, LL3

(12) "He Will Do for You"
[V. F. Stewart]
RR1, LL3

November 8, 1956—Recording session: Nashville (4 Star)
Patsy Cline—lead vocal; *most likely*: Harold Bradley—acoustic guitar, Owen Bradley—piano, Farris Coursey—drums, Don Helms—steel guitar, Tommy Jackson—fiddle, Grady Martin—electric guitar/fiddle, Bob Moore—acoustic bass.

(13) "Walkin' after Midnight"
[Don Hecht, Alan Block]
PCC, RR1, LL1, 1PC

(14) "The Heart You Break May Be Your Own"
[Tiny Colbert, Bob Geesling]
PCC, LL2

(15) "Pick Me Up on Your Way Down"
[Burton Levy, Glenn Reeves, Mae Boren Axton]
PCC, LL1

(16) "A Poor Man's Riches (or a Rich Man's Gold)"
      [Burton Hilliard, Milton Delugg]
      PCC, LL1

April 24, 1957—Recording session: New York City (4 Star)
Patsy Cline—lead vocal, musicians—unknown, background
vocals—unknown male vocal group (vocal group absent from song
no. 20). Session was *most likely* recorded at Pythian Studio.

(17) "Today, Tomorrow and Forever"
      [Don Reid]
      PCC, RR2, LL2

(18) "Fingerprints"
      [Don Hecht, W. O. Fleener, W. S. Stevenson]
      RR1, LL2, 1PC

(19) "A Stranger in My Arms"
      [Charlotte White, Virginia Hensley*, Mary Lou Jeans]
      RR1, LL2

(20) "Don't Ever Leave Me Again"
      [Lillian Claiborne, Virginia Hensley*, James Crawford]
      PCC, LL3, 1PC

* These are Patsy's two songwriting forays—using her maiden name
of "Virginia Hensley."

April 25, 1957—Recording session: New York City (4 Star)
Patsy Cline—lead vocal, musicians—unknown, the Anita Kerr Singers
[Anita Kerr, Dottie Dillard, Louis Nunley, Gil Wright]—background
vocals. Session was *most likely* recorded at Pythian Studio.

(21) "Try Again"
      [Bob Summers, Jerry Le Fors]
      PCC, RR1, LL2

(22) "Too Many Secrets"
[Bobby Lyle]
PCC, RR3, LL3, 1PC

(23) "Then You'll Know"
[Bobby Lyle]
PCC, RR1, LL1, 1PC

(24) "Three Cigarettes in an Ashtray"
[Eddie Miller, W. S. Stevenson]
PCC, RR1, LL3, 1PC

May 23, 1957—Recording session: Nashville (4 Star)
Patsy Cline—lead vocal; *most likely*: Hank Garland—electric piano,
Grady Martin—electric guitar, Jack Shook—acoustic guitar, Harold
Bradley—piano, the Anita Kerr Singers [Anita Kerr, Dottie Dillard,
Louis Nunley, Gil Wright]—background vocals.

213

(25) "That Wonderful Someone"
[Gertrude Berg]
PCC, RR2, LL2, 1PC

(26) "In Care of the Blues"
[Eddie Miller, W. S. Stevenson]
PCC, RR3, LL3, 1PC

(27) "Hungry for Love"
[Eddie Miller, W. S. Stevenson]
PCC, RR2, LL2, 1PC

(28) "I Can't Forget"
[W. S. Stevenson, Carl Belew]
PCC, RR2, LL2, 1PC

(29) "I Don't Wanna"
(Remake of song no. 8)
[Eddie Miller, W. S. Stevenson, Durwood Haddock]
RR3, LL2, 1PC

(30) "Ain't No Wheels on This Ship (We Can't Roll)"
[W. D. Chandler, W. S. Stevenson]
RR3, LL2, 1PC

December 13, 1957—Recording session: Nashville (4 Star)
Patsy Cline—lead vocal; *most likely*: Hank Garland—electric piano,
Grady Martin—electric guitar, Bob Moore—acoustic guitar, Farris
Coursey—drums, Owen Bradley—piano/organ, unknown—vibes,
the Anita Kerr Singers [Anita Kerr, Dottie Dillard, Louis Nunley, Gil
Wright]—background vocals.

(31) "Stop the World (and Let Me Off)"
[Carl Belew, W. S. Stevenson]
RR2, LL1

(32) "Walking Dream"
[Hal Willis, Ginger Willis]
RR3, LL3

(33) "Cry Not for Me"
[Don Hecht, Jack Moon]
RR2

(34) "If I Could See the World (Through the Eyes of a Child)"
[Sammy Masters, Richard Pope, Tex Satterwell]
PCC, RR2, LL2

February 13, 1958—Recording session: Nashville (4 Star)
Patsy Cline—lead vocal; *most likely*: Hank Garland—electric piano,
Grady Martin—electric guitar/electric bass/banjo, Bob Moore—
acoustic bass, Buddy Harman—drums, Floyd Cramer—piano,
unknown—horns, the Anita Kerr Singers [Anita Kerr, Dottie Dillard,
Louis Nunley, Gil Wright]—background vocals.

(35) "Just out of Reach (of My Two Open Arms)"
[V. F. Stewart]
PCC, RR2, LL3

(36) "I Can See an Angel"
[Kay Adelman]
PCC, RR2, LL2

(37) "Come on in (and Make Yourself at Home)"
(Remake of song no. 6)
[V. F. Stewart]
LL1

(38) "Let the Teardrops Fall"
[C. C. Beam, C. L. Jiles, W. S. Stevenson]
PCC, RR3

(39) "Never No More"
[Rita Ross, Alan Block]
PCC, RR3, LL3

(40) "If Only I Could Stay Asleep"
[Ethel Bassey, Wayland Chandler]
PCC, RR2, LL1

January 8, 1959—Recording session: Nashville (4 Star)
Session Time: 5:00 P.M.—8:30 P.M.
Patsy Cline—lead vocal, Hank Garland—electric guitar, Grady Martin—electric guitar, Harold Bradley—6-string electric bass, Bob Moore—acoustic bass, Buddy Harman—drums, Floyd Cramer—piano, the Jordanaires [Gordon Stoker, Hoyt Hawkins, Neal Matthews, Jr., Ray Walker]—background vocals.

(41) "I'm Moving Along"
[Johnny Starr]
PCC, RR3

(42) "I'm Blue Again"
[C. C. Beam, C. L. Jiles, W. S. Stevenson]
PCC, RR2, LL2

(43) "Love, Love, Love Me Honey Do"
[C. C. Beam, C. L. Jiles, W. S. Stevenson]
PCC, RR3, LL1

January 9, 1959—Recording session: Nashville (4 Star)
Session time: 2:00 P.M.—5:00 P.M.
Patsy Cline—lead vocal, Hank Garland—electric guitar, Grady Martin—electric guitar, Harold Bradley—6-string electric bass, Bob Moore—acoustic bass, Farris Coursey—drums, Floyd Cramer—piano, the Jordanaires [Gordon Stoker, Hoyt Hawkins, Neal Matthews, Jr., Ray Walker]—background vocals.

(44) "Yes, I Understand"
[C. C. Beam, C. L. Jiles, W. S. Stevenson]
PCC, RR2, LL2

(45) "Gotta Lot of Rhythm in My Soul"
[Barbara Vaughn, W. S. Stevenson]
PCC, RR3, LL3

July 3, 1959—Recording session: Nashville (4 Star)
Session time: 12:30 P.M.—3:30 P.M.
Patsy Cline—lead vocal, Hank Garland—electric guitar, Grady Martin—electric guitar, Bob Moore—acoustic bass, Buddy Harman—drums, Floyd Cramer—piano, the Jordanaires [Gordon Stoker, Hoyt Hawkins, Neal Matthews, Jr., Ray Walker]—background vocals.

(46) "Life's Railway to Heaven"
[Arranged by W. S. Stevenson]
PCC, RR2, LL3

(47) "Just a Closer Walk with Thee"
[Arranged by W. S. Stevenson]
PCC, RR2, LL1

January 27, 1960—Recording session: Nashville (4 Star)
Patsy Cline—lead vocal, Hank Garland—electric guitar, Grady Martin—electric guitar/fiddle, Jimmy Day—steel guitar, Harold Bradley—6-string electric bass, Bob Moore—acoustic bass, Buddy Harman—drums, Floyd Cramer—piano.

(48) "Lovesick Blues"
[Irving Mills, Cliff Friend]
PCC

(49) "How Can I Face Tomorrow?"
[C. C. Beam, C. L. Jiles, W. S. Stevenson]
PCC

(50) "There He Goes"
[Eddie Miller, Durwood Haddock, W. S. Stevenson]
PCC, LL1

(51) "Crazy Dreams"
[C. C. Beam, C. L. Jiles, W. S. Stevenson]
PCC, LL1

Note: The above recording date marks the final session Patsy recorded while under contract to Bill McCall and 4 Star Records.

November 16, 1960—Recording session: Nashville (Decca)
Session time: 2:30 p.m.—5:30 p.m.

Patsy Cline—lead vocal, Hank Garland—electric guitar, Randy Hughes—acoustic guitar, Ben Keith—steel guitar, Harold Bradley—6-string electric bass, Bob Moore—acoustic bass, Doug Kirkham—drums, Hargus "Pig" Robbins—piano, the Jordanaires [Gordon Stoker, Hoyt Hawkins, Neal Matthews, Jr., Ray Walker]—background vocals.

(52) "I Fall to Pieces"
[Hank Cochran, Harlan Howard]
PCC, PCS, GH, 2PC

(53) "Shoes"
[Hank Cochran, Velma Smith]
PCC

(54) "Lovin' in Vain"
[Freddie Hart]
PCC

August 17, 1961—Recording session: Nashville (Decca)
Session time: 2:00 P.M.—6:00 P.M.
Patsy Cline—lead vocal, Grady Martin—electric guitar, Randy Hughes—acoustic guitar, Walter Haynes—steel guitar, Harold Bradley—6-string electric bass, Bob Moore—acoustic bass, Buddy Harman—drums, Hargus "Pig" Robbin—piano; string section: Brenton Banks, George Binkley III, Lillian Hunt, Suzanne Parker—violins, Cecil Brower—viola, Byron Bach—cello; the Jordanaires [Gordon Stoker, Hoyt Hawkins, Neal Matthews, Jr., Ray Walker]—background vocals.

(55) "True Love"
[Cole Porter]
PCC, PCS, 2PC

(56) "San Antonio Rose"
[Bob Wills]
PCC, PCS, 2PC

(57) "The Wayward Wind"
[Stan Lebowsky, Herb Newman]
PCC, PCS, 2PC

(58) "A Poor Man's Riches (or a Rich Man's Gold)"
(Remake of song no. 16)
[Milton Delugg, Bob Hilliard]
PCC, PCS, 2PC

August 21, 1961—Recording session: Nashville (Decca)
Session time: 7:15 P.M.—11:15 P.M.
Patsy Cline—lead vocal, Grady Martin—electric guitar, Randy Hughes—acoustic guitar, Walter Haynes—steel guitar, Harold Bradley—6-string electric bass, Bob Moore—acoustic bass, Buddy Harman—drums, Floyd Cramer—piano/organ, the Jordanaires [Gordon Stoker, Hoyt Hawkins, Neal Matthews, Jr., Ray Walker]—background vocals.

(59) "Crazy"
[Willie Nelson]
PCC, PCS, GH, 2PC

August 24, 1961—Recording session: Nashville (Decca)
Session time: 1:45 P.M.—5:45 P.M.
Patsy Cline—lead vocal, Grady Martin—electric guitar, Randy Hughes—acoustic guitar, Walter Haynes—steel guitar, Harold Bradley—6-string electric bass, Bob Moore—acoustic bass, Buddy Harman—drums, Hargus "Pig" Robbins—piano, Floyd Cramer—organ, the Jordanaires [Gordon Stoker, Hoyt Hawkins, Neal Matthews, Jr., Ray Walker]—background vocals.

(60) "Who Can I Count On?"
[Sammy Masters]
PCC

(61) "Seven Lonely Days"
[Earl Shuman, Alden Shuman, Marshall Brown]
PCC, PCS, 2PC

(62) "I Love You So Much It Hurts Me"
[Floyd Tillman]
PCC, PCS, 2PC

(63) "Foolin' Around"
[Harlan Howard, Buck Owens]
PCC, PCS, 2PC

(64) "Have You Ever Been Lonely (Have You Ever Been Blue)"
[Peter De Rose, George Brown]
PCC, 2PC

August 25, 1961—Recording session: Nashville (Decca)
Session time: 2:30 P.M.—6:30 P.M.
Patsy Cline—lead vocal, Grady Martin—electric guitar, Randy Hughes—acoustic guitar, Walter Haynes—steel guitar, Harold Bradley—6-string electric bass, Bob Moore—acoustic bass, Buddy Harman—drums, Hargus "Pig" Robbins—piano, Floyd Cramer—

organ, the Jordanaires [Gordon Stoker, Hoyt Hawkins, Neal Matthews, Jr., Ray Walker]—background vocals.

(65) "South of the Border (Down Mexico Way)"
[Michael Carr, Jimmy Kennedy]
PCC, PCS, 2PC

(66) "Walkin' after Midnight"
(Remake of song no. 13)
[Don Hecht, Alan Block]
PCC, PCS, GH, 2PC

(67) "Strange"
[Mel Tillis, Fred Burch]
PCC, PCS, GH, 3PC

(68) "You're Stronger than Me"
[Hank Cochran, Jimmy Key]
PCC, PCS, GH

December 17, 1961—Recording session: Nashville (Decca)
Session time: 7:10 P.M.—10:40 P.M.
Patsy Cline—lead vocal, Grady Martin—electric guitar, Randy Hughes—}acoustic guitar, Walter Haynes—steel guitar, Harold Bradley—6-string electric bass, Bob Moore—acoustic bass, Buddy Harman—drums, Floyd Cramer—piano, Bill Pursell—organ, the Jordanaires [Gordon Stoker, Hoyt Hawkins, Neal Matthews, Jr., Ray Walker]—background vocals.

(69) "She's Got You"
[Hank Cochran]
PCC, PCS, GH, 3PC

February 12, 1962—Recording session: Nashville (Decca)
Session time: 7:15 P.M.—10:45 P.M.
Patsy Cline—lead vocal, Grady Martin—electric guitar, Randy Hughes—acoustic guitar, Ray Edenton—rhythm guitar, Walter Haynes—steel guitar, Harold Bradley—6-string electric bass, Bob Moore—acoustic bass, Buddy Harman—drums, Floyd Cramer—

piano, Bill Pursell—organ, the Jordanaires [Gordon Stoker, Hoyt Hawkins, Neal Matthews, Jr., Ray Walker]—background vocals.

(70) "You Made Me Love You (I Didn't Want to Do It)"
[Joe McCarthy, James V. Monaco]
PCC, 3PC

(71) "You Belong to Me"
[Pee Wee King, Redd Stewart, Chilton Price]
PCC, PCS, 3PC

(72) "Heartaches"
[Al Hoffman, John Klenner]
PCC, PCS, 3PC

(73) "Your Cheatin' Heart"
[Hank Williams]
PCC, PCS, 3PC

February 13, 1962—Recording session: Nashville (Decca)
Session time: 7:15 P.M.—10:45 P.M.
Patsy Cline—lead vocal, Grady Martin—electric guitar, Randy Hughes—acoustic guitar, Ray Edenton—rhythm guitar, Walter Haynes—steel guitar, Harold Bradley—6-string electric bass, Bob Moore—acoustic bass, Buddy Harman—drums, Floyd Cramer—piano, Bill Pursell—organ, Charlie McCoy—harmonica, the Jordanaires [Gordon Stoker, Hoyt Hawkins, Neal Matthews, Jr., Ray Walker]—background vocals.

(74) "That's My Desire"
[Helmy Kresa, Carroll Loveday]
PCC, 3PC

(75) "Half as Much"
[Curley Williams]
PCC, 3PC

February 15, 1962—Recording session: Nashville (Decca)
Session time: 7:15 P.M.—11:45 P.M.
Patsy Cline—lead vocal, Grady Martin—electric guitar, Randy

Hughes—acoustic guitar, Ray Edenton—rhythm guitar, Walter Haynes—steel guitar, Harold Bradley—6-string electric bass, Bob Moore—acoustic bass, Buddy Harman—drums, Floyd Cramer—piano, Bill Pursell—organ, Charlie McCoy—harmonica; string section: Brenton Banks, Cecil Brower, Solie Fott, Lillian Hunt, Verne Richardson—violins; the Jordanaires [Gordon Stoker, Hoyt Hawkins, Neal Matthews, Jr., Ray Walker]—background vocals, Bill Justis—arranger.

(76) "Lonely Street"
[Carl Belew, W. S. Stevenson, Kenny Sowder]
PCC, 3PC

(77) "Anytime"
[Herbert "Happy" Lawson]
PCC, 3PC

(78) "You Were Only Fooling (While I Was Falling in Love)"
[Larry Fotine, Billy Faber, Fred Meadows]
PCC, 3PC

(79) "I Can't Help It (If I'm Still in Love with You)"
[Hank Williams]
PCC, 3PC

February 28, 1962—Recording session: Nashville (Decca)
Session time: 7:15 P.M.—11:15 P.M.
Patsy Cline—lead vocal, Grady Martin—electric guitar, Randy Hughes—acoustic guitar, Ray Edenton—rhythm guitar, Harold Bradley—6-string electric bass, Joe Zinkan—acoustic bass, Buddy Harman—drums, Floyd Cramer—piano; string section: Brenton Banks, Cecil Brower, Lillian Hunt, Verne Richardson—violins; Howard Carpenter, Ed Tarpley—violas, Byron Bach—cello; the Jordanaires [Gordon Stoker, Hoyt Hawkins, Neal Matthews, Jr., Ray Walker]—background vocals, Bill McElhiney—arranger.

(80) "You're Stronger than Me"
(Remake of song no. 68)
[Hank Cochran, Jimmy Key]
PCC, PCS, GH

(81) "When I Get Through with You (You'll Love Me Too)"
[Harlan Howard]
PCC

(82) "Imagine That"
[Justin Tubb]
PCC, PCS

(83) "So Wrong"
[Carl Perkins, Danny Dill, Mel Tillis]
PCC, PCS, GH

223

September 5, 1962—Recording session: Nashville (Decca)
Session time: 2:00 P.M.—6:00 P.M.
Patsy Cline—lead vocal, Grady Martin—electric guitar, Randy
Hughes—acoustic guitar, Ray Edenton—rhythm guitar, Harold
Bradley—6-string electric bass, Bob Moore—acoustic bass, Buddy
Harman—drums, Hargus "Pig" Robbins—piano; string section: Rita
Faye Wilson—autoharp, Cecil Brower, Solie Fott, Nancy Hearn,
Lillian Hunt—violins, Howard Carpenter, Verne Richardson—vio-
las, Byron Bach—cello; the Jordanaires [Gordon Stoker, Hoyt
Hawkins, Neal Matthews, Jr., Ray Walker]—background vocals, Bill
McElhiney—arranger.

(84) "Why Can't He Be You?"
[Hank Cochran]
PCC, PCS, GH

(85) "Your Kinda Love"
[Roy Drusky]
PCC

(86) "When You Need a Laugh"
[Hank Cochran]
PCC

(87)   "Leavin' on Your Mind]
       [Wayne Walker, Webb Pierce]
       PCC, PCS, GH

September 10, 1962—Recording session: Nashville (Decca)
Session time: 2:00 P.M.—5:00 P.M.
Patsy Cline—lead vocal, Grady Martin—electric guitar, Randy Hughes—acoustic guitar, Ray Edenton—rhythm guitar, Harold Bradley—6-string electric bass, Bob Moore—acoustic bass, Buddy Harman—drums, Hargus "Pig" Robbins—piano, Bill Pursell—organ; string section: Cecil Brower, Lillian Hunt, Verne Richardson, Michael Semanitzky—violins; the Jordanaires [Gordon Stoker, Hoyt Hawkins, Neal Matthews, Jr., Ray Walker], Millie Kirkham—background vocals, Bill Justis—arranger.

(88)   "Back in Baby's Arms"
       [Bob Montgomery]
       PCC, PCS, GH

(89)   "Tra Le La Le La Triangle"
       [Marijohn Wilkin, Fred Burch]
       PCC, PCS

(90)   "That's How a Heartache Begins"
       [Harlan Howard]
       PCC

February 4, 1963—Recording session: Nashville (Decca)
Session time: 7:00 P.M.—10:00 P.M.
Patsy Cline—lead vocal, Grady Martin—electric guitar, Randy Hughes—acoustic guitar, Ray Edenton—rhythm guitar, Harold Bradley—6-string electric bass, Bob Moore—acoustic bass, Buddy Harman—drums, Floyd Cramer—piano, Bill Pursell—organ; string section: Brenton Banks, George Binkley III, Solie Fott, Lillian Hunt, Martin Katahn—violins, Howard Carpenter, Cecil Brower—violas, Byron Bach, Gary Williams—cellos; the Jordanaires [Gordon Stoker,

Hoyt Hawkins, Neal Matthews, Jr., Ray Walker]—background vocals, Bill McElhiney—arranger.

(91) "Faded Love"
[John Wills, Bob Wills]
PCC, PCS, GH

(92) "Someday (You'll Want Me to Want You)"
[Jimmy Hodges]
PCC

(93) "Love Letters in the Sand"
[J. Fred Coots, Kick Kenny, Charles Kenny]
PCC

February 5, 1963—Recording session: Nashville (Decca)
Session time: 7:00 P.M.—10:00 P.M.
Patsy Cline—lead vocal, Grady Martin—electric guitar, Randy Hughes—acoustic guitar, Ray Edenton—rhythm guitar, Harold Bradley—6-string electric bass, Bob Moore—acoustic bass, Buddy Harman—drums, Floyd Cramer—piano, Bill Pursell—organ; string section: Brenton Banks, George Binkley III, Solie Fott, Lillian Hunt, Wilda Tinsley—violins, Howard Carpenter, Cecil Brower—violas, Byron Bach, Gary Williams—cellos; the Jordanaires [Gordon Stoker, Hoyt Hawkins, Neal Matthews, Jr., Ray Walker]—background vocals, Bill McElhiney—arranger.

(94) "Blue Moon of Kentucky"
[Bill Monroe]
PCC

(95) "Sweet Dreams"
[Don Gibson]
PCC, PCS, GH

(96) "Always"
[Irving Berlin]
PCC

February 6, 1963—Recording session: Nashville (Decca)
Session time: 7:00 P.M.—10:00 P.M.
Patsy Cline—lead vocal, Grady Martin—electric guitar, Randy Hughes—acoustic guitar, Ray Edenton—rhythm guitar, Harold Bradley—6-string electric bass, Bob Moore—acoustic bass, Buddy Harman—drums, Floyd Cramer—piano; string section: Brenton Banks, George Binkley III, Solie Fott, Lillian Hunt, Wilda Tinsley—violins, Howard Carpenter, Cecil Brower—violas, Byron Bach, Gary Williams—cellos; the Jordanaires [Gordon Stoker, Hoyt Hawkins, Neal Matthews, Jr., Ray Walker]—background vocals, Bill McElhiney—arranger.

(97) "Does Your Heart Beat for Me"
[Russ Morgan, Arnold Johnson, Mitchell Parrish]
PCC

(98) "Bill Bailey, Won't You Please Come Home"
[Hughie Cannon]
PCC

February 7, 1963—Recording session: Nashville (Decca)
Session time: 7:00 P.M.—10:00 P.M.
Patsy Cline—lead vocal, Grady Martin—electric guitar, Randy Hughes—acoustic guitar, Ray Edenton—rhythm guitar, Wayne Moss—6-string electric bass, Bob Moore—acoustic bass, Buddy Harman—drums, Floyd Cramer—piano; string section: Brenton Banks, George Binkley III, Solie Fott, Lillian Hunt, Martin Katahn, Mildred Oonk, Verne Richardson—violins, Howard Carpenter—viola, Byron Bach, Gary Williams—cellos; the Jordanaires [Gordon Stoker, Hoyt Hawkins, Neal Matthews, Jr., Ray Walker]—background vocals, Bill McElhiney—arranger.

(99) "He Called Me Baby"
[Harlan Howard]
PCC

(100) "Crazy Arms"
[Chuck Seals, Ray Price]
PCC

(101) "You Took Him off My Hands"
[Harlan Howard]
PCC

(102) "I'll Sail My Ship Alone"
[Henry Bernard, Henry Thurston, Lois Mann, Morry Burns]
PCC

PATSY CLINE'S THIRTY-THREE KNOWN "LIVE" RECORDINGS

Note: These recordings are listed in the order they have been released, on the three albums on which they are available. The musicians are mostly unknown, since no one retained the personnel logs for these sessions.

"Patsy Cline: Live at the *Opry*" (MCA Records/1988)

(L1) "A Church, a Courtroom, and Then Goodbye"
[Eddie Miller, W. S. Stevenson]
June 16, 1956

(L2) "I've Loved and Lost Again"
[Eddie Miller]
June 16, 1956

(L3) "Walkin' after Midnight"
[Don Hecht, Alan Block]
December 14, 1957

(L4) "Lovesick Blues"
[Irving Mills, Cliff Friend]
April 2, 1960

(L5) "How Can I Face Tomorrow"
[C. C. Beam, C. L. Jiles, W. S. Stevenson]
April 29, 1960

(L6) "Loose Talk"
[Freddie Hart, Ann Lucas]
August 12, 1960

(L7) "Crazy Dreams"
[C. C. Beam, C. L. Jiles, W. S. Stevenson]
August 12, 1960

(L8) "There He Goes"
[Eddie Miller, Durwood Haddock, W. S. Stevenson]
September 3, 1960

(L9) "Lovin' in Vain"
[Freddie Hart]
July 7, 1961

(L10) "I Fall to Pieces"
[Hank Cochran, Harlan Howard]
July 7, 1961

(L11) "She's Got You"
[Hank Cochran]
March 23, 1962

(L12) "Crazy"
[Willie Nelson]
March 23, 1962

"Patsy Cline: Live, Volume Two" (MCA Records/1989)
Note: The following album is composed of songs recorded for radio broadcast on military radio programs.

(L13) "Strange"
[Mel Tillis, Fred Burch]
Spring 1962

(L14) "When Your House Is Not a Home"
[Roger Miller]
June 1960
(also on PCC)

(L15) "Turn the Cards Slowly"
[Sammy Masters]
Summer 1956

(L16) "Yes, I Know Why"
[Webb Pierce]
Summer 1956
(also on PCC)

(L17) "Side by Side"
[Harry Woods]
August 13, 1961
(also on PCC)

(L18) "Come on in (and Make Yourself at Home)"
[V. F. Stewart]
Summer 1956

(L19) "Stupid Cupid"
[Neil Sedaka, Howard Greenfield]
September 1960
(also on PCC)

(L20) "The Wayward Wind"
[Stan Lebowsky, Herb Newman]
Summer 1956

(L21) "For Rent"
[Jimmie Loden, Jack Morrow}
Summer 1956
(also on PCC)

(L22) "Shoes"
[Hank Cochran, Velma Smith]
Spring 1962

(L23) "Stop, Look and Listen"
[George London, W. S. Stevenson]
Summer 1956

(L24) "Just a Closer Walk with Thee"
[Arranged by Red Foley]
August 13, 1961

"The Patsy Cline Collection" (MCA Records/1991)
Note: This four-CD/four-cassette boxed set also contains the following live and radio transcription performances unavailable anywhere else.

(L25) "I'm Walking the Dog"
[Cliff Grimsley, Tex Grimsley]
August 1954 (radio transcription)

(L26) "It Wasn't God who Made Honky Tonk Angels"
[J. D. Miller]
August 1954 (radio transcription)

(L27) "Loose Talk"
[Freddie Hart, Ann Lucas]
September 1960 (radio transcription)

(L28) "Come on in (and Make Yourself at Home)"
[V. F. Stewart]
December 2, 1961 (live in concert)

(L29) "A Poor Man's Riches (or a Rich Man's Gold)"
[Bob Hilliard, Milton Delugg]
December 2, 1961 (live in concert)

(L30) "Bill Bailey, Won't You Please Come Home"
[Hughie Cannon]
December 2, 1961 (live in concert)

(L31) "Leavin' on Your Mind"
[Wayne Walker, Webb Pierce]
January 15, 1963 (radio transcription)

(L32) "Tennessee Waltz"
[Pee Wee King, Redd Stewart]
January 15, 1963 (radio transcription)

(L33) "Just a Closer Walk with Thee"
[traditional]
date unknown (live at the Ryman Theater)

PATSY CLINE'S SEVENTEEN PERFORMANCES ON ARTHUR GODFREY'S SHOWS

Note: These recordings appear listed in the order they have been released. The dates are as per the liner notes accompanying this package.

"Patsy Cline: Discovery!" (Lost Gold Records; Enfield, England EN1 1SJ/Virgule 1994)

(AG1) "Walkin' after Midnight"
song with dialogue from "Arthur Godfrey's Talent Scouts"
January 21, 1957

(AG2) "I Don't Wanna"
from Godfrey's radio program
January 8, 1958

(AG3) "Then You'll Know"
from Godfrey's radio program
October 24, 1957

(AG4) "Don't Ever Leave Me Again"
from Godfrey's radio program
January 10, 1958

(AG5) "Three Cigarettes in an Ashtray"
song with dialogue from Godfrey's radio program
October 22, 1957

(AG6) "In Care of the Blues"
from Godfrey's radio program
January 14, 1958

(AG7) "Your Cheatin' Heart"
    from Godfrey's radio program
    January 8, 1958

(AG8) "The Man Upstairs"
    from Godfrey's radio program
    January 10, 1958

(AG9) "Stop the World (and Let Me Off)"
    from Godfrey's radio program
    January 13, 1958

(AG10) "Try Again"
    from TV's "Arthur Godfrey and Friends"
    April 23, 1957

(AG11) "Walking Dream"
    from Godfrey's radio program
    January 9, 1958

(AG12) "Too Many Secrets"
    from Godfrey's radio program
    October 25, 1957

(AG13) "Down by the Riverside"
    from Godfrey's radio program
    January 14, 1958

(AG14) "Come on in (and Make Yourself at Home)"
    from Godfrey's radio program
    January 14, 1958

(AG15) "Ain't No Wheels on This Ship (We Can't Roll)"
    from Godfrey's radio program
    January 16, 1958

(AG16) "Hungry for Love"
    from Godfrey's radio program
    January 16, 1958

(AG17) "Walkin' after Midnight"
    song with dialogue from TV's "Arthur Godfrey and Friends"
    April 26, 1957

ALPHABETICAL LISTING OF PATSY'S 102 "STUDIO" RECORDINGS

(30)   "Ain't No Wheels on This Ship (We Can't Roll)"
(96)   "Always"
(77)   "Anytime"
(88)   "Back in Baby's Arms"
(98)   "Bill Bailey, Won't You Please Come Home"
(94)   "Blue Moon of Kentucky"
(3)   "A Church, a Courtroom, and Then Goodbye"
(6)(37)   "Come on in (and Make Yourself at Home)"
(59)   "Crazy"
(100)   "Crazy Arms"
(51)   "Crazy Dreams"
(33)   "Cry Not for Me"
(11)   "Dear God"
(97)   "Does Your Heart Beat for Me"
(20)   "Don't Ever Leave Me Again"
(91)   "Faded Love"
(18)   "Fingerprints"
(63)   "Foolin' Around"
(45)   "Gotta Lot of Rhythm in My Soul"
(75)   "Half as Much"
(64)   "Have You Ever Been Lonely (Have You Ever Been Blue)"
(99)   "He Called Me Baby"
(12)   "He Will Do for You"
(14)   "The Heart You Break May Be Your Own"
(72)   "Heartaches"
(1)   "Hidin' Out"
(4)   "Honky Tonk Merry-Go-Round"
(49)   "How Can I Face Tomorrow?"
(27)   "Hungry for Love"
(36)   "I Can See an Angel"

233

(19)   "A Stranger in My Arms"
(95)   "Sweet Dreams"
(25)   "That Wonderful Someone"
(90)   "That's How a Heartache Begins"
(74)   "That's My Desire"
(23)   "Then You'll Know"
(50)   "There He Goes"
(24)   "Three Cigarettes in an Ashtray"
(17)   "Today, Tomorrow and Forever"
(22)   "Too Many Secrets"
(89)   "Tra Le La Le La Triangle"
(55)   "True Love"
(21)   "Try Again"
(2)   "Turn the Cards Slowly"
(13)(66) "Walkin' after Midnight"
(32)   "Walking Dream"
(57)   "The Wayward Wind"
(81)   "When I Get Through with You (You'll Love Me Too)"
(86)   "When You Need a Laugh"
(60)   "Who Can I Count On?"
(84)   "Why Can't He Be You?"
(44)   "Yes, I Understand"
(71)   "You Belong to Me"
(70)   "You Made Me Love You (I Didn't Want to Do It)"
(101)   "You Took Him off My Hands"
(78)   "You Were Only Fooling (While I was Falling in Love)"
(73)   "Your Cheatin' Heart"
(85)   "Your Kinda Love"
(68)(80) "You're Stronger than Me"

PATSY CLINE'S ORIGINAL ALBUMS ON DECCA/MCA RECORDS

With the exception of Patsy Cline's first three singles on Coral Records, the majority of her releases were on Decca Records, which has since been purchased by MCA Records. The following is a list of Patsy's albums and compilations, all of which are available on compact disc. The one oddity is the RCA Patsy Cline and Jim Reeves album, on which a posthumous "duet" was created in the studio; the rest of the album is filled with the two performers' solo hits. On the "Always" and "Sweet Dreams" albums, for several cuts the original music was stripped away and new instrumentation is heard behind Patsy.

1. "Patsy Cline"
    (Decca/MCA Records)
    Release date: August 5, 1957

2. "Patsy Cline Showcase"
    (Decca/MCA Records)
    Release date: November 27, 1961

3. "Sentimentally Yours"
    (Decca/MCA Records)
    Release date: August 6, 1962

4. "The Patsy Cline Story"
    (Decca/MCA Records)
    Release date: June 17, 1963

5. "A Portrait of Patsy Cline"
    (Decca/MCA Records)
    Release date: November 2, 1964

6. "Here's Patsy Cline"
    (Vocalion/MCA Records)
    Release date: 1965

7. "Patsy Cline's Greatest Hits"
    (Decca/MCA Records)
    Release date: March 13, 1967

8. "Country Great"
    (Vocalion/MCA Records)
    Release date: 1969

9. "Always"
    (MCA Records)
    Release date: 1980

10. "Greatest Hits" by Patsy Cline and Jim Reeves
    (RCA Records)
    Release date: 1981

11. "Remembering" by Patsy Cline and Jim Reeves
    (MCA Records)
    Release date: 1982

12. "Today, Tomorrow and Forever"
    (MCA Records)
    Release date: 1985

13. "Sweet Dreams" movie soundtrack
    (MCA Records)
    Release date: 1985

14. "Stop, Look and Listen"
    (MCA Records)
    Release date: 1986

15. "Songwriter's Tribute"
    (MCA Records)
    Release date: 1986

16. "The Last Sessions"
    (MCA Records)
    Release date: 1988

17. "Live at the *Opry*"
    (MCA Records)
    Release date: 1988

18. "Commemorative Collection"
    (MCA Records)
    Release date: 1988

19. "Live, Volume Two"
    (MCA Records)
    Release date: 1989

20. "The Patsy Cline Collection"
    (MCA Records)
    Release date: 1991

PATSY CLINE'S SINGLE RELEASES

Patsy's singles are listed below by their release date. The bracketed figures (i.e., [#1 country/#12 pop]) indicate the song's peak chart positions in *Billboard* magazine. In some instances, both the "A" side and the "B" side of individual singles charted.

1. A: "A Church, a Courtroom, and Then Goodbye"
   B: "Honky Tonk Merry-Go-Round"
   (Coral Records/July 20, 1955)

2. A: "Hidin' Out"
   B: "Turn the Cards Slowly"
   (Coral Records/November 5, 1955)

3. A: "I Love You Honey"
   B: "Come on in (and Make Yourself at Home)"
   (Coral Records/February 5, 1956)

4. A: "I've Loved and Lost Again"
   B: "Stop, Look and Listen"
   (Decca Records/July 8, 1956)

5. A: "Walkin' after Midnight" [#2 country/#12 pop]
   B: "A Poor Man's Riches (or a Rich Man's Gold)" [#14 country]
   (Decca Records/February 11, 1957)

6. A: "Today, Tomorrow and Forever"
   B: "Try Again"
   (Decca Records/May 27, 1957)

7. A: "Three Cigarettes in an Ashtray"
   B: "A Stranger in My Arms"
   (Decca Records/August 12, 1957)

8. A: "I Don't Wanna"
    B: "Then You'll Know"
    (Decca Records/November 18, 1957)

9. A: "Stop the World (and Let Me Off)"
    B: "Walking Dream"
    (Decca Records/January 13, 1958)

10. A: "Come on in (and Make Yourself at Home)"
    B: "Let the Teardrops Fall"
    (Decca Records/June 2, 1958)

11. A: "I Can See an Angel"
    B: "Never No More"
    (Decca Records/August 18, 1958)

12. A: "If I Could See the World (Through the Eyes of a Child)"
    B: "Just out of Reach (of My Two Open Arms)"
    (Decca Records/September 9, 1958)

13. A: "Dear God"
    B: "He Will Do for You"
    (Decca Records/December 15, 1958)

14. A: "Yes, I Understand"
    B: "Cry Not for Me"
    (Decca Records/February 23, 1959)

15. A: "Gotta Lot of Rhythm in My Soul"
    B: "I'm Blue Again"
    (Decca Records/July 20, 1959)

16. A: "Lovesick Blues"
    B: "How Can I Face Tomorrow"
    (Decca Records/March 7, 1960)

17. A: "Crazy Dreams"
    B: "There He Goes"
    (Decca Records/August 1, 1960)

18. A: "I Fall to Pieces" [#1 country/#12 pop]
    B: "Lovin' in Vain"
    (Decca Records/January 30, 1961)

19. A: "Crazy" [#2 country/#9 pop]
    B: "Who Can I Count On" [#99 pop]
    (Decca Records/October 16, 1961)

20. A: "She's Got You" [#1 country/#14 pop]
    B: "Strange" [#97 pop]
    (Decca Records/January 10, 1962)

21. A: "When I Get Through with You (You'll Love Me Too)"
    [#10 country/#53 pop]
    B: "Imagine That" [#21 country/#90 pop]
    (Decca Records/May 7, 1962)

22. A: "So Wrong" [#14 country/#85 pop]
    B: "You're Stronger than Me"
    (Decca Records/July 16, 1962)

23. A: "Heartaches" [#73 pop]
    B: "Why Can't He Be You"
    (Decca Records/October 8, 1962)

24. A: "Leavin' on Your Mind" [#8 country/#83 pop]
    B: "Tra Le La Le La Triangle"
    (Decca Records/January 7, 1963)

25. A: "Sweet Dreams" [#5 country/#44 pop]
    B: "Back in Baby's Arms"
    (Decca Records/April 15, 1963)

26. A: "Faded Love" [#7 country/#96 pop]
    B: "Blue Moon of Kentucky"
    (Decca Records/August 5, 1963)

27. A: "When You Need a Laugh" [#47 country]
    B: "I'll Sail My Ship Alone"
    (Decca Records/October 28, 1963)

28. A: "Your Kinda Love"
    B: "Someday You'll Want Me to Want You"
    (Decca Records/February 20, 1964)

29. A: "That's How a Heartache Begins"
    B: "Love Letters in the Sand"
    (Decca Records/April 27, 1964)

30. A: "He Called Me Baby" [#23 country]
    B: "Bill Bailey, Won't You Please Come Home"
    (Decca Records/September 14, 1964)

31. A: "Just a Closer Walk with Thee (part 1)"
    B: "Just a Closer Walk with Thee (part 2)"
    (Kapp Records/February 19, 1965)

32. A: "Your Cheatin' Heart"
    B: "I Can't Help It (If I'm Still in Love with You)"
    (Decca Records/March 15, 1965)

33. A: "South of the Border (Down Mexico Way)"
    B: "San Antonio Rose"
    (Decca Records/July 6, 1965)

34. A: "I Love You So Much It Hurts Me"
    B: "Seven Lonely Days"
    (Decca Records/November 8, 1965)

35. A: "Shoes"
    B: "Half as Much"
    (Decca Records/March 28, 1966)

36. A: "You Were Only Foolin' (While I Was Falling in Love)"
    B: "Lonely Street"
    (Decca Records/July 18, 1966)

37. A: "That's My Desire"
    B: "Foolin' Around"
    (Decca Records/December 12, 1966)

38. A: "You Took Him off My Hands"
    B: "Does Your Heart Beat for Me?"
    (Decca Records/March 20, 1967)

39. A: "Hidin' Out"
    B: "Have You Ever Been Lonely (Have You Ever Been Blue)?"
    (Decca Records/July 24, 1967)

40. A: "True Love"
    B: "Love, Love, Love Me Honey Do"
    (Decca Records/December 4, 1967)

41. A: "Always"
    B: "Pick Me Up on Your Way Down"
    (Decca Records/April 29, 1968)

42. A: "You Made Me Love You (I Didn't Want to Do It)"
    B: "Too Many Secrets"
    (Decca Records/August 5, 1968)

43. A: "Anytime" [#73 country]
    B: "In Care of the Blues"
    (Decca Records/November 11, 1968)

44. A: "Crazy Arms"
    B: "The Wayward Wind"
    (Decca Records/March 10, 1969)

45. A: "Crazy"
    B: "Your Cheatin' Heart"
    (MCA Records/May 14, 1973)

46. A: "I Fall to Pieces"
    B: "He Called Me Baby"
    (MCA Records/June 25, 1973)

47. A: "Crazy Arms"
    B: "Pick Me Up on Your Way Down"
    (MCA Record/August 6, 1973)

48. A: "Walkin' after Midnight"
    B: "South of the Border (Down Mexico Way)"
    (MCA Records/October 15, 1973)

49. A: "Life's Railway to Heaven" [#98 country]
    B: "If I Could See the World (Through the Eyes of a Child)"
    (4 Star Records/March 1978)

50. A: "Always" [#18 country]
    B: "I'll Sail My Ship Alone"
    (MCA Records/August 1, 1980)

51. A: "I Fall to Pieces" [#61 country]
    B: "True Love"
    (MCA Records/November 1980)

52 A: "Have You Ever Been Lonely (Have You Ever Been Blue)?"
    [this is a posthumous "duet" between Patsy Cline and Jim
    Reeves, generated in the recording studio] [#5 country]
    B: "Welcome to My World" [Jim Reeves, solo]
    (RCA Records/August 1981)

243

53. A: "I Fall to Pieces" [this song is a posthumous "duet" between
    Patsy Cline and Jim Reeves, generated in the recording studio
    [#54 country]
    B: "So Wrong" [Patsy Cline, solo]
    (MCA Records/May 1982)

54. A: "Sweet Dreams"
    B: "Blue Moon of Kentucky"
    (MCA Records/October 1985)

Bibliography

Books

Behind Closed Doors: Talking with the Legends of Country Music, by Alanna Nash (New York: Knopf, 1988).

Coal Miner's Daughter, by Loretta Lynn, with George Vecsey (New York: Warner Books, 1976).

Complete Directory to Prime Time Network TV Shows, 1946–Present (Third Edition), by Tom Brooks and Earle Marsh (New York: Ballantine Books, 1985).

Country Music Almanac, by Tom Biracree (New York: Prentice Hall, 1993).

Elvis (Revised Edition), by Albert Goldman (New York: McGraw Hill, 1981).

Encyclopedia of Television Series, Pilots and Specials, 1937–1973, by Vincent Terrace (New York: New York Zeotrophe, 1986).

From the Heart, by June Carter Cash (New York: St. Martin's Press, 1987).

Get to the Heart: My Story, by Barbara Mandrell, with George Vecsey (New York: Bantam Books, 1990).

The History of American Bandstand, by Michael Shore, with Dick Clark (New York: Ballantine, 1985).

Kilgallen, by Lee Israel (New York: Dell, 1979).

Patsy, by Margaret Jones (New York: HarperCollins, 1994).

Patsy Cline, by Ellis Nassour (New York: Leisure Books, Dorchester Publishers, 1985).

Rock Encyclopedia, by Lillian Roxon (New York: Tempo Books, 1974).

Rock Movers and Shakers, by Dafydd Rees and Luke Crampton (New York: Billboard Books, 1991).

Rock On, by Norm N. Nite (New York: Popular Library, 1977).

Rolling Stone Encyclopedia of Rock and Roll, by Jon Paraeles and Patricia Romanowski (New York: Rolling Stone Press, 1983).

Top Pop: 1955–1982, by Joel Whitburn (Menomenee Falls, Wisc.: Record Research, Inc., 1983).

Willie, by Willie Nelson, with Bud Shrake (New York: Pocket Books, 1989).

LINER NOTES FROM CD BOXED SETS

"The Complete Patsy Cline" (MCA Records, 1991)

"Elvis: The King of Rock and Roll" (RCA Records, 1992)

"Songs of the West" (Rhino Records, 1993)

VARIOUS ISSUES OF THE FOLLOWING MAGAZINES AND NEWSPAPERS

Arizona Daily Star

Associated Press

Billboard

Country Music

Country Style

Goldmine

Music Reporter

Nashville Banner

New York Times

The Tennessean (Nashville, Tennessee)

People

USA Today

The Washington Star

VIDEOTAPES

"The Real Patsy Cline" (Hallway Productions, Inc., 1989)
"Remembering Pasty Cline" (Hallway Productions, Inc., 1994)

TELEVISION PROGRAMS

"The Women of Country Music" (CBS-TV, 1992)
"Biography" (Arts and Entertainment TV, 1994)

MOVIES

Coal Miner's Daughter (Producer: Bernard Schwartz, Universal Pictures, 1980)
Sweet Dreams (Producer: Bernard Schwartz, Tri-Star Pictures, 1985)

247

Index

250

253